far, far
better
things

far, far better things

A Memoir of Surrendering the American Dream and Finding a Better One

CINDY DEBOER

credo
house publishers

ISBN: 978-1-62586-312-6

Cover design by Lindsay Sisson
Interior design by Frank Gutbrod
Editing by Vanessa Carroll

Printed in the United States of America
First edition

To my love and my greatest adventure—Paul.
From the patter of four tiny pairs of feet to grandparenting joys,
from passport stamps to a westside crack house,
from shared holy moments to painful lessons
learned side by side—
you are my favorite chapter in this beautiful, God-written story.

"There are far, far better things ahead than any we leave behind."
C. S. Lewis

Contents

Prologue

It's not a subtle knock.

The subzero winter winds whistling through the gaps around our former crack house's century-old windows suggest that the forceful, desperate nature of the knock is warranted.

For some odd reason, even though it's well past his bedtime, my handsome, larky husband is still in his favorite chair, one eye open, cocooned in a cozy red chenille blanket. Typically, he begins to "rest his eyes" around 9:30 p.m. and heads upstairs to bed around 10:00. I'm his polar opposite (in oh, *so* many ways). When the clock strikes midnight, I kick off my glass slippers and pounce on all the things I merely thought about doing throughout the day and stay surprisingly productive well past 2:00 a.m. Tonight, at 11:30 p.m., I'm nestling into our couch that's tucked into our front bay window and trying to choose which Jimmy to laugh with before I get some work done. Since the bay window juts out a couple feet onto our large front porch, I am positioned in clear view of the front door—a mere ten feet away. When the forceful knocker jolts me to attention, I glance over my left shoulder through the shadeless bay window and see the young man at the door. He sees me too, and our eyes meet.

He immediately gives me the universal sign of someone who is cold (hugging himself and shivering), then the universal sign of hunger (holding fingers to his mouth as if possessing a morsel of food), and then the universal sign of prayer/begging (clasping hands together, bowing toward me).

I nonchalantly look at Paul and say, "There's a cold and hungry young man at our door. I think you should answer it."

Paul cracks open the front door. "Can I help—?" the young man nearly bowls Paul over as he rushes in. He gives Paul a bear hug and launches into a long spiel describing weeks of unfortunate circumstances. His speech is so disordered that it's difficult to understand most of it. But he manages to convey a few key points: He's from Sudan. He's homeless and penniless and is wearing all his earthly belongings. He assures us he isn't a bad guy and has never done anything wrong but that he had only wanted to sleep in the doorway of a nearby church when someone in the neighborhood called the police on him. He says he's terrified of going to jail so he started running and when he saw our lights on, he was sure Allah had directed him to us. He says his name is Abdellah, which rests easy on our Arabic-tuned ears, but he says we can call him Daniel.

Paul's legendary discernment skills conclude Abdellah/Daniel is an okay guy and invites him in to get warm. The young man's smell enters the room before he does. It's not a smell I recognize, which frustrates me because I pride myself in having an uncommonly elevated olfactory sense. Although his eyes are bloodshot and he's not steady on his feet, I easily rule out alcohol and weed (smells I'm well acquainted with—this is a college town, after all). Plus, his body movements are too twitchy and jittery for someone baked. He might be tweaking, but as a psych nurse, I've seen many psychotic patients exhibit bizarre behaviors resembling a tweaker—so I'm just not convinced. To my dismay, it would be days before I'd successfully remove that indistinguishable odor from our home.

But I don't care about that.

Abdellah/Daniel's manners predicate himself and he kicks off his mud and snow-caked shoes but misses our entrance rug and the melting snow creates a significant muddy puddle on our refurbished wood floors.

But I don't care about that.

Abdellah/Daniel plops down in the only nice chair we own and as his smelly, visibly dirty body sinks into the chair, about fifty old crusty Cheerios fall from his grimy neck onto the floor around him. I watch as he repeatedly rubs his mucky hands up and down the light beige cloth arms of the chair. *Yeah, not looking too likely I'll get that thing clean after this . . .*

But I don't care about that.

There was a time I would have cared. As in, big-time cared. I well remember the person who would have freaked out to have a late-night homeless visitor, let alone a Muslim man, in her home. I can vividly recall how clean floors, new stylish furniture, and a magazine-worthy home that emanated perfection and wealth were vitally important to that person. I remember how she justified all the excess. In fact, she had an answer for everything—especially when it came to how God thinks.

She's gone now, but I still remember her.

Just like my former self, life in Morocco is a distant memory, and France but a fading shadow, yet both places and their people are indelibly tattooed on our interiors (our family of six)—so much so that we sometimes unintentionally shock people here in Michigan.

Sometimes we say things that take people aback. Sometimes we travel to places where people around here say you should never go. Sometimes we have new and different ideas about what to believe than many of the others in this conservative, church-soaked area. And sometimes we do things—(perhaps letting an unhoused Muslim stranger into our home late at night?)—that our family and friends warn us may be stupid or dangerous.

But I don't care about any of that anymore, either.

⁂

It's clear Abdellah/Daniel isn't going to leave on his own accord. We spend at least an hour getting to know one another. We feed him dinner. He asks for seconds. I see Paul giving me a familiar look from across the room. He knows how I love to analyze mental illnesses, and with that glare, he's telling me to diagnose the man and prescribe an appropriate response. But Abdellah/Daniel is a baffling mixture of behavioral abnormalities, and I just can't decide what's more prevalent: substance abuse or mental dysfunction or if it even matters.

What I do care about today, however, is that we do right by Abdellah/Daniel.

With three spare bedrooms in our empty nest and a soul thick for justice, I chastise myself for even considering sending Abdellah/Daniel back out in the cold. And yet, most of my sensibilities are steering me toward that option. I can tell from Paul's look, he's in agreement with me that this man is not well—for one reason or another. However, if I know Paul at all (which I do, better than anyone on the planet) he'll also agree with me that there's simply no way we're not going to help this troubled soul.

Eventually, Abdellah/Daniel asks if we'll take him to the hospital. He mumbles something about "out of medication" and this resonates with me. I think of the many patients I've cared for at the psychiatric hospital who suffer severe relapses in mental illness if they stop their medications. We load up Abdellah/Daniel with a sack of food, a coat, a warm blanket and new gloves. Paul drives him to the Emergency Department, gives him our phone number if he should ever need help again, and pulls him in for a hearty hug goodbye. We never hear from Abdellah/Daniel again.

Sitting in my stinky living room post the late-night visitor, I realize there is no place in the world I would rather live than right here, right now, in this part of this city, with this man, living out our faith as best we know how, amid our relatively new Jesus community who unanimously believe following the Rabbi looks the same way we do.

I am barely a shadow of my former self.

Today, living on the "less desirable" side of Grand Rapids, we are not at all the same people who, for the first twelve years of our marriage, lived hell-bent on pursuing the "more desirable" things in life. In those early days—the days before God did a little surgery on our souls—we not only bred children, we bred those two thieves named "perfectionism" and "competitiveness." That incarnation created a life of busyness, hustle, strive, push, jealousy, grind, exhaustion, sweat, and sacrifice. "Getting ahead" seemed to be our guiding principle while we ignored the ever-present painful and hollow ache in our souls telling us we were made for so much more. We couldn't shake the disrupting thoughts telling us life didn't have to be so hard. Telling us we have choices, and we don't have to careen to our deaths entirely exhausted from trying to convince the world we have everything under control, that our family is admirably adorable and accomplished, and that our lives are pure Instagram perfection. We always tried to bury those disrupting thoughts because no one enjoys being disrupted. But burying those thoughts simply left us with the terrifying fear that life was passing us by while we waited for the courage to do something about it.

I now believe with all that's in me that God longs to grant each of us that elusive courage to do something about it. That if we ask, God will remove our fear, fill our hollow aching souls, and show us a path to life with meaning. Dear friends, please know how deeply and profoundly I believe in you, in me, in us—to find the courage to walk that path.

If you've ever felt that you were meant for more, you were. A life of far, far better things awaits you.

Let's do this thing.

CHAPTER 1

Bunny Chasers

"There is more to life than increasing its speed."

MAHATMA GANDHI

As I sit crisscross on the floor in the sunroom of our custom-built home with the pungent smell of new paint and carpet still lingering thick, I'm flummoxed by what I see. The large bank of west-facing windows is not now, and will never be, capturing the descending afternoon wintertime sun. How in the world did this get missed? I was adamant that this house would get as much sunlight as possible since Michigan offers us so little.

When this home only existed on paper, I stood out on the property at every time of day in rain, sleet, snow, and sunshine to ascertain the best angle for the house. I pored over the blueprints to ensure every window was perfectly positioned to capture maximum daylight. We even added six unnecessary windows just to, you know, be sure. I made it clear to everyone involved how important sunshine was to me. And yet, somehow these sunroom windows are doing a dismal job on this November afternoon.

Who wasn't paying attention when we said we were only going to build our dream house once so everything needed to be perfect? Someone screwed up here, and I feel my neck color changing from pink to red as I contemplate who. The architect? No. He simply put down on paper precisely what I told him to. The builder? No. Our builder, also our dear friend, built precisely what the architect drew up.

This little sunshine debacle is my own fault. I'm mortified I missed it.

Then, an epiphany: transom windows! Such a simple fix! All we need to do is extend our already tall windows further upward to the top of our ten-foot ceilings so when the winter sun begins its descent in the western sky, they'll be perfectly poised to capture daylight sooner.

I mentally give myself congratulatory applause for my designing acumen. Now, if I can just find a way to convince the hubby that ripping open walls in a brand-new home and spending maybe another $20,000 when we were already significantly over budget is a wise move, it'll be a done deal. Our home will be perfect at last. After all, I'm sure we can afford it. That's all that matters, anyway, I tell myself.

As I plan my justification conversation with my sweet and too-generous husband, I realize what I'm doing. I'm chasing that elusive perfection again—always reaching for something that's just outside my reach.

Oh Cindy, how quickly you forget. Do you remember nothing of our little chat in the woods in Germany just a few months ago?

Walking back into our custom cherrywood kitchen, I reflexively gather Buzz Light Year and a bunch of matchbox cars and dump them in the toy box. I pause in front of the arched window above our kitchen sink that faces west to massive fields of wheat, freshly planted and still green. The wind is doing a weird thing. Instead of blowing in one direction, it's going back and forth, back and forth. The wheat looks like it's shaking its head at me—probably recognizing my materialism. I stare for a long while at our gorgeous rolling landscape—fields of corn, wheat, and pastureland—land we purchased from my husband's parents on the back half of their farm. It's the most idyllic piece of property: ten acres on a quiet country dirt road and no neighbors within shouting distance. Not only is it the most perfect piece of dirt, but it's also located in the perfect village, with the perfect schools and our perfect little church. I'm having a hard time accepting that just ten minutes ago my house was perfect, too, and yet now, not quite. I don't know if I should laugh or cry. I'm just so tired. So very tired of trying to get everything right. I wish I knew how to let it go. I wish I knew how to stop the madness. I'm not sure I'd try it, but I do wish I knew how. I can only imagine a life where I'm not always chasing, striving, and pursuing perfection. My head spins at the thought. It just seems impossible.

As I try to imagine it, my thoughts are interrupted by how badly I really want those transom windows and our sunroom to be sunnier. Why is it so bad to want that?

It often feels like God and I are in a tug-of-war. I deeply desire something—this house, a trip, new furniture, a swimming pool, etc. When I get it, I cherish it, and believe that I truly do see it as a benevolent gift from God. But then God tugs at my heart and I think maybe he's telling me I love the new thing too much. I apologize to God, who says, "Okay, you're forgiven." Then I vow to stop wanting new things so much. Yet, like an addict returning to old habits, I clutch my little must-haves list as if it were the Gospel of John and traipse off to Target, Home Goods, Home Depot, or some remote, dusty antique shop to procure my dopamine rush. And no matter how many things I can cross off that must-have list, there are always more to add.

What I'd really like is for God to just leave me alone for a while so I can revel in the achievement this beautiful home represents. Like a heavy backpack at an amusement park, I'd like to just check God at the entrance. I don't want any more tugging at my heart where I wonder if that's God nudging me to pull back and somehow do life differently. I'm kind of sick of feeling like God is trying to tell me something.

A Scripted Life

I remember walking into church on Sunday morning the week Paul had been elected to serve on our church's consistory (church board). Our pastor's wife stopped us in the narthex and randomly asked if Paul's suit was new. I wondered how she knew! Paul responded, "Well, as a matter of fact, it is!" The pastor's wife beamed and said, "I knew it! I have a theory and it's never failed me yet! Whenever a young man is voted on to the consistory, three things always follow: a baby, a new car, and a new suit. Since you're expecting a baby soon, and you've just bought a new car, I just knew you'd be wearing a new suit too!"

Because, you see, Cindy, there is a certain script to life—and you've been given your logical, predicted role. Don't question it. Stick to the script.

Paul and I were very good actors; we excelled at sticking to the script. We liked that comfortable, familiar path, and it seemed like that's what everyone wanted from us, anyway. But like those greyhounds at the dog races who chase a rubber bunny around a circular track, we too were racing around a track to nowhere. Chasing, chasing, chasing. Not once, not ever, did anyone tell us the bunny we were chasing was a fake. I wish someone had been brave enough to warn us: *"You might catch it, but you'll get a mouthful of rubber disappointment!"*

It was about that same time, barely ten years into marriage, that I remember thinking the hard parts of life must certainly be behind us now. We had worked hard to accumulate a good amount of money and things, and I assumed the real work, or any other challenging aspect of life, would certainly all be a part of our past now. I believed we had arrived. We were still so young, but our conversations were dotted with topics of passive income, early retirement, and wealth management. We were poised to just kind of "coast" from that point until Jesus came. We justified our coasting by noting how hard we had worked to get there. After all, we ascertained, God doesn't want us feeling guilty for our achievements and blessings, does he? We made thankfulness our panacea and vowed never to stop thanking God for all our good gifts.

In true American fashion, arriving comes with a trophy. By many people's standards, the pinnacle of success is when we're able to buy or build the dream home. We chose to build it. With nary a pause, we began the nearly two-year journey of thinking, dreaming, shopping, drawing, scheming, building, changing, fighting, crying, and shopping some more for that total misnomer of a thing called a dream home. The project became all-consuming. It seemed like all our conversations for two years centered on "The House." How big should it be? What do you think of white houses, dear? Will white look the best in that big open field? What about when the field is covered in snow? Knobs or pulls for bathroom drawers? Hardwood or tile in the kitchen? Cherrywood or painted cabinets? Paint or paper? Twenty years of debt or thirty?

It soon became clear to me that every single minuscule decision made when building a house—from the size of the baseboards to the shingles on the roof—comes in three categories: good, better, and best. I still don't know how someone who grew up thinking creamed peas on toast was a delicacy, who spent blistering-hot summer days playing in the leech-infested creek that fed Mud Lake, and who wore imitation Gloria Vanderbilt jeans sewn by her mother, could develop an eye for high-end home design years before HGTV was even a thing, but it's one of the many inexplicable plot twists in my life. For every decision for our new home, I would invariably choose that which was best.

And so it began.

Paul learned, by necessity, the quiet art of nodding his head up and down, and occasionally he'd pipe in for good measure: "Just keep track of where we're at—I don't want to go over budget." My silly husband! Go over budget? Who meeeee? She who cannot even balance the checkbook? To be honest, I never once checked our budget. I think we unofficially went about $100,000 over what we had planned. Unbelievably, Paul never got angry with me. He'd just quietly reply, "Well, I guess this is something we'll only do once, so let's not have regrets." There was some serious reckless spending as I lived to ensure we didn't have regrets.

Every day, while our house was under construction, I'd check in at the work site to make sure every detail was exactly the way we (read: I) wanted it. I was obsessed with making that house perfect. PERFECT! I must have annoyed the hell out of the guys working for us. I knew nothing about home construction, but I considered myself the General Contractor. I constantly made those guys re-do things, un-do things, and just do more things.

I couldn't get enough of the feeling that we (again, read: I) were building such a gorgeous home that masterfully reflected our success, education, wealth, and status. I dreamed of the envious looks on the faces of my family and friends when they would eventually behold the wonder.

I imagine Frankenstein probably had similar feelings when he created his monster.

One Thing More

One day, on the way to inspect the dream home, I was feeling exceedingly proud. It was a good hair day and I thought my tight black sweater made me look thin and sexy. Our two boys (our only kids at the time) had had a good morning, and I was thinking Paul and I probably deserved a Hollywood gold star for our parenting. My life couldn't be more perfect. We were at the top of our game, and I knew it. I opened the sunroof of our shiny new SUV as I pulled out onto the street because my blonde hair looks the best in the sunshine. I turned the radio up loud and wondered how many people I passed envied me and my car. I could feel my heart pick up its pace as I neared the construction site. It was like a drug for my ego to be building one of the larger homes in our mostly farming community, and I got a buzz from the dopamine euphoria. I spent that five-minute drive stroking my ego for having finally arrived. We were building an impressive new house: check. My husband was successful, handsome, and charming: check. We had two cute, witty, and talented young sons: check. And even though we were pretty young, we already had everything money could buy—cars, clothes, a lake house with boat, vacations—check, check, check, and check. My big ego could barely fit in my big SUV.

And then a very unexpected thing happened.

I looked down at my hands on the steering wheel and my wedding ring caught my eye. The precious, hand-carved stone Paul had personally chosen, was now, after ten years of marriage and ten years of morphing fashion, looking a bit outdated. *Almost*, I thought, *ugly.*

I wanted to cry. Everything in my life was so perfect—except, now, this. This diamond just seemed unacceptable for someone who has it all put together so, so, so perfectly. I made a mental note to hit Paul up for a new diamond ring as soon as the dust had settled from moving. And I thought, "Then everything will be perfect. That will certainly be the last thing I'll ask for. I can't imagine ever wanting another thing because I'll have everything I've ever wanted!"

I cannot say for certain, because it's impossible for humans to confirm this for each other, but I think I heard from the divine. I felt something deep on the inside—like a "ping," but not a pain, a "cringe" but not a cramp. It was other-dimensional and outside of the realm of my five senses. I felt for a moment I was going to vomit, yet I knew I wasn't sick.

I don't think this was *actually* the first time God tried to speak to me, because I now believe God speaks to us thousands of times each day in thousands of different ways. I just think this day in the car was the first time I noticed it. It sounded, or, more accurately, felt like these words: "The ring won't really be the last thing, will it? Will you ever stop chasing, Cindy? It's such an endless, dangerous game—because, for you, you don't really mean you want just one thing, what you really mean is you want just one thing more. Always *just one thing more . . .*"

I believe God spoke to me that day in my car. Not necessarily an audible voice—but I knew I had been given an important, life-altering message and there's just no other explanation for who sent it. The problem, however, is that I just did not want to hear it. This message didn't fit my script.

I jacked the volume up on the radio and drove on, hoping to forget what had just happened.

The radio paused, then the all-too-familiar first notes of a song I knew by heart rang out. I nearly veered into oncoming traffic as I lunged to shush my accusing radio. It was a song called "One Thing" by Rich Mullins, my favorite Christian musician of all time. I knew all his songs by heart.

His lyrics pummeled me: *"Everybody I know says they need just one thing. But what they really mean is they need just one thing more. . . ."*

Unbelievably, even this didn't convict me. It just made me mad at God, and I switched the radio off hoping it would switch God off too. It felt like God was toying with me, batting me around for no good reason—like a cat bats a mouse around just to torture it. I told God exactly that and that I didn't think this is what love looks like.

You would think if the Creator of the Universe took time out of his busy schedule to talk to you and give you some instructions on life, you'd listen. You would think. But not me. Like a cheating spouse who leads a double life, I kept that encounter with God a secret for a terribly long time. I especially didn't want Paul to know because I feared he'd suggest it might be a good idea to listen to the voice of God and obey.

I just really, really wanted a new diamond ring and feared if I told anyone that quite possibly the Creator of the Universe spoke to me about materialism, it might jeopardize getting one. I truly believed once I got a new ring, I'd never ask for anything else.

Ever. The ring was my one thing. Then, I vowed, I'd listen to God no matter what.

Chasing, Chasing, Chasing

Reflecting on our first decade of marriage, our priorities were evident by how we spent our time, money, and energy: raising the best, smartest, athletic kids, advancing our careers, enjoying nice possessions, taking several great vacations each year, stockpiling sufficient wealth for retirement, and keeping lots of friends around who will join us in the appreciation of all these amazing "blessings." Of course, Paul and I were far too virtuous Christians to verbalize such worldly, carnal goals. Instead, had anyone asked, we would have said our one priority in life was to love the Lord our God with all our heart, soul, mind, and strength. But if a tree is indeed known by its fruit, we were not living what we said we believed. Our lives reflected two people hell-bent on making more and more money so we could spend *it* on bigger and better things and some fine day give *it* all to our four spoiled children.

The problem with all of *it*, however, is that *it* will never be enough. We will forever be chasing, chasing, chasing.

And when you're raised like me, with a dad who makes you feel like you will never be enough, the chasing, chasing, chasing is significantly amplified.

CHAPTER 2

My Own Pa Ingalls and His Disappointing Half-Pint

"Children begin by loving their parents, as they grow older they
judge them; sometimes they forgive them."

OSCAR WILDE

"Diane! Heidi! Follow me! Let's make a house underneath the picnic
table and pretend to cook a meal with grass, weeds, and dirt!"

"Why? That sounds stupid," my two younger sisters reply in
chorus. *Oh, why don't these two have any imagination?*

"It will be fun! We can pretend we're Amish preparing a feast
for a barn-raising!"

"No. We're tired of being Amish. You always want us to be
Amish, and the Amish are boring. Let's play softball!" *They always
want to play softball but I'm tired of softball. Softball is boring.*

"Okay. Well, then, how about this! Let's turn the picnic table
into our stage and play Donnie and Marie! We can create a whole
show and perform it for Mom!"

"I get to wear the white go-go boots!" declares Diane. *I got
'em! These two are suckers for Donnie and Marie.*

Wearing our flair-leg hip-hugger pants and purple sparkly shirts Mom bought us at the thrift store, we grab two electric knives and a curling iron, which will serve well as our handheld microphones. I pause at the screen door and watch the two of them bolt into the backyard, Kool-Aid mustaches, summer sun in their hair, not a care in the world. I love these two with all that is in me. Together, our little trio contemplated the most important things in life: Why did Laurie marry Amy March and not Jo? Should Anne of Green Gables have married Gilbert? Which of our two Grandmas makes the best mashed potatoes? And why can't we have creamed peas on toast for lunch every day?

Pam, the oldest of our tribe of four girls, is a hard one for me—aloof, preferring horses over people and sports over boys. I don't understand any of that nonsense. Our two younger sisters give her the respect due a firstborn as well as equal "play time." I do not. Pam mostly rolls her eyes at me. Or beats me up. I try to stay away from Pam.

But these two precious pawns? They are my projects— the little people with whom I get to deposit whatever I want. I have their brains, beliefs, and passions to mold and shape as I choose, so I choose to teach them how to read and write poetry, that Louisa May Alcott probably had our family in mind when she wrote *Little Women,* and that the barn loft could become anything we imagined it to be: a small-town diner, a fancy lady's house with maids and butlers, a school classroom, a dance floor, or even the Eiffel Tower. Of course, they'll eventually become their own people and start doing what they really enjoy, which is play sports, but all these growing up years, whenever I have the chance, I demand their allegiance as I craft their play and develop their imaginations. The silliness is overcoming us as we rehearse all the parts of "I'm a Little Bit Country, and I'm a Little Bit Rock 'n Roll."

I don't remember who suggested it, but we decided we needed a better stage. A bouncy one, for some odd reason.

We jack the sugar content higher by grabbing a few Oreos on the way back indoors. We head toward Dad and Mom's queen-size bed in their seventies blonde paneled bedroom. This is a far, far better stage for our Donny and Marie (and Marie) Show.

With increasing exuberance, we hold hands, jump up and down in a circle and sing all the lyrics we know—*I'm a little bit country, and I'm a little bit rock 'n roll. I'm a little bit of Memphis and Nashville with a little bit of Motown in my soul . . . (something, something, something). I'm a little bit country, and I'm a little bit rock 'n roll.*

Suddenly the air in the room grows cold on this hot summer day. Just like in the movies—we sense a presence before it arrives. Steps at the doorway. A large frame. Not good. The smaller frame would have gone easier on us. No way this is going to end well.

Without pause or a warning, Dad grabs me by one arm and lifts me so high my feet are dangling above the bed. He whacks my bottom forcefully, repeatedly, more times than necessary, the way I remember it.

Why? Why, Dad, why? Why do you sometimes seem so far away that I don't even know if you're real? Why are you sometimes happy and funny and joyfully suggest we all play softball together and tickle us on the way out the door? Why do you sometimes, out of nowhere, blow up and terrify us? I don't understand, Dad. I don't know how to behave around you.

Dad

Dad was an amazing athlete in his younger years, as were his brothers. Like many small-town heroes, people in our hometown of Hudsonville knew their names. Many still do. But not always for noble reasons. The Hudsonville High School students of the late fifties remember the time Dad felt he got a bad call from the referee in a basketball game, so he slammed the ball so hard on the gym floor, it bounced up and hit the ceiling. He swore at the referee after receiving the much deserved technical foul and was then evicted from the game. Legend has it you could hear him swearing the whole way down the hall to the locker room.

A former high school classmate of my dad's recounts the time school had been dismissed early due to heavy snowfall. Just for fun, dad dared two of his friends to be pulled behind his car by ropes while on snow skis. They took the dare and dad pulled his buddies right down the center of 32nd Avenue, the main road in Hudsonville. With dad's head craning out the open window and looking back at the skiers, and the heavy snowfall limiting visibility, he never noticed the two pranksters watching from the sidewalk. They quickly took advantage of this prime opportunity to take my dad down a few notches (perhaps deserved?). They unloaded a fusillade of snowballs at his head. Dad slammed on the brakes so hard his skiers flew right into the back of his car. Dad leaped out of his car and gave those pranksters a pounding and, I'm told, the two of them never got a single slug in. My storyteller pauses here and just shakes his head. "Your dad! Oh my, could he ever get mad! Your dad was something else!"

Unfortunately, for my sisters and me, we reaped what he'd sown by attending the same high school and church that Dad did growing up. Before we even had a chance to prove otherwise, our last name alone harkened our teachers to potential temper and anger issues. I remember walking into my Sunday school class at the beginning of seventh grade and the teacher—a short, hunched lady in her eighties with gray hair coiled high like a beehive—took one look at me and groaned, "Another Visser. Great." My dad left us quite a legacy. And even though he was gifted seventy-five years on planet earth, it still wasn't enough time for him to learn how to contain his anger.

The jumping-on-the-bed day he spanked me so hard, so many times, I threw up. I don't remember if he spanked the other two. He may have, but I don't remember it. I threw it all up—red Kool-Aid, Oreo cookies, and half-digested hot dog chunks—all over their new white chenille bedspread, which angered him even more, so he spanked me again. As Mom frantically tried to clean the pink and red puke out of the bedspread, I ran down the hall to the bathroom. And when I threw up the remaining hot dog chunks all over the tan tweed carpet in the hallway, Dad spanked me a third time.

I fled to my room and bawled into my pillow. I remember thinking, "I must be sick. Surely, this is the flu. Dad wouldn't spank me so hard I'd puke, would he?" But I woke up the next morning completely illness-free.

It's weird how memories are unique to the beholder—how some are permanently wallpapered to the inner rooms of our psyche while others are almost instantly vaporized. My sisters, while acknowledging dad's angry outbursts and volatility, mostly remember his silly side and enthusiasm in rehashing every one of our sporting events. I mostly remember the spankings and being fearful of his irrational anger. I'm not entirely sure if that speaks more to his poor character or mine. But as the four of us compared notes on our childhood, it became glaringly obvious that children can live under the same roof, with the same parents, yet experience quite different childhoods.

I know it's so unoriginal to have daddy issues. And sometimes I feel bad acknowledging my own because I realize there are far worse degrees of family messed-upness than ours. Yet, I share this part of my story because it came close to crippling me for life, and I long to help young women avoid the same pain. Daddy trauma can be a huge impediment to healthy development and wholeness. I harbored unnecessary and unresolved resentment well into my adult life which only made me miserable—not him. I loved my dad. But I also hated him. I was afraid of him while simultaneously trying to please him. And because I was a good church girl who knew God was our Father and we were his children, I projected that same fear and feelings of inadequacy on God. To me, God was also not approachable. God was also distant but demanded obedience. God was also big and scary, but I was supposed to enjoy his presence. God was also someone who demanded full allegiance to receive his love, and so I figured that's what I'd do: play sports. Er, I mean, do Jesus-y things.

God and my dad were all tangled up in my head, and I believed I had to earn both of their love and attention. Consequently, I often felt unloved by both of them.

My Pa

Ours was a sheltered, slumbering, mid-western farming village called Forest Grove that sat just to the south of Hudsonville, the nearest almost-city. I know what you're thinking—that sounds just like Laura Ingalls in her little country town of Walnut Grove! Yes! Back then, I wanted everyone to think that too, because I so wanted us to be one and the same. As the second-born of four daughters in a conservative Christian family, I felt a strong kinship to Laura Ingalls Wilder, or "Half-Pint," who was also the second-born to Pa and Ma Ingalls. I read every one of her books and would have had to be in a coma to miss an episode of the TV show. Monday nights, 8:00 p.m. on NBC, I could always be found snuggled up in my brown faux leather beanbag with a bowl of Hudsonville's vanilla ice cream with Hershey's syrup on top. I couldn't wait for Mondays. Watching *Little House on the Prairie* made me dream of having Pa Ingalls as my father.

Tuesdays were second best because at 8:00 p.m., we watched *Eight Is Enough* on ABC. I sometimes imagined Tom Bradford as my dad, but he just didn't make the cut for my fantasy father team. There were two areas where I was truly proud of my dad— his rugged good looks and athleticism. Daddy Bradford had neither. Despite his kindness, he was short, bald, unathletic, and hiked his pants too high. I wanted a dad who'd make the popular girls at school jealous. Pa Ingalls for the win.

In Walnut Grove, Ma and Pa Ingalls, along with their four daughters took the horse-drawn buckboard wagon to the white, one-room church building every Sunday morning. They would wave to all their friends and neighbors along the way, happily greeting the other worshippers with a hearty, "Good mornin' there, neighbor!" Wearing their Sunday best and their ever-present smiles, the six of them just emanated love for one another and their fellow mankind.

Similarly, every single Sunday of my life my dad and mom drove my three sisters and me to our country church in Forest Grove—with a few distinct differences, however. Our buckboard was a cream-colored, rusted-out Pontiac Caprice; my dad snarled at us if we were running late; and I'm unsure of the sincerity of our "Sunday smiles." Because I was the only one who liked to fuss with my hair and make-up (my sisters didn't care about such things), I often made Dad wait. Dad hated to be late. He waited for me in the driveway with the car running, obnoxiously honking the horn, and always threatening to leave without me. We were never late, just less early than Dad wanted to be. He wouldn't even look at me when I made us less early; he just stared out the car window in obvious disgust. I'm not sure what our family emanated as we drove up to church, but the smoke coming out of my dad's ears didn't feel like love to me.

I always imagined Pa Ingalls coming home from work smelling like fresh sawn wood from working at the sawmill paired with a hearty dose of earth, wind, and sun from the hours spent plowing his fields. I'd imagine him giving me a big bear hug. I'd bury my head in his chest to inhale that manly scent. My dad, conversely, smelled a hideous combination of fiberglass from his boat factory job, Kent Premium Lights, and Maxwell House instant coffee. When he came home, I worried I wouldn't be able to hold my breath long enough for a hug. I worried for naught. Dad never gave me a hug when he came home from work.

I think the reason I stopped watching *Little House* reruns entirely was because Pa Ingalls had a special place in his heart for Half-Pint. The disparity between our two stories just hurt too much because, in my world, it felt to me like Dad loved our Mary, Carrie, and Grace more than Half-Pint.

All three of my sisters, to my dad's great satisfaction, were stellar athletes. They could have played any sport they wanted to, but we all played the Big Three (according to Dad): basketball, volleyball, and softball. My sisters received accolades and recognition at our school, in the region, and even in the state. Me? My basketball teammates once voted me as "Best Hair."

Still, almost all my evening memories from our growing-up years include some form of after dinner sports activity. We shot hoops in the driveway as soon as fall basketball tryouts were announced. We played three-on-two late into the evening until the mosquitos or a jammed finger forced our retreat. Winter came and ushered in volleyball season and that's all we talked about for months. When it was too cold to play sports outside, we watched them on TV: the Tigers, Lions, Pistons, Red Wings, University of Michigan, Michigan State—we didn't have strong team allegiances in our home, just a holy reverence for sports in general. In early spring, before the snow had fully disappeared, we broke out the ball gloves and warmed up our arms in the muddy grass. All spring and summer long we played softball in the side yard of our little brown brick ranch—the corner of the old sandbox for first base, the half-dead lilac bush for second base, the willow tree third. A white square painted on the side of the house for the strike-zone allowed us to forego a catcher. By utilizing ghost runners, we were able to make two teams between the five of us. Mom rarely came out there to play ball with us. I never thought about it much. We just figured sports weren't her thing.

Unlike the other three, I was a dreamer—often lost in a fictional universe located exclusively in my head. I liked to sing and dance and write and play the piano. Mostly, I enjoyed things my sisters generally didn't. Maybe even for that reason. And yet, I played sports. Every sport. Which is a funny little lie I tell myself and everyone else. In truth, I rarely "played" the sport; I mostly watched from the bench. I didn't totally suck as an athlete but was probably just good enough to make the team in a medium-sized school with a medium-quality athletics program.[1] And it wasn't that I hated playing sports—I just wasn't great at them like my sisters, so I always felt inferior. As a family, we spent nearly every meal talking about sports, analyzing the nuances of the game, what we could do to improve our performances, why our coaches had their heads up their asses, and why, if my dad were coach, we'd be winning.

Dad rarely came to my choir concerts, high school musicals, or Hudsonville High School's famous music revue shows. He didn't visit the local churches where I was often asked to sing for special music. He didn't ask me about the books I was reading or the stories I was writing. It was hard for Dad to know how to talk to me because my world was painfully foreign to him and because my sports world was painfully boring and small (from all that bench sitting). Conversely, the other girls always had interesting, exciting, victorious things to share! I felt all my dad could see when he looked at me was the weakest link in his little tribe of female athletes. I always believed I was his biggest disappointment in life.

I never understood, until it was too late, that the exorbitant amount of time spent playing sports with us girls was Dad's way of saying, "I love you." I wanted more from him. I wanted the actual words. I wanted the hugs. I wanted more attention. I've been hard on my dad for many years now because I didn't understand then what I now know. I didn't understand that he wasn't trying to hurt me. I didn't understand how I had interpreted his hurt as rejection, which resulted in shame. Shame is such a nasty, yet prevalent, by-product of a botched Christian faith that leads you to believe you are broken beyond repair and will never be good enough—which is exactly the lie I had bought.

Never good enough.

I wore my perceived rejection from Dad like a weighted, musty, oversized wool coat on a hot summer day. A coat, however odd this may sound, that I refused to take off.

Looking back, I so wish I had had the capacity to give Dad the mercy and grace he needed for simply doing his best. I never got a chance to tell him that. As a parent now, I understand how impossibly hard this parenting gig is and that we're all just barely hanging on out here like Titanic survivors clinging to a floating door in the frigid Atlantic. This job is all on-the-job-training, and even if you believe you've at least earned a passable C-, your kids might grow up and tell you all the things you did wrong and grade you much lower. They'll probably even suggest you flunked the class. This is just how parenting works. I see now that we're all operating out of our own woundedness and a past we can do nothing about and the quicker we learn to extend mercy to those who contributed to those wounds, the quicker we'll have peace. I didn't learn this soon enough. My dad went home to Jesus before I ever gathered the strength to forgive him.

Dad had definitely acquired his own wounds in his complicated life, and I, the "sensitive one" simply felt those repercussions most acutely.

I had no way of knowing those repercussions from our conflicted relationship would push me into the arms of other men and haunt me well into my adult years.

CHAPTER 3

Despicable Me

"The wound is the place the light enters you."

RUMI

I was a teenager having sex. A lot. And I liked it.

Many people do not think teen sex is one of the worst sins. Perhaps that is because they need to justify it in their own lives, or perhaps it's because they were not raised like me where everyone understood there to be five cardinal sins: abortion, homosexuality, adultery, divorce, and sex outside of marriage (quite possibly in that order). All other sins were barely worth mentioning. At least I don't remember ever discussing them. I didn't know there was any shame in lying, cheating, gossiping, or coveting all the rich girls' clothing; but I was certain I was damned to hell because I was a teenager having sex. I could have probably murdered someone and felt less guilt.

I do not know, exactly, how we came to understand this hierarchy of sins. I do not remember my parents ever verbalizing it to us—it was just *known*. It could have been the hushed tones used in relaying juicy information so we pious would know better "how to pray for one another." It could have been the huddled whispers and brazen stares as certain girls walked into church—girls whose reputation we questioned. Perhaps it was purely based on the amount of time given to gossip on the topic. We just didn't talk about Mike's porn addiction, Dave's workaholic tendencies, Beth's temper with her children, or Sue's careless spending habits. I'm not sure if we didn't know about these things or just didn't care. In my ultra-conservative pocket of the Midwest during those flagrant purity-culture years, we mostly cared that you don't have sex before marriage, that you don't get pregnant, and that you get to wear that white dress.

While growing up, there was one thing for which I believed with everything in me: My dad would disown me if I got pregnant. He never said those words. But I felt deep in my bones it was intrinsically true. I lived my life believing that if I ever screwed up, especially in this way, I would have to face the irrational, uncontained fury of my father. And I feared his condemnation far more than God's when I was a teen having sex.

Prior to all the sex, I was the quintessential good girl. I loved mama, Jesus, and America too. I was even crazy 'bout Elvis, horses, and my boyfriend too.[2] As a good Christian girl, I was faithfully following that irrevocable script for my life and didn't have the pluck or predisposition to question it.

So I just proceeded to follow the formula that seemed all too clearly laid out for me: college, career, marry the nice Christian boy next door, kids, money, church, success, community status, etc.

And they all lived happily ever after, right? I mean, that's how it always works, doesn't it?

Apparently, I'm no Cinderella.

My perfectly scripted life was right on track when I started high school. As a mere lowly freshman, I dared to dream about one of the most handsome and sought-after senior guys in our high school—my Paul. Apparently, I caught his eye too. Our first conversation happened at church youth group, which would be funny if it weren't so sad. We both knew, without a doubt, we had to date a good church kid. For both of us, our faith had been so ingrained that a non-churchgoer was out of the question.

I was desperate to fill that gaping hole in my heart left vacant by Dad when I met Paul. To me, it felt like all Dad could see was the athlete I wasn't. With Paul, well, let's just say he wasn't exactly looking at my basketball skills.

He affirmed me in ways I'd never heard before. Before Paul told me so, I didn't know I was worth anything. I didn't believe my thoughts, dreams, desires, and goals mattered. Paul told me they did and encouraged me to run hard after them. I felt complete for the first time in my life. But, to be honest, I was so young and so naive that I would have listened to anybody who had come along at the time and told me what I wanted to hear. How do I know Jesus loves me? Because he sent me Paul when, as insecure as I was, I probably would have followed Jim Jones all the way to the Kool-Aid stand. The only two things I knew for sure were that Paul was handsome and he loved Jesus—like Tom Cruise and Ritchie Cunningham having a baby. For me, the conclusion was simple: Search over. I was smitten. Beyond weak-in-the-knees. Beyond cute teenage crush. I found myself *relinquished* to Paul.

Girl in the Pew

As high school marched on, the perfect script for my perfect life started to veer off the rails. I felt like the queen of Sheba when Paul would pick me up in his baby-blue vintage 1966 Chevy Chevelle every Saturday night and whisk me away for $5 prime rib at Mr. Steak. He taught me fancy things I thought only rich people knew—like how to order steak (I'd never eaten one in my life until dating Paul) and how to play golf. I taught him less costly things like how to appreciate music and see God in nature. He laughed at my incessant talking, and I loved having my own private listener. We'd sing all the wrong lyrics to Benny and the Jetts and debate which Michael was best: Jackson or W. Smith. Then we'd drive to some remote field south of Hudsonville, park the car on the tractor trails, climb in the back seat, and forget all the rules.

I went to Planned Parenthood to get put on birth control pills because my doctor, a Christian pediatrician, refused to put a child on the pill.

Yes, that nice churchgoing girl that sits next to you in the pew, who sings in the choir, who serves in Sunday school, who babysits your children, whose family votes a straight Republican ticket regardless of who's running or what they stand for, who despises abortion and marches in rallies against Planned Parenthood and who volunteers at the homeless shelter, well, she's got a dirty little secret. And believe me, she feels dirty. Yet every Sunday, she'll walk down the center aisle in her pretty pink dress and sit eight rows from the back, piano-side, and smile so brightly and confidently you'd never guess those deep, dark secrets, would you? And in the one place where she should be able to go and unload her guilt and confusion and struggles, she feels the most glaring condemnation.

That "she" was me. And that same "she"—writhing with pain as she hides her secret sin, whatever it may be—is sitting next to you in your church pews today. I guarantee it.

I believed our church and it's Reformed[3] tradition held the corner on all that was true and right in Christianity and everyone else just fell a little short. But that led me to believe we were the only Christians held to that impossibly perfect standard while also assuming other churches, denominations, and faith-practices just probably weren't as holy. Consequently, I believed people (me!) in the Reformed tradition were constantly letting God down and other Christians were awarded more mercy than we were. It would be many, many years before I discovered, with great relief, this false Christian "gospel" which overemphasized morals and underemphasized God's redeeming work actually saturated most of the American Christian culture in the eighties and nineties—Catholics and Protestants alike. Many teen girls, like me, suffered for decades under the weight of a Christian culture that offered us an insufficient and unbalanced view of sex and prioritized purity above all else.

For me, being a churched female teen in the eighties sucked. I loved my guy. I really did—at least as well as a fifteen-year-old knows how. And since I never once doubted his love for me, our relationship had simply blossomed like all romantic relationships eventually do. But with every single youth group meeting and every single youth rally screaming at us how abstinence, purity rings, and safe boundaries are all God cares about (Go ahead, teens, snort your brains out with some premium blow! Just don't have sex!) and that obedience in this one area of our lives is what ultimately brings us closer to God, I could only assume I had let God down beyond reconciliation. *How could God love someone as despicable as me?*

Breaking Up

Paul and I dated throughout my four years of high school, but I got scared when he mentioned marriage. He had finished college, secured a sweet job, and felt ready to "settle down" just as I was entering college. I felt rushed. I had barely had a meaningful conversation with another boy besides Paul, let alone dated one. I had skipped dances, proms, class trips, and parties at Hudsonville High just to be with Paul and hang out with him at the local Christian college where all good Reformers, if they could afford it, attended. When I started college in our fifth year of dating (at the cheaper local public university where us less fortunate Reformers usually attended), I met many interesting young men—all who could have cared less that there was a boyfriend back home. I was more than just a little bit curious. I really wanted to—needed to—date other guys.

Two months after beginning college, I broke up with Paul and started dating like it was my job. The first time a guy started making a physical advancement toward me, an hour-long debate ensued in my head in the span of a few seconds. *Come on! Have some fun! Life isn't meant to be bound by rules! Besides, you're already forgiven. You are not the sum of your mistakes anyway. Live a little!* But also: *There's a better path. And you know it. Your parents weren't crazy. They were* right! *They emphasized the dangers of promiscuity because it's that* destructive! *Don't do it. Don't let them and everybody else down.*

In those critical, life-changing seconds, after hearing the defense and the prosecution, my closing argument to myself went like this: *What does it matter anyway? You're already ruined, damaged goods. You've already let God and the whole world down, and that can never be undone. You've already sealed your eternal destination in hell and you should have been honest about that and flushed that purity ring down the toilet years ago. Besides, who will ever know, anyway?*

I cried myself to sleep that night. And I remember thinking, *Well, God knows. God knows what I did.*

All a Blur

I was certain I was now a slutty girl like those I'd judged in high school. In my growing-up, black-and-white Christian world, there were only two kinds of girls: good and bad, and I had always been the good girl. You were either in or you were out—and I was always in. I had completely justified a sexual relationship with my Paul because I was sure we'd marry one day. It never dawned on me that sexual impropriety with him might someday be problematic. I never even considered that perhaps those bad girls I'd judged in high school were perhaps working through their own woundedness. My view of sin, God, and damnation left no variation for woundedness. You did not get a pass or even a smidge of leniency for things done to you like childhood trauma, abuse or neglect, or even growing up in poverty. I wholeheartedly believed the Republican mantra: "You make your bed; you lie in it," which suggests we're all solely responsible for our outcomes. I was not taught empathy for those lacking my same extensive privileges presenting me with a huge leg up on favorable outcomes. To me, there were sinners and there were good people. Sin is sin is sin, and bad sinners deserve hell. That's just the way it is.

I still wanted to be a follower of Jesus, but was so deeply wounded, confused, lost, and lonely. All I could feel was shame and condemnation. I was doing bad things—the things I had been taught were the worst—and God felt extremely far away, if present at all. I felt as if I now had no choice but to stay in the camp of the condemned. I didn't know who to turn to for help in this dark season of life. There were still many people in my life (outside of college friends) who should have been safe and whom I could trust and rely on for acceptance and forgiveness. And yet, I didn't believe, nor did I feel, they were safe.

Though no one knew what I was going through, by the sheer nature of all that had been taught to me and said to me over the years, I felt condemned by all of them.

I turned to alcohol to escape the guilt of my promiscuity. It's not like I hopped on the Betty Ford freeway or anything, but I did try a few onramps. Many weekends were just a blur from all the partying. I worked weekends as a nurse's aide at a local nursing home. I remember dragging my butt into work the morning after partying and popping Ibuprofen all day long for my hangover headache. Mondays brought heaping loads of self-condemnation, followed by more self-loathing. Hanging out with new friends who didn't judge me helped a little. They were all behaving badly, so it lured me into believing our sick behavior was not sick at all. We mocked the kids who wouldn't have fun like us—kids like the former me.

A former honors student, my grades were plummeting. I hated everything about me, but I repeated my new narrative over and over hoping I'd eventually believe it: *Life is supposed to be fun! Be wild! Be crazy! Drinking just makes life exciting! You're the life of the party now! Don't sweat it!*

I knew in the back of my mind that this narrative was untrue, and I was torn and confused. I thought about dropping out of college to escape it all. I thought about moving to Colorado (mountains seemed like an appropriate challenge) and starting life over. I thought about just running . . . running, running, running as far away as I could get from me.

My Atheist Democrat Roomie

I had two roommates in college. One was my longtime friend from high school, Mary, and the other was our new friend from the east side of the state, Shawn. Mary was a solid student, every coach's dream athlete, and a loyal friend. Mary only ever had one steady boyfriend whom she would later marry. I had no doubt Mary would have my back in a crisis. Shawn was a wild child, who liked to drink, smoke, and chase the boys. She was from the east side of Michigan—the blue side. People now think of Michigan as a purple state and that's because my side—West Michigan—is red. Really red. It's so deeply red, so densely Christian, and so conservative in West Michigan that it is often referred to as the "Bible belt" of the North. I once read that our county is the most philanthropic county in the whole country. In our town of Hudsonville, we pray in the public schools, we pray at city meetings and everyone at the local Panera Bread is either praying, having coffee with their preacher, or plotting how to convert non-Christians. Our prayer meetings hold prayer meetings.

Shawn comes from the more eclectic part of our state, where great corporate wealth exists side-by-side with hard-working automotive industry employees who have come from all over the globe. Unlike my side of the state, on Shawn's side they don't make the joke that there is a church on every street corner. Shawn's dad was some kind of big deal in the car industry, so Shawn was a rich, alcohol-loving Democrat who didn't go to church. Shawn was basically everything I wasn't.

When I freaked for a day about the possibility of being pregnant, logic told me to talk to Mary. But my fear led me to Shawn. One thing I knew about Shawn—as someone who didn't live with a lot of "Thou Shalt Not's" in her life—she wouldn't judge me. After class on a fall, football-weather kind of day, I practically ran across campus eager to talk to Shawn, who was waiting for me back at our apartment. I needed to be freed from my secrets before they ate me alive. I confessed everything to Shawn and told her of my fear.

"Cindy! Are you serious? *You?* Who? When? How? Okay, I know how, but *you*? Really?" Shawn was as shocked as I was.

I crumbled and burst into tears. The sound of my confession and Shawn's response made the awfulness even more real. And my atheist Democrat roomie ran to me, enveloped me with open arms, and I soaked her white Bob Marley t-shirt with tears and black mascara. I poured out all the details to her—the guilt, the shame, the regret—but most of all the terror of an unplanned pregnancy. I grabbed Shawn's shoulders and violently shook her while insisting I could not, would not, would never, ever, *ever*, be able to have a baby now, and no one must ever know. Ever. "I don't think you understand how this is life and death for me. It's just completely unacceptable for me to be pregnant. No one in my family or church gets pregnant out of wedlock. Especially me. Do you hear me, Shawn? No one can ever know about this!"

"Cindy, it's gonna be okay," Shawn reassured me. Like a mother consoling her child who had just run out in front of a car, she stroked my head and said, "It's okay. You're gonna be okay. I love you. You're still a good person. Really. It's okay." I felt so known and loved in that moment and finally, for the first time in a long time, I felt safe. Shawn truly cared for *me* and wanted to help me navigate perhaps the biggest mistake I've ever made in a way that preserved *me*. I clearly remember thinking: *I probably need to reevaluate my beliefs about Democrats.* And then she added this: "I'll take care of you and make sure your life isn't ruined. If it's true, I know of a great abortion clinic in Detroit. I'll take care of everything, and no one ever needs to know."

No one. Will. Ever. Know.

It turned out I wasn't pregnant. But the truth doesn't change because of that fact. The truth—one that so many of us lucky girls will never confess—is this: I would have had an abortion had I been pregnant. No doubt about it. For someone so emphatically pro-life, I was also emphatic that a baby at this point in my life—from a virtual stranger, no less—would have been the death of me. Because I was also very pro-my-life. I never had an abortion. But I get why some girls do. I still believe abortion ends a life and grieves the heart of God. But I get why some girls feel "One of us must go. There's no possible way forward for both of us." I would have rather died than face an unwanted pregnancy and tell my dad, my pastor, and my community. I know it was only a twenty-four-hour span or so, but that's the most suicidal I've ever been in my life and it was utterly terrifying. I had even taken inventory of all the pills in our apartment and researched if they would be "enough."

In my world, Christianity, Republican, abstinence until marriage, and pro-life were like a polygamous marriage impossible to separate. I could not conceive that anyone would ever dare deviate from that foursome. Therefore, as someone who lost her virginity so young, didn't even stop with just one partner, and even contemplated abortion, I felt as if I'd descended into the next level of Dante's inferno.

To this day, I'm still not certain how I shut down my Charlie Sheen alter ego and found my way back to me. If I had to guess, I think God heard the prayers of my mom and Paul's mom—two people who actually pray when they say they're going to. I certainly wasn't praying for myself. I also just grew weary of hangover puking in our apartment toilet we never cleaned. I got tired of wiping saggy, elderly butts at the nursing home on weekends and watching that hard-earned paycheck get flushed down the tuition toilet as I nearly flunked out of college. I got tired of casual dating and wondering if guys really did have only one thing on their mind. I was also so very, very tired of self-hate. It's so exhausting.

Miraculously, I just decided one weekend to stop drinking. I never learned to like beer, so as my funds ran low and beer was all a poor college kid like me could afford, some of my motives to stop drinking were financial. On the heels of that decision, I also stopped chasing guys. I finally realized those two things were absolutely murdering my grades. I'd dreamed of being a nurse my entire life and the thought of flunking out of college gutted me. Before long, I was back on the Dean's List. Soon after that, I found a sweet new job as a phlebotomist at our city's biggest hospital. In a matter of a few weeks, hope returned, and I felt the former, truer version of myself reemerging. A few weeks after that, I made the best phone call of my life. I called Paul.

Wounds

I'd never stopped loving Paul—but clearly needed a whopping dose of maturing before I could understand him. It was a world-class miracle he took me back. I still can't believe it, and I still lose my breath when he walks into the room.

We faced a colossal problem, however. Paul lived in another city about an hour away during my freshman year of college and so we had had minimal contact. He had no idea what a train wreck my life had been during that year. And I never told him. When we started dating again, I knew I'd need to reconcile my past, so I immediately began asking God for forgiveness figuring that should do the trick. Of course, God forgave me, but it was more complicated than that.

My life turned into a washing machine: Wash. Rinse. Repeat. Over and over and over I would confess, and God would cleanse me of the evil that haunted me. I believe God heard me, and I believe God forgave me, but I just couldn't believe I'd become clean. I couldn't *get* clean, I think, because I refused to fully *come* clean. Sometimes cleansing requires more than just a confession to God.

I could not find the strength to confess to Paul. The enemy of our souls wanted to keep that little secret in the dark, so it would grow into a wound too big to heal. I now know a secret between spouses can never result in good. Never.

August 22, 1986—Paul and I were married and I'm not being melodramatic to say it was the happiest day of my life. However, to get his approval for marriage, we had to look our Pastor squarely in the eye during our premarital counseling session and promise him we were virgins. He would have refused to marry us otherwise. On the way back to our car after that meeting, I asked Paul how he felt about lying to the pastor. He tried to comfort me by saying, "You know, I think it would be more of an issue if we weren't actually marrying each other. Since it's always been just you and me, I don't think it's a big deal."

He had no idea how his words stung me because he knew nothing of my big deal.

When the bridal consultant presented an ever-so-slightly-off-white wedding dress and suggested I'd be on the cutting edge of style with it ("Pure white dresses are so blasé," she said), I knew it was the dress for me. It was beautiful, for sure, but I dared not wear pure white, anyway. I just couldn't shake the condemnation. It was such a subtle deviation in color that I secretly hoped no one would notice.

On the day of our wedding and only a few short hours before the ceremony, I was walking up the basement steps about to enter the sanctuary for photos when our pastor met me, grabbed me by the arm, and pulled me aside with an uncomfortable force.

"Cindy," he probed, with an unsettling sternness in his voice, "I'm sorry to confront you with this now. But it's crucial that I know the truth. Why aren't you wearing a white dress?"

Again, I looked that man in the eye and lied: "It means nothing, Pastor. I thought off-white was simply more elegant and looked better with my skin tone. That's all." So the wedding happened and people gushed over us and told us weird things like we reminded them of Cinderella and Prince Charming, or a Precious Moments figurine, or a wedding cake topper. We were Hudsonville's little darlings and, I guess, because everyone kept saying it, we were living the dream.

But our marriage began embedded with lies. There were wounds and hurts done to each other and wounds and hurts done apart from each other. But wounds are something our families and church community just didn't discuss. We're better at pretending we don't have any, covering them up with unnaturally white smiles, and overcommitting at church. And yet, as is common knowledge in Nursing 101, when you keep wounds covered and hidden in the dark, they grow and fester and become full-blown infections. I didn't realize how imperative that knowledge of wound care would be to understanding the infectious, destructive wounds caused by keeping hidden sins. By undisclosing my past to Paul, I caused far, far more damage than if I'd brought it into the light and just dealt with it.

For twelve years we thought we had a great marriage. For twelve years we thought we were killing it even though, at times, we wanted to kill each other. We thought we were good Christians living a decent enough life. We thought that as long as we went to church, tithed a bunch of money, and kept a dusty Bible on the bookshelf, we were at least keeping up with the status quo. But in reality, the lies at the foundation of our marriage had created a chasm between the two of us and between us and God. Every year we'd give more and more of ourselves at church, but were actually growing farther and farther apart from God. We were not okay. We were not whole and healthy, but just couldn't see it.

I didn't know it at the time, but wholeness requires one to deal with their whole past.

God began the unraveling of my perfect, tidy life by yanking me halfway around the globe.

CHAPTER 4

My Mother-in-Law May Be a Saint, but She Ain't No Sherwin Williams

*"Many a small thing has been made large
by the right kind of advertising."*

MARK TWAIN

In the early years of our marriage, I worked as an RN in the intensive care unit (ICU) at the biggest, most prestigious hospital in Grand Rapids. We were a proud gaggle of bad-ass nurses caring for the sickest patients in West Michigan: abdominal aortic aneurysms, triple bypass surgery, gunshot wounds, life-threatening injuries from car accidents. (ICU nurses, by definition, are a little—okay, a lot—cocky.) Our patients were often in that liminal space between life and death, requiring constant bedside attention. We rarely stepped away for bathroom or meal breaks, let alone socializing.

It took me off guard when out of nowhere, a Christian coworker whom I'd never really taken the time to know, approached me and asked if I'd be interested in going on a short-term mission trip to Germany. Would I? Would I ever! It wasn't the mission trip part that excited me so much as the chance to see Europe! The purpose of the trip was simply to provide childcare at a missions conference. Every other year, church-planting missionaries from all over Europe gathered in Germany for a five-day conference where they received encouragement, shared experiences, and received a little reprieve from their kids. My friend, Annette, and I would provide five days of programming for the twenty-five or so youth ages thirteen to eighteen.

Our team of ten women from Michigan would travel together first to Black Forest, Germany, for the conference, spend a couple of days touring Germany, and close out our trip with a few days in the Netherlands. I had always wanted to see the Netherlands, our family's homeland, as both sets of my grandparents were first-generation immigrants. I simply thought this trip seemed too good to refuse. Without a single prayer I told her: "Sign me up!"

I had no idea what I was getting into.

Something grabbed hold of me that first week in Germany. Something reached down inside of me and pulled and nudged and jabbed and twisted. It was so very strange for me to experience this invasion of a part of me that I really like to control all on my own, thank you very much. But I couldn't help being drawn in.

All these years later, looking back at this time, I think I know what happened: Someone took it seriously when I asked five people to pray for me on this mission trip. Back then, I thought when people said they were "praying for you," they meant it about as sincerely as when we run into an acquaintance at the grocery store and blurt out, "Hey! How are you?" We don't really want them to answer the rhetorical question and would prefer them to just roll that shopping cart right on by. I didn't know people meant it when they said they'd pray for me!

I never expected the trip to Germany to rattle my world so profoundly. I naively believed it was going to be just a trip to Europe. I was blindsided by the spiritual maturity of the kids we served and was utterly unprepared to lead them. However, partnering with Annette made it less scary and together we rose to the challenge. We'd stay up until the early morning hours with these kids and discuss esoteric questions I'd never before contemplated. Questions like:

- How can I know the voice of God in my life? How do I know it's not my own inner voice?
- Do you ever feel overwhelmed with all the demands on your life that you think some of them may be from Satan? (Is being busy a sin?)
- Do you think non-scriptural ancient texts have things to teach us about God and shouldn't we be studying them too?
- Does God's will for my life have to be the same as my parents?

Although I'd attended church my entire life, I'd never sat in a circle of friends and talked about God. My whole Christian community—family, friends, church—were much more reserved with their faith and we just didn't talk about spiritual things. We didn't pray together (save the token mealtime and bedtime prayers), and we never talked about the beliefs, fears, and doubts surrounding our faith. We just knew we were all Christians—as far as our little eyes could see—and that was that. Nothing to discuss.

I had always believed the sum of my faith was a singular verbalization of "I believe," and that got me in. After that, there just wasn't a need to talk about it. I said the prayer. My salvation was secure. I simply knew that some glad morning this life would be over and I'd fly away to a shore someplace in heaven— hallelujah by and by! What did it matter how I lived now? Why did we need to talk about it?

I remember staring into the big brown eyes of our days-old firstborn child and thinking, *Wow! How I've previously underestimated and under-experienced God! I had no idea life could be this rich—full of all these new thoughts, feelings, hopes, dreams, and wonder.* Every night in Germany, similar thoughts whirled around in my mind. Although I've always loved travel, challenges, and new discoveries, this was different. This was the deep down change that occurs when you meet people who open you up to a whole new way of viewing the world and God and you absolutely know that both now and forevermore you will never be the same.

Calling Home

Midway through our week in Germany I was finally able to make a long-distance phone call to Paul after several days of failed attempts. It'd be many years before anyone heard of Skype, Facetime, or Zoom, so when the phone call finally went through, I started to cry. It was so good to hear his voice. I know I started rambling on and on about this surreal experience and these incredible kids. I was finally in Europe! *And these kids— these amazing kids—they talk to God like he's here in the room! I don't even know how to pray with them . . . They're so smart! They speak foreign languages and know more about politics, geography, and religion than I do . . . did I already tell you how amazing they are?*

And somewhere in our conversation, I must have paused to take a breath, and Paul said he had a couple of important questions for me regarding our house. *Oh yeah—back to my American reality—we're in the midst of building our "dream house." I almost forgot.*

I think there was something about the central sound system (I wasn't really listening) that needed clarifying from me. Then he asked if I'd be upset if his mother changed our interior paint color. We were nearing the end of this arduous building journey, and had reached the painting stage. Before leaving for Europe, I picked out all the paint for every room and figured no decisions would need to be made until I returned. It probably would have been less scary for Paul to tell me the whole thing burned to the ground than to tell me that his mother thought the paint color I'd chosen was too light so she "darkened it up a bit."

Perhaps it seems like a minor misdemeanor—but for me, the queen of the building project, someone overruling one of my decorating decisions should have been a criminal offense. For the past year, I looked like a homeless gypsy living out of her SUV with the entire back seat and hatch loaded down with carpet and tile samples, paint samples, furniture fabric swatches, and wood-stain samples to ensure no matter where the day would take me, I'd be ready to make seamless decorating decisions. I even drove hundreds of miles all over West Michigan to find the perfect black kitchen light fixtures and the exact bisque-colored toilets to match the spectacular bathroom wallpaper. For a year, I never left home without my house binder which had become more precious than my

Bible as it held hundreds of magazine clippings that captured the look I wanted, contractor conversations and quotes, and years of designing notes from touring the Parade of Homes. I obsessed over making sure this home flowed in every sense of the word. In my mind, I hadn't missed a detail and had no doubt my paint colors were on point.

Worth noting here is that my mother-in-law was practically a saint. She was a dutiful, hard-working, loving wife and mother, and all who knew her commented on her gentleness and faithful prayer life. But, bless her heart, one thing my mother-in-law was never going to be was a guest at a Sherwin Williams design party. She was never going to see her home headlined in *House Beautiful*. And yet, while I was halfway around the world, she had the audacity to suggest to Paul that I had made an erroneous choice in paint color!

But that's not the incredible part of this story. This is: In the middle of the Black Forest in Germany in the winter of 1995, I clearly heard Paul's questions and yet, out of my mouth came this: "I could care less." It even caught me off guard—but still, I meant it. At that moment, the whole idea of a large dream home and the obsession of making it perfect, right down to the location of outlets, seemed like the most useless expenditure of my time and energy and life, and I truly didn't care anymore. I was exhausted from caring so much about a *thing*.

This may seem shocking, because it was pretty late in my life to finally have this thought, but I remember thinking: *People are probably more important than things.*

Paul was dumbfounded. Had he heard me correctly? As he was catching his breath from gasping, I repeated, "You guys just do whatever you want. It doesn't matter to me."

I felt as if I had slayed a dragon with that statement. It lay dead at my feet and finally, for the first time in nearly two years, I didn't have its fiery breath blowing in my face. I felt free.

Night Prayer

I tossed and turned in bed that night—sweating, freezing, somewhat nauseous in the German cold. I knew I wasn't physically sick. I finally got up and walked outside. Snowflakes peppered my hat, gloves, and coat and paused on my eyelashes before mixing with my tears. The entire landscape covered in a bright blanket of snow made it feel like someone had left a light on just for me. Perhaps someone had.

I wandered around the ministry campus for over an hour— the only sound was the crunch of the snow beneath my boots. I wanted to reach out to God, but didn't exactly know how. I didn't know if I was praying or just crying or if those two things are the same . . . *What have I become, God? What are we doing with our lives? Meeting these kids, learning to pray, finding you outside the borders of America—what are you telling me? Why does this experience feel significant and suddenly that new house, which was previously the most important thing in my life, doesn't? Has the dream house been a sort of place holder—just something we used to fill space in our lives because we lacked more meaningful and significant things to do? What if out of boredom, I made an insignificant thing significant? Do I make small things big things? Is that who I am? I wonder—are we created to need something significant in our lives, but when it's not there, we'll fill that hole with anything we can find? I wonder if these missionaries at this conference spend as much time thinking about houses and cars and vacations as I do. Are their lives so full of meaningful work there's no room for the wasting of time on little things? I wonder if they would have gotten as upset as I did over recent events in my life: like Josiah not getting the teacher I wanted, or the dispute with the lady at church who disagreed with me on daycare funding, or the coworker who gossips about me. Oh God! Did I make those little things big things because my life lacks depth?*

The crunching snow didn't answer me, but oddly, I felt heard for the first time in a long time.

It was only the beginning, but it was the start of a revolution. Paul and I were about to start our revolt against a lie the enemy had sold us: that the more money and the bigger/better/nicer things you have, the happier you'll be and that the pursuit of those things is a perfectly acceptable, even commendable way to spend the eighty or so years God gives you on this planet. The enemy of our souls had us convinced that filling our lives with small things (building houses, buying cars and cottages, exhaustive levels of kids' activities to ensure their success and college scholarships) was a good and full life, simply because we were busy. He had us believing that there was no room for bigger things (loving those unlike ourselves, for starters) because we were too busy. He had us believing, and our culture had affirmed it, that chasing after stuff and success and the subsequent elevation of our status was a worthy goal in life.

The revolution began with me that night in Germany, but just because I had some powerful revelations didn't necessarily mean there was an immediate transformed life. Those insights in Germany were merely the seeds.

But, apparently, I grow a slow garden.

CHAPTER 5

Death by Gravel

"Death is not the greatest loss in life. The greatest loss in life
is what dies inside us while we live."

NORMAN COUSINS

We did, in fact, move into our dream home just a few weeks after Germany.

Like all the good Christians around us, we consistently acknowledged that our achievements, our accumulating wealth, and our carefree and comfortable lives were entirely blessings from God.

However, a gnawing ache in our souls grew into a nagging question. A question no one else in our middle-class Christian circle seemed to be asking, at least not of us, anyway. We thought maybe we were going crazy because we just couldn't shake it: "I wonder what we might have been blessed *for*?"

It's seldom asked—by Christians, or anyone else for that matter—because the answer is implied: We've been blessed for *us*, of course. God insists we enjoy these blessings! And so Paul and I did. We set our dreams high, achieved them all, and then set out to repeat that lovely Christian phrase for the rest of our lives: "We're just so very, very blessed."

It's weird to be so young and saturated in blessings, yet not sure where to go from there. Upon acquiring our dream home, all our dreams had come true.

So what's left after that?

Set of Coasters

After considerable thought and sleepless nights, I concluded that since we'd now arrived, we were essentially left with three choices:

1. We could ask ourselves if perhaps we'd just been dreaming too small and then simply go and dream some bigger dreams. This would, most certainly, result in chasing after more, bigger, better, and faster things. Because there will always be someone to chase who has more, we could always just dream bigger.

2. We could ask ourselves if this is all there is to life. Maybe we could even ask God if there is more to life than all this chasing after stuff and success. What if we asked God our aching question: *What have we been blessed for?* We knew there had to be some brave souls who chose this option, but at this point in our lives, Paul and I had yet to meet them.

3. Or we could choose the well-trodden path of option number three. We could coast out the rest of life—just ride it out to the end. No challenges, no problems. Just all our stuff and us—oh, and lots of traveling, relaxing, and socializing too, but always busy, busy, busy. It would be the life Huxley prophesied for our culture in *Brave New World*—our utopia being a place of no worries, no need

to even think—just coast. Coasting would be weekends at the lake, Detroit Tiger games, John Mayer concerts, John Grisham novels, travel softball teams, blueberry picking, and picking our noses. And probably millions of other pleasurable things too. Always with pleasure. The phrases "something to do" and "just killing time" would be our mottos. And Jesus would be right there beside us, of course—folded neatly and tucked into our back pocket in case of emergencies like cancer or miscarriage or stupid neighbors who erect their privacy fence eleven inches onto our property. But really, we'll never have to put our feet to the pedals again. We're just coasting till Jesus comes.

For a long time, I lacked the courage to ask Paul what choice he would make. I didn't want to risk it. He had been asking the hard questions more and more frequently, and I was afraid he'd pick the second option. Deep down I wanted choice number three. I didn't want to jeopardize it by inviting his conscience into the discussion.

I still have no idea why, but God refused to let Paul and me remain a set of coasters.

Torrential Downpour

We've been living in the dream home for exactly ten days, and I love it more than I think I've loved anything (even the alternate paint color my mother-in-law chose has grown on me). I haven't entirely forgotten the transformation I experienced in Germany, but I mostly just keep it pressed down, hidden, and ignored. I want to enjoy our new beautiful home without guilt, so forgetting Germany would be best.

In our new, beautiful home, I feel wealthy, envied, and on top of the world. Who wouldn't want to feel this way? Everyone who comes over to see the house gives it glowing reviews: "You thought of every detail!" "Did you hire a professional decorator?" (I love this question because, no, I am the only decorator) "Who drew up this floor plan?" (Again, great question because, again, it's just me). But I do find myself making excuses for the things that aren't done yet: a paved driveway, a finished basement, and a barn. I tell people we just didn't have time to get it all done and that we're going to tackle those projects soon. Which, I decide, isn't a lie because whenever I (carefully) suggest these "add-ons" to Paul as necessary improvements to our already perfect home, I know he'll agree to them anyway.

It's a cold and rainy Saturday, and Paul's working again. We didn't come by any of our wealth easily. No lotto winnings, no inheritance, no crotchety old neighbor leaving us millions upon her death because we were the only people who gave her attention and would occasionally bring her warm, homemade banana bread. No, none of that kind of fortune. Any financial wealth we had was a result of Paul's hard, hard work. Evenings, weekends, all four seasons, very little vacation. Accountants, especially of the public variety, work long, hard, relentless hours, which explains why I was parenting alone again on this particular Saturday.

I do not particularly enjoy getting groceries with both boys in tow. At three and five years old they are too big for the grocery cart but too young to trust they'll follow me closely. They ask for donuts, fruit roll-ups, and matchbox cars, and my overstressed brain can't take all the distractions. But we're out of everything, and it can't wait until Monday. After loading up the back of my SUV with a week's worth of food, we drive home in a torrential downpour. I turn onto our long, winding gravel driveway but don't make it very far. The rain has created a huge washout impassable by car. We have no choice but to make a run for it.

"Hey guys! What do ya say we run in the rain and call it our bath for today? We're gonna get ridiculously wet, but it's gonna be fun!"

We scream and laugh like toddlers experiencing the ocean for the first time. We enter the house totally drenched and giddy with joy. The boys shed their wet clothes and run to their rooms to get dry clothes, but I head back out in the rain to retrieve the groceries. After three trips up and down our long, winding driveway, I've finally retrieved all the groceries and proceed to put them away. When I'm done, I look outside to see if the rain is still destroying our driveway. It is. But at the washout area, I see my father-in-law's red pickup truck. Harvey, my seventy-year-old second dad, is out in the pouring rain digging a culvert so he can lay a large drain pipe underneath our driveway. I'm mortified. Harvey was diagnosed with multiple myeloma just one year prior. We rarely thought of him as sick because he was the healthiest looking cancer patient ever. But still . . . it's *cancer*.

I call Paul at work.

"Hey, hon. You'll never guess what your dad is doing. He's out in the rain putting a drainpipe in our driveway! I couldn't make it up our driveway today because of a washout and he must have watched me from across the field bring the boys and all our groceries up to the house in the rain. Not even twenty minutes later and he's here fixing it!"

"Gah! Dad! Why is he so darn stubborn? He knows I can do that! And I'd rather do it myself. But no, even with cancer, if there's work to be done, he's gonna do it! I guess we should just be thankful he's doing so well on this break from chemo that he's able to do things like this again."

"Yeah, I guess."

So I watch Harvey finish the culvert.

Harvey DeBoer

It should have been a red flag when we didn't see Mom and Dad DeBoer in church the next morning. They never miss church. We assumed they were visiting another church because that's the only excused absence in the church attendance world.

The blinking yellow light on our answering machine indicated we'd missed four calls while at church. Paul listened to the messages—they were all from his mother. They didn't make it to church because Harvey woke up with severe back pain. Paul and I rolled our eyes at one another. Of course. If you're seventy years old and you shovel gravel for hours in the pouring rain, your back just might hurt the next day.

But the second message left by his mom made us stop and pause. "Hey kids. I ended up taking dad to the hospital. He started breathing kind of funny from the pain. He doesn't look so good."

Within minutes, we had our faithful next-door-neighbor babysitter, Amy, walking over to watch the kids while we scooted off to the hospital. By the time we arrived, the medical team had already admitted Dad to the ICU. *Odd*, we thought. *ICU for a little back pain?*

We found our way to the ICU and immediately had a change of attitude. The doctors, nurses and technicians were frantically working on Dad—securing multiple IV lines, a urinary catheter, and a central-heart monitoring line. Mom was in the corner, clutching Dad's coat and shoes, skin pale and gray, looking smaller than I remembered her to be. One of the residents pulled us aside and explained Dad had sepsis, a systemic infection of the blood. The back pain wasn't only from digging the trench in our driveway but from an undetected kidney infection. About a month prior, Harvey's oncologist had put him on steroids to carry him through the weeks of suspended chemo. Steroids are notorious for making one feel extremely energetic, strong, and invincible. I get why professional athletes are drawn to them. Steroids had completely camouflaged Harvey's brewing kidney infection. The resident explained Dad was about to be intubated, so we needed to take a quick moment to say hello, but then we needed to give the team space and step out of the room.

Dad's eyes were huge. He looked scared, and Harvey DeBoer is never scared. He gripped Paul's arm so tightly, he left marks. We told him we loved him and we would be right back as soon as the ventilator was comfortably assisting his breathing.

We never saw Dad alive again.

He died from septic shock and shoveling gravel in the rain. It was 12:21. A palindrome number. No matter how you look at it, forward or backward, it's still the same. Harvey's sudden death felt like that—a palindrome we desperately wanted to write another way, but it's impossible. Forward or backward, it's death. We stood in the hospital hallway for what seemed like hours, trying to make sense of it. We didn't want to leave. If we left, that made it real.

Driving up our long winding driveway, Paul and I didn't need to say a word. Our smooth driveway with its new culvert screamed at us like a bullhorn evangelist on a street corner: "Idiots! You spent the last year of your lives thinking about nothing but this house. REPENT! The one person who was the proudest of your accomplishments just literally laid down his life so you wouldn't have a washed-out driveway! REPENT, you sinners!"

We were ten days into living the dream. Ten days of people telling us how #blessed we were. Ten days of feeling on top of the world because we had a newer, bigger (perhaps the biggest?), nicer (perhaps the nicest?), and more beautiful (perhaps the most beautiful?) house than most people our age and most others in our lives. Ten days of believing we had found true happiness.

But now. Now? The same feelings I had in Germany came flooding back. This house, once again, suddenly means nothing to me. I might even hate it. Now? I'd gladly take a single-wide in the local trailer park if it meant we could have Harvey back.

We laid in bed arm-in-arm the night of Harvey's funeral—the pungent smell of fresh paint still thick in the air of our two-week-old home. Our crisp four-hundred-count sheets that matched our duvet that matched our paint that matched our carpet suddenly felt cold, grating, and unwelcoming. Only a few nights prior I had lain in this exact spot and reveled in the luxury—so proud of our new home that felt like a five-star luxurious hotel or an upscale Sandals resort. Tonight, it felt like a stranger—someone who lied to me and betrayed me. Someone who told me I'd be happy here. And now I never knew greater sadness.

Paul's salty tears rolled down onto my face. He so rarely cries. My broken heart didn't know how to comfort his. I wanted to say something healing and hopeful, and my mind was reeling with possibilities. I chose silence. There were no words. There's nothing to say to make sense of a father/husband/grandpa/brother dying way too soon. There was no denying we all needed him here on earth, but God said, "No. I'm taking that angel to join me now."

After a long stretch of silence, Paul said this to me: "What's the point of all this, anyway? I mean, why do we work so hard? What in the world are we here for? It feels like life is like a train ride. Sometimes people hop on. Sometimes people hop off and the rest of us keep going. And no matter how hard we try, we do not have any say as to when we get off the train. And yet, it seems to me, we do get to decide how fast we want it to go. Why do we insist on riding the fast train, Cindy? Always trying to get somewhere faster than everyone else? What are we doing with our one life, and could we possibly be missing something because we're going too fast?"

His words hung in the air like a thick fog. I think we both had some ideas to answer his rhetorical questions but were afraid to say them out loud. After an unbearable silence, we contemplated the meaning of life and wondered if we were close to the mark or missing the target entirely. We posited that if life is just a game to see who gets the farthest ahead, experiences the most successes, and has the nicest stuff, well then, we were doing fairly well and might even be winning. But then we agreed that on the day you bury one of your parents, it feels like an utterly stupid game to play.

We had just spent nearly an entire year—the last year Paul's dad was on this earth—completely engrossed in building a house. We had just spent all our time, money, and energy for a year on a freaking thing—but now, a person—our dad, for goodness' sake—is gone forever and we're well aware there are no do-overs. We pleaded with God and said if we'd known Dad was going to die, we wouldn't have wasted so much time on such a foolish pursuit. But who can know these things? How can we ever know if we're poor stewards of our limited time in this one precious life if we're never told just how much time we actually have?

Between sobs, I eked out a prayer for the two of us:

"Dear God, what are we doing here? What's the purpose of this life anyway? How is it that we do not know the answer to that question? God, you gotta show us. You just gotta. We feel so lost right now and we cannot continue living this way."

For weeks we moped around worse than a couple of teens who had just broken up. We were disoriented and unable to make decisions. We were devastated by Paul's dad's passing, but it was our conversation on how we were spending this one chance at life that haunted us.

No matter how many times we'd say it—"People are more important than things"—the truth is, we weren't living it. We continually found ourselves spending the bulk of our days buying things, taking care of those things, talking about buying the next thing, or pushing ourselves harder to just, you know, "get further ahead," whatever that means.

The passing of Paul's dad convicted us that we were not living what we said we believed. We just lacked the courage to do anything about it.

The Last Thing List

How can such a stinging revelation lose its potency so quickly? Like eating a whole cake only a week after signing up for Weight Watchers, we far too rapidly forgot the conviction Dad's passing had made upon us. It affected some random choices and actions for a few weeks, maybe a few months at best. But then we forgot, and everything went back to the way it had always been.

Merely six short months after Paul's dad died, I thought the 2,200 square feet of our main level felt tight and began plans to finish off the lower level to double our living space. We finished off the lower level and spared no expense: home theater, second kitchen, custom window treatments, and new furniture. I felt some temporary euphoria because, yes, of course, four thousand square feet felt more like the size of home we deserved. *Most definitely this was good and right. Successful people should live in at least four thousand square feet.*

I thought I had reached my final "need" and now our home was truly perfect and now I'd be happy forever. But then . . .

Just a few months later, we were in the midst of an abnormally hot and humid Michigan summer. I wanted a swimming pool in the worst way and justified it six ways to Sunday. A swimming pool would unite our family, bring us closer to our friends, provide an excellent backdrop for parties, and keep our kids strong and healthy all summer. I *knew* all this to be true so there was no way anyone could have convinced me otherwise. We could afford it. I wanted it. And it would serve us and others well. *Serving others! See God! See how I think about others?* What else was there to think about?

I remember the left side of Paul's face twitching a little when I suggested a pool. He said, "But we have a cottage on a lake! Cottage owners don't need swimming pools too." I launched into my hundred reasons why they absolutely did and barely let the guy get a word in edgewise. In the end, he had no option but to acquiesce. I was good at this. We put in a pool a month later. Surrounded by a huge deck. And new landscaping. And new patio furniture. Because, you know...

We both insisted that was the last project. Finally. Our house was complete. We were totally content.

That's what we said, anyway.

But we lied.

The last thing list continued to grow: a barn, a pond, a hot tub, those pesky transom windows in the sunroom that I still dreamed of, a split-rail fence around the property, a dry-walled and painted garage, a finished storage room above the garage, relocating our laundry room . . .

Greed and Grumbling

I remember hearing a sermon during this time about the grumbling Israelites in the Bible's Exodus account (Exodus, chapters 1–20) and why that story is so relevant for us today. God's people, the Israelites, were so miserable in Egypt, that they grumbled to God and begged for release from captivity. And so, after much ado (significant understatement) and assistance from Moses, they were finally released. You'd think they'd be so grateful. But no, within weeks they were grumbling because they were hungry. Then they didn't like the food God sent and grumbled some more. Then they grumbled for better water. Those silly Israelites had such terrible short-term memory! How quickly they had forgotten everything God had done for them. Our pastor pointed out that similarly Christians today are wont to forget all God has done for them and often spend more time grumbling than in thanksgiving.

Walking out of church that day I felt a little numb. I didn't want to be like the grumbling Israelites. I believed I was content. Er, I wanted to be content. I didn't like the feeling in my gut suggesting my life looked more like the opposite of contentedness. Truth be told, my life was practically a poster child for discontentment. As we walked to the car, it even felt like the sunshine was exposing me—like a spotlight announcing, "This one! This one here! Israelite! Israelite! Liar! Liar!" We climbed into our fancy car, and

Paul, in his sweet passive way, just had to ask, "What'd you think of that sermon today? Did you feel the same conviction I did about contentment?"

I fought back. I most definitely felt it, but I just knew I couldn't—wouldn't—separate myself from that beautiful house because other than that week in Germany, the few weeks after Paul's dad died, and now some random moments at church, the house just felt so right, so normal, so accepted, so good. I didn't want to give any credence to owning a beautiful house as problematic. So I said, "No, I don't really think we have an issue with contentment. I mean, I see people everywhere far more discontent than we are and amassing a whole lot more than we do. I think if we had to lay it all down, and give it up for some reason, we would. I don't think we're attached to our stuff, so I think that means we're content."

And then Paul gave one more short comment before we laid this conversation to rest, "But maybe . . . maybe if we were content, we'd just stop. Stop moving forward. Stop trying to have it all."

Nothing was solved that day. We drove the rest of the way home in silence and drove up the long, winding driveway to our big, beautiful house.

And I thought to myself, "I'd sure like a porch swing out on that wraparound porch. I picture it in black."

Unhealthy Home

On my more virtuous days, I'd reflect on my time in Germany and our conversation from the day Paul's dad died and suggest to Paul we might have bought a societal lie that suggests the pinnacle of a good life is a beautiful, brand-new home. I'd sometimes suggest we should sell the house and live more simply. I'd sometimes accuse the house of driving a wedge between us and God. Most days, however, I was far less virtuous. Because most days, I took an enormous amount of pride in our stunning new home and would conveniently forget what I'd learned in Germany and that it was this stupid house that killed Harvey.

There were times when either wealthy or important people were coming over, and I was thrilled to show off our impressive home. I wanted to fit in with that crowd, and a gorgeous home was really the only way they could see we were doing pretty okay. There was still a part of me that wanted to be perfect and have the best at everything.

Then there were other days—harder days—when certain other people were coming over, and Paul and I would struggle with embarrassment over that big white house. Embarrassment from having too much. We had spent so freaking much money on a thing, while some of our friends struggled just to pay their rent and feed their kids each month. It all felt so very wrong on those days. How could I face my neighbor who struggled to keep her kids in snow boots and, without even using words, essentially say to her, "I'm sorry I can't help you with that. I've got to have all this. I've got to have high ceilings and cherrywood floors and a home theater more than your kids need boots." We went from pride to embarrassment and back again.

We never landed in a place of healthy acceptance of that house. And here's the thing: I don't think we were supposed to land there. I don't believe that for us we could accept that house and simultaneously be healthy.

As much as we wrestled with owning that house, it took us a long time to figure out what to do about it. That place held some kind of magical power over us, and we just weren't strong enough to resist it. It's a powerful thing when the world has convinced you that being sick is normal.

But the foundation we had built our marriage on—wealth accumulation, status, success, and winning the race—was starting to crack. That was a good thing because it was built on sand, and if you had even a single gold star sticker after your name on the Sunday School attendance board, you knew that if the foolish man builds his house upon the sand, the rains come down and wash it all away.

We were going to have to start over. We were going to have to rebuild the very foundation of our marriage, or we were going to lose it all to the storms of life.

To wake us up, shake us up, and school us on building healthy foundations, God plopped my butt down at a pregnancy resource center.

CHAPTER 6

The Confession

"Not everything that is faced can be changed,
but nothing can be changed until it is faced."

JAMES BALDWIN

For all the wrong reasons, I decided to volunteer at a local Christian crisis pregnancy center. I believed all good Christian wives of accomplished husbands volunteered somewhere. I didn't care at all where I volunteered. It could have been giving tours at one of the city's art museums, serving on the board of the local symphony, or helping third graders with reading. I just needed to appear significant and impressive at the occasional cocktail party when conversation turned to philanthropy.

In my little world, Christian wives held certain status markers not unlike our Sunday School gold stars that helped us compare ourselves to one another: attend Bible studies 2.5 times per week, lunch at Panera Bread 3.5 times per week (each time with a different influential friend), shop 10.5 hours per week, and volunteer .5 days a week. I didn't need a paycheck, heaven's no! I had stepped away from my nursing career after child number two came along, believing this, too, brought me great favor with God. In fact, to me, having a paying job at the time would have made Paul look weak. So volunteering made us all look good. I liked the pregnancy center gig because I just knew abortion was wrong even though I couldn't explain why any better than that. So I figured, how hard could it be? I'd simply tell young girls in our city why abortion is so sinful (quite possibly the worst of all, for those ascribing to the same sin hierarchy of my upbringing) and save them from making such a tragic mistake. Never mind that I was totally prepared to abort my own child if I had ended up pregnant from some yahoo in college. That fact didn't seem to enter my consciousness.

Looking back, I shudder because I was that woman. The woman striving to be the perfect Christian—or at least desiring the appearance of one so as to convince everyone else. So plastic. So phony. So dang perfect on the outside. I was The Simpson's Mrs. Lovejoy. Dana Carvey's church lady. Dirty Dancing's disapproving nags sitting in the corner. Footloose's Reverend Moore.

Most Christians, like me, silently believe this funny little thing about teen sex, premarital sex, extramarital sex, and abortion: You're only guilty if you get caught. If you're one of the lucky ones like me, you can point your bony, little condescending, condemning finger all the rest of your life if you want to. No one ever has to know.

I walked into the Pregnancy Resource Center (PRC) for the first time on a brisk autumn day. Red and orange leaves blew into the foyer with me while the ubiquitous ring-a-ling of the ancient doorbell let the staff know I had arrived. My heart was pounding, but I couldn't fathom why. I told myself: *You're so meant to do this kind of work.*

I planned to be the volunteer nurse one day a week, figuring I'd tell all these scared and careless pregnant girls they must take their prenatal vitamins and, for heaven's sake, stop smoking, drinking, and using illicit drugs! However, when I called for my phone interview, the director said I'd still need to go through the counselor training as well because, she said, I would invariably be giving counseling services as well.

I arrived early for the first of three days of counselor training. I took a seat in the back of the room so I could size up the rest of the class and make fun of the Pollyanna do-gooders who had never sinned in their lives. A nun dressed in her full habit took a seat next to me. She surprised me—I wasn't expecting nuns. I didn't think Catholics did good works. The closest I had ever come to a nun was watching Sally Field play one on TV. I didn't know real nuns actually interacted with the world. I thought they just piously prayed all day at the convent.

With soft praise and worship music playing in the background, our instructor waited for us in the conference room. Cookies and bottled water were beautifully displayed at the center of the tables. I was softening up to the place. I generally like any place that serves good cookies.

After a brief introduction and a heartfelt prayer of invocation, our instructor began: "You know, I'm sure it's safe to say many of you are volunteering here because you believe that abortion is wrong. You believe you need to talk girls out of having an abortion, and you want to learn the tools to do so effectively. While we, as a ministry, do truly value the sanctity of human life, and pray that someday we will see an end to all abortions, there is something we value even more importantly here at the PRC: prayer. If Christ isn't at the center of all we do, we are nothing.

Without prayer, we have nothing to offer the women who come in through our doors and we have no hope to extend to them. And, of great importance, you need to realize that somewhere around 80 percent of the women who come through these doors will not, in fact, be pregnant. They often come for the free pregnancy test. We will be doing far more abstinence counseling than abortion counseling. Our greatest ministry is to love on these women no matter their story or circumstance and simply share with them God's plan for their lives, including a biblical approach to sexuality."

Busted.

My mind reeled out of control; I hardly heard anything after that. I began dreaming up lies to get me out of there and to find a way out of volunteering at this stupid, Pollyanna place.

All I could hear was my own condemning voice in my head shouting: *Hypocrite, hypocrite, hypocrite. You cannot possibly step into that counseling room and help young girls navigate issues like premarital sex, promiscuity, STDs, AIDS, etc. when your own sex life has been such an epic fail.* My dirty little secret suddenly grew a life all its own—head, torso, and long arms that squeezed me so tight I thought I might pass out. I knew at that moment I either had to kill that beast or it would kill me. I knew there was no way I could enter that counseling room and pretend to know about God's design for sexuality. The only thing I knew for sure was that I had done it all wrong. Miserably wrong. I would never want anyone to follow the same path I had taken because it was still, even twelve years later, causing me enormous shame, pain, and heartache, as well as creating a wedge in our marriage.

But I couldn't help but feel something supernatural had brought me through these doors, and something outside of myself kept me in my seat. Was it the nun sitting next to me? Do they have some kind of superhuman Jedi-mind trick powers? Why, of all the seats in this room, did she have to sit next to me? I suddenly had a strange thought: *What if . . . What if my past sexual sin and my understanding of the enormous fear of getting pregnant by someone I didn't love could actually help girls feel safe with me? Me, of all people. What if the perfect Christian middle-aged woman who saved her virginity until marriage, who never watches an R rated movie, who never listens to Nirvana, and who always votes a straight pro-life ticket no matter who the buffoon is, would actually struggle to connect with girls at this clinic? What if they felt more comfortable with someone a bit more, shall we say, seasoned like me?*

Would it? Could it, God? Could it be that my story might help someone else sort out their own story?

I experienced a flicker of hope. Maybe my wounds, sufferings, and mistakes can be redeemed. My heart raced as I wondered if I had been divinely appointed to be here, at the Pregnancy Resource Center in Grand Rapids, Michigan, at this time in history, with my own painful story, because God wanted to actually *use it.*

Seriously, God? Is this how you move? Can you take our worst pain and make something good of it?

But my very next thought was this: *If I'm going to take the plunge here—to dig deep enough to be vulnerable and share my painful past with these girls, I must first share my secrets with Paul. He deserves to know what I've been hiding from him all these years.* For twelve years my secrets were only shared between me, God, and my roommate Shawn. I had decided long ago that I would carry those secrets with me to the grave, believing I was protecting Paul. I thought loving him well meant not telling him. Even the thought of coming clean to Paul made me sick. All these years I had believed, wrongly, that I would simply die if Paul knew the truth about my past—and yet, the reality was, I was slowly dying by keeping it from him. I did not know our marriage couldn't be everything God meant for it to be because we were keeping secrets.

If I was going to find new life here and have any hope of helping the lives of these young girls, then I'd have to die to the old me—the me who was hanging on to lies.

Prayer Room

On the second evening of our training at the PRC, the instructor concluded the night with an exercise in contemplative reflection. On a large poster-sized sheet of paper she used her own life as an example and she drew a tree. She showed the path of her life as she grew up, the different branches representing different developments in her life. Then she drew one completely dead part of the tree—where no green existed—and she said this was her turning point, representing the time she was raped by her father's friend. She wept as she shared her painful past. And yet, standing before us was the most confident, beautiful, restored, and redeemed human being. Her testimony to God's miraculous work of healing and redemption brought every single one of us to tears.

Then came the assignment. We were to go off alone to a quiet space somewhere in the center and bring with us our poster paper. On it we were to draw something—a picture, a map, a diagram—anything that represented our own life's journey. We were to try and summarize where we have come from, where we are now, and where we believe God is calling us. Specifically, she wanted us to ask God how that personal journey had led us to the PRC.

I went off by myself and quickly headed upstairs. Everything was dark. During the daytime, this area was a bustling materials ministry where maternity clothes, diapers, and formula are given to women in need. Right next to the materials room there was a door. A door with the little plaque: "Prayer Room." *Poetic*, I thought. I walked in and walked right into the presence of God. Now, philosophically, I know God is everywhere. I know the meanings of omniscient, omnipotent, and omnipresent from all those years of Sunday school and catechism. But God was thick in that room—I had never felt anything like it before. I didn't realize it, but I was about to have an encounter that would change me forever, and just like Saul, I would be given a new name. First, like a dutiful schoolgirl with an assignment, I pulled out the sheet of paper to begin my life map. But I never drew a thing. Instead, an almost other-worldly force pulled me to the ground and for the first time in my life, I prayed from my knees. I just started talking at first—telling Jesus everything he already knew and about how this center and this instructor were really messing with me. Then I pleaded, asking what I was supposed to do. And I heard God's response. Clearly.

Years before *Eat, Pray, Love*, where Elizabeth Gilbert describes her transcendent experience at the Ashram in India, I was having one of my own in a little prayer room in Grand Rapids, Michigan—I just had no clue what it was. As my body shivered uncontrollably, I knew somewhere deep down in my soul what I was being told to do next.

I was alone and I'll never know if the Creator of the Universe had communicated to me audibly or not, but it was yet another moment when I could feel my answer. It was just like the time in my car when I wanted a new diamond ring. This time, the message God gave me was this: "It's time to leave this shame behind you. You already know what you need to do. You need to confess to Paul. It's the only way out, Cindy. And I will go with you." I can't say for sure the words came to me in that form or order, or if they were even in English. It was as if I aroused a new level of consciousness—a sleeping member of the crew on my life's ship just finally woke up and started talking. He had always been there, of course, down in the bowels of my ship, but I didn't know I could access him and thought I'd only have to wake him to quiet a life-threatening storm. But here God was, so very present even in this, *My Embarrassing and Atrocious College Sex Scandal.* And He wanted nothing more than to set me free.

I wept awhile, imagining Jesus holding my head. Then my head felt lighter, as if it really were being held up. *It's as if someone else is here,* I thought. I have no idea how long I was in that prayer room—it seemed like a flash, and it seemed like an eternity. It felt like I stepped outside of myself and outside of time and space and bounced around the galaxies for a while. It's not like I saw stars and planets and angels or anything like that—it's just that for a moment I didn't feel anchored to the earth, as if gravity had lost its pull on me. It was weird. It was other-worldly. And I knew I had been touched by the Father. That's all. I just knew.

I walked into that prayer room feeling as if "guilty" were tattooed on my forehead and would forever define me.

I walked out of that room feeling truly forgiven for the first time.

I returned to the conference room just as our group gathered in a circle for the final exercise of the evening. One by one, we took turns sitting in the middle of the circle and our instructor prayed over us. She shared positive and encouraging comments for each person. Things like, "Lord, you have made Sharon so passionate and yet so tender. May she use those gifts to your glory as she passionately loves the girls who come through these doors." Or "Father, God, you have brought Sister Karen to the PRC for such a time as this. May her commitment and devotion to you be a source of encouragement, light, and hope for each patron she ministers to."

I was the last person to take "the chair." The instructor, uncharacteristically, paused for like two or three minutes before praying over me, which turned out to not even be a prayer. She simply said this: "I hear the word of God for my sister Cindy. These are the words of David the Psalmist: 'Search me, O God, and know my heart; try me, and know my anxieties; and see if there is any wicked way in me, and lead me in the way everlasting.'" That was it. She quoted Psalm 139:23. That was her "blessing" for me!

I looked at the instructor incredulously and blinked away the tears. Was there any way she could have known my secrets? No way! She had only met me yesterday and we hadn't had a single private conversation. I had masterly disguised this nasty past of mine from my husband, family, church, and community for over a decade. There is simply no way she could have known without having hidden cameras in the center or reading my journals! I just know the Holy Spirit led her and I now believe he leads us all on a daily basis. After I got over being a little ticked that she didn't have anything glowing to say about my skill set or personality, I realized the Creator of the Universe had spoken to me again and I had better heed Psalm 139's injunction to search my heart, expunge my wicked ways, and get on that way everlasting!

Free at Last

Oddly (because I avoid confrontation more than even raw oysters), I couldn't wait to get home and get our kids to bed so I could come free from the bondage of my secrets and tell Paul everything. I knew it would be one of the most difficult and agonizing things I'd ever do in my life and yet, even as I drove home, I already felt the weight beginning to lift. It kind of goes against common logic, but I couldn't wait to finally tell the truth to the man I loved more than anyone else in the world despite knowing he'd be crushed.

As I type this story, I am sitting in the same comfy chair I was sitting in on the night I told him. I still remember exactly how I felt, and I remember exactly the color of his skin and the look in his eyes. To say the color drained from his face when I told him would be an understatement. He turned gray. Like a corpse. He looked as if he might pass out. Then his eyes welled up with tears. *God, how I hate to see (to make) this man cry!* Without saying a word, he got up from the ottoman where he had been sitting and walked away. He couldn't quite walk upright. It looked as if someone had punched him in the gut. I guess someone did. He walked down the hallway and then disappeared into the bedroom, and I just stayed in the chair I'm sitting in now, motionless. But I prayed. Pleaded. Confessed. Cried. Trusted. I trusted that if God had taken me this far—and I had absolutely no doubt he had—he'd be faithful to complete this story in his own perfect way. Come what may.

Just a few minutes later Paul returned to the family room. He knelt on the floor in front of me, grabbed my hands, looked me in the eyes, and said, "Cindy, I love you. I have always loved you and I always will. Nothing could change that. But I need to go for a drive just to get some fresh air, and I don't know how long I'll be gone. It may be ten minutes, maybe two hours, maybe all night. But I'll be back. I promise. And I really need you to know this." He paused, reached up, and cradled my face. "I forgive you."

Busted Dam

For the first time in our married life, we talked about our past and how sex before marriage may have brought some heavy and unnecessary baggage into our marriage. Together we acknowledged we had both made many poor choices that now, even twelve years later, were compromising our marriage. Paul wept as he acknowledged he should have been protecting my heart back in high school when, instead, he captured it and then exploited my vulnerabilities.

Paul's acknowledgment of that responsibility set off a new string of emotions for me that took many months to unravel. I slowly realized I'd buried my anger toward him all these years. Even though our teenage physical relationship was entirely consensual, I was so young, that what I had wanted—had really *needed*—was someone to protect me. I finally unearthed that anger for Paul, and his parents too, for not instructing him better. For years, I had lumped all that anger and blame on my parents for not prohibiting me to date and sheltering me from obvious sexual temptation. (Haha. Had they done that, I would have snuck out of our home and had sex anyway. No doubt about it).

Paul forgave me. I forgave Paul. I forgave my parents. I forgave his parents. And slowly, painfully slowly, I worked toward forgiving myself.

That part was the hardest. I think this is the primary reason our marriage was suffering. Growing up in my Christian bubble,

I knew by heart what the Lord requires of us: To love the Lord your God with all your heart, soul, mind, and strength, and then to love your neighbor as yourself. *But what if I don't love me, God? What if I actually hate me? Then what?*

Unwilling to forgive myself, I had unknowingly created a chasm where I was unable to truly love Paul. I had enough head knowledge about Jesus, love, kindness, peace, joy, etc., that I was able to act the way I thought I was supposed to toward Paul. But I couldn't feel the fullness of love toward him because I didn't know how to love people—not without loving myself. That night, on the big comfy chair, where the tears and confessions and anger and forgiveness all flowed, it was like a gigantic, life-size dam busted open, and the healing waters were finally allowed to flow over and consume us. When I learned to accept myself, my past, my wounds, my upbringing, and my family, I learned to love myself. Only then could I really truly love Paul.

I had always believed hiding my secrets was protecting Paul from the pain and everyone else who might be hurt by it. I certainly didn't want my guilt known by my husband, let alone our children, or pastor, or the kid who packs my groceries. I didn't want to share my sinful past! It took enormous amounts of courage, but then ultimately trust, to believe God truly did want us to "go there" and that He would help us through it all. It was the hardest work we've ever had to do in our marriage.

I can see now that God had been prompting and encouraging us for years to bring our lies and secrets out into the open— we just hadn't been willing. And I can also see now how our unwillingness created a barrier between us and God. It felt like God couldn't (wouldn't) use us to do the work of His will until we were ready to do the work of dealing with our past. Paul and

I had always wanted to be about loving others—we talked about it a lot anyway—but until that evening when the dam blew open, I don't think it was ever truly possible.

I wonder now if we're not able to truly see and know the others whom God has put in our path and honestly love them until we've experienced some kind of extravagant grace ourselves. Coming clean of my terrible past made a path for Paul and me to experience extravagant grace.

People ask us all the time what finally flipped the switch that would so radically transform our lives. There was never one thing—but transparency with one another was certainly integral. Years of harboring secrets kept us from so many great things God wanted to give us—a whole and healthy marriage, an open and honest relationship with God, a message to share with other teenagers struggling with the same stuff. We longed to be distributors of God's mercy and grace, but carrying around our own secret past laden with lies and coverups prevented us from doing so.

My involvement at the Pregnancy Resource Center not only transformed me personally, it also transformed our understanding of prayer and how to do it. We started to see prayer more like a conversation with God and something we needed for survival. After I confessed to Paul, for the first time in our marriage we began praying together every night at bedtime. And I don't mean those short, pithy, mealtime prayers or cursory thank-you prayers. I mean, we *prayed* together. We'd lay arm-in-arm and pour out our hearts to the Lord together, rejoicing, lamenting, requesting, beseeching, and thanking. One prayer at a time, our marriage was restored, and we went from a good marriage to a holy union. I had no idea marriage could be so beautiful and whole, and I had to grieve the years gone by when we had settled for so much less. I made a vow to myself and before God that I would not hold this story back from others if there was any way God could use it to help other young girls from making the same horrible mistakes I did.

I had finally, painstakingly, concluded that a life that is more about honesty than perfection is a richer, freer, and far, far better life.

Kennedi

I had only been at the PRC for a few weeks when Kennedi walked in. Her strong name matched her strong facade—a gothic dress hugging her tiny frame, black kohl-circled eyes, and piercings circled the entire rim of both ears. She followed me into the counseling room and slouched down into the chair, gaze fixed on the floor. As I tried my best to get her to open up, she became more and more agitated. She repeatedly flipped her phone open and shut and never once looked up at me. Finally, I asked, "Kennedi, why did you come here? What is it you're hoping to find?" She slowly lifted her head until her dark eyes met mine.

With an emphasis on every word, she said, "I. Have. No. Idea." She drew a long pause and those hurting eyes pierced me. Finally, she hissed, "I just need a f***ing pregnancy test. Okay? Can you cut through the bullsh** and just give me the f***ing test? You cannot help me any other way. You cannot 'counsel' me out of this situation. You will never know me. You sit there in your pretty clothes, and what are you, some perfect motherf***ing princess whose husband makes a ton of money, and you work here to appease your conscience? What do you have? Like three or four perfect f***ing kids? You got a big SUV parked out back too? Just like all the rest. I know who you are. You're a f***ing perfect middle-aged, suburbanite, judgmental Christian. I know who you are, and I hate you. I hate you and everything you represent. You have no f***ing idea what my life is like or who I am. You will never understand getting pregnant from someone you barely know, having no money and no job and parents who will kill you—I mean KILL you—if they find out you are pregnant. I would rather die than be pregnant and have to tell my parents. And: *I. HAVE. NO. IDEA. WHY. I. CAME. HERE!*"

It wasn't hard to recognize a lifetime of bottled-up anger and hate, now directed at me.

Kennedi was the daughter of a well-loved local pastor. She felt she could never be who her parents expected her to be, so she adopted a completely different persona and rebelled against every dream they ever had for her.

I took about five deep breaths and then took a risk. I said, "Kennedi, you're right. I can't imagine what it's like to be you. You're dealing with a lot. But if you'll give me a chance, I want to share my story with you. I am not who you think I am. And I am really hoping you can come to trust me."

I told Kennedi about my past, and how I could have so easily been her. I could have been pregnant by someone I didn't know well. I, too, would have been terrified to tell my parents—truly terrified of their response! I told her how lies and coverups had almost destroyed my life and marriage and that God never wants us to live in the darkness and bondage of lies. I told her I may appear to be the f***ing perfect princess (and yes, I said the f-bomb, because for one, sometimes words create connections and sometimes they create barriers—I wanted a connection, and for two, once I accepted that God's mercy was big enough to cover my promiscuity, I had great confidence it would also be enough to cover my little issue with expletives), but I hate that I appear that way from external appearances, because inside I am a huge screwup who's okay today only because of Jesus and His forgiveness. I told her about getting real, being honest, and receiving Paul's forgiveness, and how, after all that, I'm finally able to love and accept others.

Long silence. Phone flipping open and shut. Open and shut. Open. Shut. Finally, eyes still fixed on the floor, she said this: "So about ten years ago you were me, and you could have been sitting in this chair?"

"Yeah. I could have been. I should have been. I don't know where I would have ended up if I had found myself pregnant. I can only hope it would have been at a place like this and not in an abortion clinic. I can only hope that someone would have reached out to help me and spoke truth to me. Kennedi, I do understand your pain and confusion."

And then I saw the slightest tremble in her shoulders. A muffled sniffle. Eventually, all-out crying. I switched seats and positioned myself beside her so I could put my arm around her. She leaned in and we both cried. We talked about options and God and fear and forgiveness.

She took a risk with me because I was no different from her. I was not like many of the other women who worked here—the good Christian women who have it all together and the kind I'd always thought I should be. I just felt so far from perfect now but also finally free to say it. That little difference opened some doors in the hearts of these young girls in crisis, to which some of my counseling peers with less colorful pasts struggled to gain access. It was truth and honesty that opened doors, not perfection. Pure redemptive work.

I became very intentional about sharing my story wherever and whenever permitted, believing that must be how God uses pain.

The strangest thing for me was this: I couldn't share my story with my own family and certainly not with people at church. Every Sunday, Paul and I and the kids marched down the center aisle, and I assumed the role of the perfect mom whose husband rises up and calls her "blessed" and whose kids wear matching clothes and always have their Bible verses memorized. I looked and behaved exactly like I always believed was necessary, like someone who never sins. Statistics say that 80 percent of evangelical young adults have had sex outside of marriage and somewhere between 60 and 65 percent of all abortions are by Christians. By all appearances, my church defied those statistics. I felt like the only sinner in a room full of saints. I would look around at all the women in our four hundred plus member church and wondered if any of them had secrets that were eating them alive. I wondered if any had had abortions. I wondered if any had had affairs. I wondered if any of those women did anything outside of their marriages that their husbands didn't know about. I wondered if they would feel as free as me if they shared. But all I could do was wonder. I never mustered up the courage to ask a single soul those questions.

CHAPTER 7

The Fallacious Fake Ficus

"God wants every local church to be the first place people think
to go when they're really messed up. Not the last."

TULLIAN TCHIVIDJIAN

At the PRC I met a young coworker named Cara. Cara was at least ten years younger than me and at least twice as wise. Cara had been working at the PRC for a couple of years and was developing some significant relationships with a couple of our regular patrons who worked in the sex trade. Many times, these women came to our center simply for a free pregnancy test. This took serious courage because they would have to endure our mandatory Christian counseling and prayer. If you're not a Christian, or even if you are but don't like hearing you're wrong, those things can be brutal.

Over many months, Cara developed a real and lasting friendship with one such girl. Eventually, Cara, like the good Baptist she was, invited this girl to church. Even Cara was shocked when the girl said, "Yes, I'd like to go."

Cara wisely decided her conservative Baptist church might not be all that welcoming to someone who kind of "looked the part." Instead, Cara took her to Mars Hill Bible Church, a new church startup in our area. I don't know the specifics of what happened at that service, but the young lady went forward and in a puddle of tears, she accepted Jesus Christ as her Savior. She went home and told her boyfriend all about it. Later that same day, the two of them called Cara and asked if she would come to their apartment to talk about Jesus. With more than just a little trepidation, Cara went down to the toughest side of Grand Rapids and met the boyfriend at the door.

I remember how Cara described the incident to me: "Cindy, this huge bald guy comes to the door—shirtless and blowing cigarette smoke in my face. His multiple facial piercings and full-body tattoo took me so off guard, I didn't even know where to look. So I looked him straight in the eyes, shook his hand, and said, 'Hi, I'm Cara, nice to meet you.' He was curious about our morning church service and had a lot of questions about how it was possible his girlfriend felt so welcome at a church. I told him it was a very open church and all are welcome. I answered their questions for like an hour. Then, this guy, who I really think was the pimp, asks me if he too, could visit Mars Hill! Cindy, I about died!"

Cara loaded up the pair in her car and took them to that evening's service at Mars Hill.

A Different Kind of Church

When Cara shared this story with me, all I could think was: *I need to belong to a church like that. I want to go where everyone is welcome—even people as awful as me.* I know if you ask most churchgoers if they would welcome a pimp and a prostitute into their church they would say, "Yes, of course!" But the reality is that the crisply painted building, the perfect lawnmower lines, the steeple, the immaculate carpet, the stained-glass windows, the organ, the pulpit, the fake Ficus trees, the Saturday-washed fancy cars in the lot, and all the suits and dresses would not be all that welcoming. Before people like Cara's friends would even cross the threshold of a place like that, they'd be uncomfortable, feel out of place, and quite possibly judged. I am not suggesting those churchy things need to be abandoned, but I do feel we need to ask ourselves, what purpose do they serve? Especially the Ficus trees.

I longed to be a part of a community where anyone—pimp or prostitute, liar or cheater, trans/queer/cis, rabbi/priest/prophet, even good-girl-with-secret-sexual-past—are always welcome and free to be real.

Not coincidentally, friends of ours were attending Mars Hill. Although they were completely oblivious to our season of life, they decided to send us the weekly sermon tapes (yes, as in, cassettes—and if you're under thirty, you'll need to ask your parents). The tapes arrived every Wednesday which quickly became my favorite day of the week.

Since we spared no expense in building the dream home, we had the most amazing central sound system with speakers in every room. My life was transformed in our laundry room while I folded underwear and listened to Rob Bell teach from Leviticus. I had never thought of Jesus as a Jew before—but, of course, He was. It was the first time I ever heard Jesus referred to as a Rabbi. It was the first time that I can remember when Paul and I—and the kids!—would spend hours discussing the sermon and pulling out our Bibles to reread things we thought we already knew. Rob's teachings truly made us pause for introspection and we didn't particularly like what we found. All we knew is that we really did believe this Jesus of Nazareth, and we really believed the literal truth of every red-letter word of Scripture. The problem with believing all that is this: If you're brave, you have to ask yourself if your life reflects those beliefs. We mustered up some courage, and we asked. And it hurt.

We were not living what we said we believed. Something had to change.

The thing about Rob Bell was that he didn't care about stepping on toes. He preached the gospel straight up, but that sometimes cut deep and took us places we didn't necessarily want to go. Most of us do not exactly enjoy having our sins exposed and will do anything to keep our secrets and avoid uncomfortableness. So it was mind-blowing that despite sermons that made us squirm, every single week more and more people came. Weird how people will endure pain to hear truth. This upstart church numbered over two thousand attendees in mere weeks and was soon dubbed the fastest growing church in America. But for Paul and me, when something's trendy, it loses its appeal. So we were quite wary of jumping on the proverbial bandwagon. For several months, we only visited Mars Hill at their evening services to hopefully remain inconspicuous. But eventually it came—the talk about leaving our home church.

Not Good Enough

For people like us, living in such a conservative rural pocket, leaving your childhood church of origin is simply a moot issue— it must never happen. Our church was like Hotel California— you can check out any time you like (we "checked out" every single Sunday), but you can never leave. All our friends went to our church. Both of our parents went to our church, as well as my three sisters and their families. My grandparents had gone to that church. This is just the way things work in this town—you follow your parents' lead, you keep the faith, you stay the course, generation after generation. It felt, to me anyway, that our lives and our destinies were all very formulaic.

We had never, up to this point, even considered we might be an exception to the formula. Although we loved the people and the community, the fact that our dark past made us feel inferior also started to make us feel more and more isolated. I would sit in the pew Sunday after Sunday and think, "There is no one here as sinful as me. No one here knows the real me."

We finally braved visiting Mars Hill for morning services. Every week we'd hear testimonies of someone God had rescued from a wretched past. I never heard stories like that before. *I* had a wretched past. *I* had a story too! I so longed to be a part of a community where I could be authentically me—wretched, but loved. Sinful, but forgiven. A quote often heard at Mars Hill was this, "May those who come disturbed, leave comforted. And may those who come comfortable, leave disturbed" (Rob Bell).

We were also drawn to the church because dressing to impress on Sundays wasn't a thing at Mars Hill. We wore jeans. The whole "honoring God by spending thousands of dollars on clothes" just wasn't working for us anymore. I think churches are a lot like the shape sorter baby toy, where each yellow plastic shape has its own specific hole in the blue and red receptacle and no matter how hard you try, you cannot get the star to fit in the trapezoid. I think all the absurd things Christians have done in an attempt to separate ourselves—labels, locations, denominations, and music preferences—completely misses the fact that we all end up in the blue and red receptacle when the game is over. Paul and I decided it was better to go searching for the hole that fit our shape than stay outside the receptacle. Every shape is good. But recognizing your own shape is hard.

About a month after we left our church, we ran into a prominent man from that congregation, and he pulled us aside, "Hey, I heard a rumor," he said. "Is it true that you two have left our church?"

"Well, yes, that's true," we replied, awaiting the interrogation.

"What's the matter? You guys think you're too good for us now?" he said, half chuckling, but looking a little too serious for us to believe he was joking.

"Actually," I said, "We're not good enough." He didn't get it. But I wasn't about to explain.

And so we left the church both of us had attended since birth. Man, how we loved that place. We loved the community, the people, the rich heritage, and the hospitality that emanates so profoundly in small, rural, close-knit settings. But from everything God had shown us—from who we once were and what He was transforming us to be—we were certain He was asking us to move on. Sometimes, we've learned, it's necessary to leave behind a good thing not for what it is, but simply for what it represents. This monumental move in our lives marked the beginning of a long series of events where God asked us to be brave, to get uncomfortable, and to keep taking the next right step.

We just had no idea how far God was going to take it.

CHAPTER 8

Money Matters

"Honor the Lord with your wealth and
with the first fruits of your crops."

PROVERBS 3:9

DeBoer, Goodyke, Kahler & Tuttle, PC, CPA exploded into the business world with dizzying speed, accompanied by exploding earnings. For the first time in my life, I could shop with reckless abandon for whatever we (I) wanted. I mean, it was all ours, right? A blessing from God, right? We were tithing 10 percent (of course!), paying all our bills, and still had plenty to spare. It's funny how no one ever challenges overspending as long as you can afford it. American Christian culture told us it was fine to spend money on things we didn't need. That, Christians posit, is not overspending. It's only considered a sin if we spend money we don't have. Christians love to preach about money and spending, and they're not one bit shy about telling the poor what they're doing wrong financially, but they rarely confront the well off to analyze their spending habits. Paul and I felt completely justified in our materialism and over-indulgence. It was, after all, within our budget. Not a single soul in our wide Christian circle warned us that this is when money starts to create trouble.

It could be in Paul's DNA (since he's adopted, we'll never know), but initially, he wrestled with the question of what's the best-good-right thing to do with our money more than I did. Even though we had everything we ever wanted or even dreamed of at that point, it still would have been SO easy to justify more (a third home, say, in a sunny place) or bigger (moving upward to an even *more* impressive primary dwelling) or better (a fancier car perhaps—a BMW? Mercedes?), because, let's face it, there will always be another rung a little higher up the ladder.

Heaven knows why, but one day Paul came home and stopped me cold in the middle of chopping onions with this introspection: "You know, all my clients work so hard to make a living. Every single one of them is trading significant time and energy for their income. So I wonder, when they turn around and pay me for my accounting services, am I in some way accountable to them for how I spend it? I mean, if we could get by on less, shouldn't I charge less? Or, if that's not good or wise, then shouldn't we give more? How do I best respect my clients with the hard-earned money they compensate me with? Is it possible that overspending—whatever we define that as—is unethical because it devalues the person who worked so hard to pay me my fees?"

I felt a lump in my throat. It made a little too much sense. I wasn't sure I liked where this was headed. I knew we could live on less; I just didn't want to.

That's not the point, is it God? Why would we ever want to live on less? Isn't it okay to charge what you're worth in the service industry? Shouldn't we make as much money as we are able? Dear Lord, this is a panicky moment for me . . . If you're a good Republican like I think you are, don't you want us to work like dogs, earn as much as humanly possible, and stimulate the economy to a point where even those on the lowest rung of the economic ladder receive some nebulous benefit? You know, job creation, trickle-down, and all that stuff . . . As long as we're stimulating the economy, we can keep the excess, isn't that right? That's how it works, right God? Right?

Mistress Money

I always felt Paul's accounting firm wasn't charging enough. Their fees were lower than average, yet I knew their reputation as fair and honest accountants (not to mention good-looking) was above average. I looked at Paul's anguish and could see he was struggling with his epiphany.

Since we couldn't agree on what God was teaching us about our finances, Paul dealt with it by doing more pro bono work for pastors, missionaries, and families who couldn't otherwise afford accounting services. Still, he made a very decent income. It was definitely more than we needed, so I stayed drugged up on shopping.

To be honest, everything in our lives was bulging: our closets, our garage, our basement, our bank accounts, and our egos. I just didn't understand that unless you're Elon Musk, there will always be someone who has more. As soon as I believed we had everything I could ever want, I'd play the comparison game and discover someone who had more, which would remind me of that one thing more I just had to have.

I couldn't see at the time how cruelly seductive money is and how she winds her strong, slithering hands around our skinny throats in such a sensuous fashion, she makes us think we like being choked. No wonder Jesus spent so much time warning us about her.

Wild Souls

On a cold, snowy March Sunday, I pathetically whined to Paul on our way out of church. "How in the world can Sam and Becky afford that BMW? They can't make that much money! We certainly make more than they do! I don't get it!" My competitiveness was baring its ugly fangs. I wanted the nicest house in our area, the best husband, the best job, the best children, the best of everything. I was nearly winning on all fronts. But driving out of church, Sam and Becky won the competition of nicest car and this was not okay with me. I sunk my fangs into the narrative as I droned on about how two college educated professionals certainly earn more than two laborers who didn't even have letters behind their names. Paul made some little comment under his breath about how I would be shocked if I saw the W-2s he sees. I pushed him a little—wanting to know more about the W-2s he sees. But Paul is nothing if not trustworthy and would never divulge even a hint of confidential information.

Back at home with the kids distracted, Paul cornered me in the kitchen. He seemed too serious for a kitchen talk, but leaned in and said, "Cindy, things are not always what they appear to be. I know that probably better than anyone. I get a front row seat to the reality of people's finances. W-2s don't lie. I'm not suggesting this is the case with Sam and Becky, I don't know their situation and I don't care. I just know many times what you see is only a smoke screen." He explained that, interestingly, there are many people with lots of money that no one would believe judging from outward appearances. He said the converse is true as well—

that there are many people who appear to be made of money, but in reality, struggle financially. They may be living on credit, or spending money from future or potential profits, or simply juggling payments from week to week, but they're actually quite broke.

"Bottom line, Cindy, is that many people who appear wealthy are not, and many who do not appear wealthy, actually are."

Really? Is this true, Lord? Are there people out there who spend more money than they make? This explains so much! Does this mean I should not covet their possessions because they don't own them anyway? How come I never figured this out before?

My parents had always lived within their means, as did Paul's, as have Paul and I. So I had wrongly projected that value onto everyone else too. Paul was teaching me so much about money and the dangers of it.

"I think I know who you're talking about who looks poor but is actually well off. It's the VanDerBosDerBergDeVelds!" (I may have changed their Dutch name here slightly to protect the guilty). "I know what they do—live like paupers as they secretly get rich. They never tip at restaurants; they barter for every service and even turn down Girl Scout Cookies and the neighborhood kids' lemonade stand because they're so friggin' stingy! I've heard that Mrs. VanDerBosDerBergDeVeld stashes extra ham sandwiches in her purse at funerals and freezes them for later! Mom and dad mocked those rude Dutch people who are rich simply from being obnoxiously miserly. I have no interest in being like that, hon."

"Quite the contrary, Cindy. There are those who have independently, apart from an inheritance, worked hard and done quite well for themselves and yet, in humility, feel no need to let the world know about it. They're just very quiet about their choices. It's entirely different from stingy Dutch folk."

Yet the real cluster bomb that sent its shrapnel into every area of our finances came from yet another type of client Paul occasionally encountered. He described a renegade band of folks who were more the exception than the rule but who fascinated him the most. He said there are these wild souls who, whether they have a lot or a little, hold their finances so loosely they just don't worry or really even care if they gain or lose significant amounts of money. These revolutionaries feel free enough to even make jokes about financial loss, taxes, college tuition, and business failures. Money held no power over them. One man said to him, "Paul, to me, the only reason to try and make more money is simply so I can give more away. Nothing brings me greater joy." Paul told me those who held their money loosely were not necessarily wealthy, just not enslaved to it. He recalled a family whose income was probably below the poverty line and yet they tithed 30 percent! *Thirty freakin' percent!*

These people somehow lived out a changed heart when it came to their finances. They believed their spending habits really mattered, and so instead of spending all their time trying to make more, more, more, they spent most of their days figuring out ways to give, give, give. They lived a life of extravagant generosity—whether they could "afford to" or not.

A Different World

My Paul is wicked smart when it comes to finances. After explaining these different kinds of people to me, he added this nugget: "If more of us would live like those few clients of mine— those who live with their finances held loosely—wow, what a different world this would be."

"How so?" I asked.

Paul used a quote from our pastor to make his point: "The world doesn't have a resource problem, Cindy, it has a distribution problem. Imagine humanity being driven not by self-advancement but instead by the love and care for others. What would that look like, Cindy? Just imagine it."

He went on a bit of a tangent after that. I picked up most of it, but sometimes his rantings on economics, finances, and taxes leave me in a fog. What I do remember has stuck with me ever since. He told me that even though our political views were increasingly leaning left, he still believed small government and lower taxes were best, but added this: "Capitalism without benevolence will never work—because capitalism ultimately relies on greed. Greed may stimulate the economy, but it is not of God and it neglects our responsibility to those in need. Our American hearts have become too self-centered and so as a country we've become less and less benevolent. That's the heart of the problem with our failing Capitalistic system. A famous guy once said, 'Where your treasure is, there will your heart be also.'" Paul can be a little cheeky at times.

I had always thought we'd be rich one day (whatever that means in the minds of the middle-class). My excitement had mounted as we inched forward on that continuum. I dreamed endlessly of the bigger cottage, the nicer house, the better car, and the more elaborate vacations, and I was well aware all these things were probably within our reach. But as Paul described these changed heart people to me and challenged me to imagine ourselves living out that narrative, I thought, "Hmph. Perhaps that is a better life story. It would be kind of cool if someday that would be the story of our lives—that we would not be remembered for all that we attained, but all that we gave."

l didn't realize what I was suggesting, but by using the word *someday*, I was essentially saying *never*. It's easier to not feel guilty about how we're living today when we convince ourselves that someday we'll do better. I didn't want to start a radical life of holding our finances loosely and extravagant generosity right away! It's easy to talk about wanting to be more generous—someday. But, in truth, it would never happen with that mindset because what I really wanted was for us to have so much extra money we could give generously from our excess. Jesus was pretty clear on this with the story of the widow's mite—a woman with almost nothing who gave sacrificially.[4] That kind of generosity can only come from a changed heart. And I wasn't there yet.

Then Christmas happened.

CHAPTER 9

A $20,000 Bonus

"A child born to another woman calls me mommy. The magnitude of that tragedy and the depth of that privilege are not lost on me."

JODY LANDERS

On the Christmas of 2000, our extended family on my mom's side gathered together for a big potluck. After dinner, my cousin Kim and her new husband Charlie set up a slideshow and gave a presentation to the whole family on their recent trip to China to pick up their newborn daughter.

I settled into my seat ready to absorb a feel-good story for the next half hour. Because Paul is adopted, we're definitely in the pro-adoption camp. Additionally, I always love a good slideshow. Throw in some sappy Christian tune, and it's all "Grab-a-Kleenex" for me.

I had no idea how this moment would impact our futures forever. Kim and Charlie shared their journey of adoption, including the flood of emotions they felt as they walked into the Chinese orphanage and were given a number that corresponded to a little baby girl.

They discovered endless halls lined with rooms, each filled with rows of cribs. Baby girl after baby girl—tiny heads flattened from neglect, their fragile bodies rarely held, their skin crawling with lice and scabies. Lying in a wooden crib-manger full of hay, and wearing no bottoms or diapers, these seraphic infants were largely abandoned to rot in their urine and feces like animals. Kim and Charlie waded through this baby hell to find their assigned number on a crib where their new little daughter lay waiting.

My guts churned from their story. All these infants. None wanted. They were in the way. Disposable. They were girls in a country that only honors sons and only lets you have one child. But there was good news for this one cherished, angelic child. She was adopted by two loving parents that day and the story of her life took a dramatic, upward turn.

Upon returning home, Charlie shared how one Sunday at church, a friend of theirs challenged their decision to adopt internationally. He said things like, "I've always heard foreign-born adopted kids have enormous identity issues and are never really able to adjust. You guys pretty much just wasted $20,000 and there are at least a hundred better things you could have done with your money." And then he drove away in his brand new $50,000, four by four truck.

Kim and Charlie went on to adopt four more kids.

$20,000

Paul and I had three children at this point in our lives. When Andy was seven and Josiah five, Grace Evelyn exploded into this world batting her big brown eyes and just about everything else that got in her way. She was a lively dose of upheaval to all things controlled in the DeBoer home. Adding a third child was a gigantic leap for

Paul and me because we had declared to Jesus and everybody we were going to stop after having the boys. We believed two kids to be just the right amount of comfortable and easy—two things we highly valued. Two kids are affordable. Two kids meant man-to-man defense. Two kids—two boy kids, in particular—play nicely together. And our first two boy kids slept well. Our first two boy kids hardly fought and knew how to pick up after themselves. Life was a lovely level of bliss with two boy kids.

Grace, well, she just came bursting onto the scene, flipping her middle finger at any hope whatsoever for peace and calm. Bye-bye bliss.

Although Grace trailed her brothers by five years, she believed she could (and should) hang with them in all their exploits. Consequently, she pestered them relentlessly. The sound decibels in our home skyrocketed with Grace. She didn't sleep through the night—at all, for that matter. She was a chubby kid like her mama, yet she never ate! She would get so distracted creating masterpieces with her plate of food—chicken nugget castles, green bean forests, smashed pea lakes with carrot swimmers. Grace's food spent most of its time on the plate, her face, or the floor.

She played with her food but didn't play with toys. She'd use her legendary imagination to bang pots and pans like a rock star, empty cupboards for hideouts, flip furniture for forts, unfold the neatly folded towels to make lily pads, tip potted plants over to create a jungle, encircle herself in the fireplace screen to make a jail, and create beaches in the middle of our living room with lawn chairs, beach towels, and sunscreen. Grace's three main food groups were dirt, bugs, and Lego pieces. She was the reason we had to put the Poison Control hotline on speed dial. One time she ended up with a bead lodged in her sinus passage because she shoved it up her nose to "just see if it'd fit." Almost daily, she'd break or destroy something expensive or precious to me. Grace was noisier, messier, busier, and more expensive than both her brothers put together. I aged ten years in her first two years of life.

We had never been in a season of life when we were more exhausted.

Even still, at Kim and Charlie's adoption celebration, the same week we celebrated our Savior's birth and its ultimate celebration of life, we were splayed open to the reality of a global orphan crisis. And because God had already been working us over about our finances and wastefulness, we just couldn't help but wonder: "*What, God? Who? Us? Are you calling us to adopt?*"

The timing felt so wrong. We were tired and feeling less rich with three kids, yet at the same time, it was evident God was teaching us something new about our finances.

Ever since "the confession," Paul and I prayed together every night at bedtime and focused on this question: "What if we lived what we say we believe?" I mean, we said we believed in taking care of the poor, the orphan, the widow, and the alien in our midst. But we were doing none of those things. We said we believed in loving our neighbor as ourselves, but had been avoiding the question of "Who's our neighbor?" We said we believed people were more important than things, but things still received the bulk of our attention. In addition, the lyrics from a popular song on the radio compelled us to ask God these two questions: *What breaks Your heart, Lord?* and *What makes You cry?* So every night we'd bravely ask God to break our hearts for the same things that broke His and show us how to live like Him if He were back in human form in Hudsonville, Michigan.

And also, Jesus . . . what if You were making a lot of money? What would you do with it?

Those prayers and asking those questions revolutionized our lives. If you like your life the way it is, I wouldn't recommend it.

A simple Google search told me there were over 150 million orphans in the world. One afternoon while folding laundry I began weeping as I thought of all those babies in all those cribs in all those many countries . . . waiting . . . waiting . . . waiting . . . And in the middle of that heartbreak hurricane, God plopped $20,000 on our laps.

Seriously, God? Do you have to be so obvious?

In the accounting world there is often a lump sum of income after the long, hard hours put in over tax season. Some years we had it spent before it even arrived. This year it was spent in my head, but nothing had been bought yet. We both felt this weird, sinking feeling that we were not going to buy any *thing* with that money. We had asked for our lives to align with what we said we believed. There was no way we could take that money to pad our bank account or buy a new car or a bigger and faster boat or a nicer cottage directly on the water—all things that at one time or another I did, quite honestly, think we would do. A couple of days later, we met with the adoption agency.

People tell us all the time they would adopt too, if they could afford it. They say if they had $20,000 plop in their lap, that's what they'd do with it too. But they fail to see God has probably already plopped $20,000 in their laps. Paul's salary simply came in chunks, while most people get paid consistently from week to week. Paul often says, "I'd be happy to help any middle-class family find $20,000 in their budget. Because, most likely, it's there." When I tell people that—that my husband could look over their budget and help them find $20,000—we never hear from them again. I think they know exactly where Paul would find that $20,000 in their budget, and I think most people don't feel like giving up things like bedrooms and bathrooms with a smaller home, or daily mocha-mochas, or spring break vacations, or name brand clothing to adopt a child.

When the adoption caseworker first called to tell us we were given a referral (matched to a child) in Guatemala, I started to cry. (Surprised by that yet?) I almost missed the part where she excitedly told us, "And its newborn twin boys! I just need a response in the next twenty-four hours if you'll accept this placement!"

We had told the adoption agency we were open to any child, any country, any age, any problems or disabilities, and any gender. We just wanted whomever God wanted for us. But we secretly hoped for a girl. Hoped God would choose that for us too. We had told ourselves, and everyone else, that in our minds, adopting was no different from being pregnant—meaning the first call from the agency is equivalent to an ultrasound. *It's a boy! It's a girl! He has Down's Syndrome. She has spina bifida. Or, sit-down-before-you-hear-this, your baby has hydrocephalus and will only live a few hours.* When you're pregnant and do not believe in abortion, whatever the ultrasound reveals, you simply know it is God's plan for you. This is your child, and you will love him or her unconditionally no matter what. We believed the same to be true with adoption.

But we were wrong.

Adoption is not like being pregnant. You truly do have choices. It begins with the choice to adopt. Then, domestic or international? Same race or different? Physical deformity, or no? Handicapped? Boy? Girl? When you're adopting, you actually may choose these things and that's okay. That's adoption. And it includes the choice we had never once considered: twins. We hoped for one girl. They called us with two boys. And we weren't ready for that decision.

I rapidly spiraled into decision-making hell. In less than a minute I had those two boys named, imagined their differing personalities, assigned and decorated their bedrooms, and pictured our five kids comprising their own basketball team. I even named it: "Grace and the Cuatro Hermanos." On the one hand, I loved the idea of having twins and having five kids in total. On the other, we liked the idea of adopting a sister for Grace since our boys were already so tight. We had also learned an interesting insight about adoption from my older sister, Pam. Years of tests, doctor visits, and failed hormone injections forced Pam and her husband Tom to face the heartache of infertility. They ended up choosing domestic adoption to bring home Samantha Joy and, two years later, Matthew Charles. Pam explained to us many adopting couples actually request twins because it usually means less paperwork, bureaucracy, and cost. Knowing this, we couldn't help but wonder if somewhere out there a lovely Christian couple was just praying to adopt twins—our twins.

We prayed too. Like crazy. We prayed for twenty-four hours but still didn't have an answer. When it came time to call the adoption agency, Paul arranged a conference call so he could be at work and I at home. I sobbed into the phone as I told Paul I just didn't have an answer and that he'd have to decide. I said, "I hope God gave you an answer. I got nothing."

What a beautiful, holy thing to have a husband you can trust.

I sat in silence on the phone while Paul explained to our case manager this placement of the twin boys just wasn't a fit for us. He explained our hope was that somewhere out there a couple unable to have biological children was praying for twins. These twins. He said we had peace about the decision. I didn't feel peaceful at all, but I did trust Paul, and I was learning to trust God.

Two weeks after we declined accepting the twins, our case manager called and told us the boys had been placed in a wonderful Christian home in Indiana where the young couple, struggling with infertility, had specifically prayed for twins. They had requested a call be made to us to thank us for listening to the voice of God and passing on the boys. I had no place whatsoever to put a God that big.

Then He got bigger.

One week after that, on March 16, 2001, we received another call from Kristin saying we were now matched to a baby girl. My heart leapt. We specifically asked God to make it crystal clear when the child he chose for us would be presented to us. We wanted to be sure. Was this *the* call? How will I know? My heart leapt higher when Kristin told me the birth mom, in atypical fashion, named the baby. She said birth moms don't usually do that because they don't want to get attached to their infant. She told us we were free to rename the child whatever we wanted, and I was so relieved because we had the name Selah Elizabeth all picked out, and I thought I was so very clever because it was in the Bible, in the Psalms, yet we had never heard anyone name their child that before. But I thought I'd go ahead and ask anyway:

"What did the birth mom name her?" I questioned.

"Yulisa Beatrice."

I choked. "Wait. What? What did you just say?"

"Yulisa Beatrice," Kristin repeated, loosening her thick Spanish accent so I could better understand. "Isn't that a beautiful name? It's not very common, though, is it? But remember, you can easily change it to whatever you want."

"Well," I said through tears, "Beatrice is actually my mother's name." I paused to let that sink in for both of us. "I think she's already been supernaturally named and that this is a sign for us."

After hanging up, in utter disbelief, I realized Yulisa, having been born one day prior, shared a birthday with Paul's dad: March 15. Harvey DeBoer adored children and he would have been thrilled beyond words that we were adopting. Another miraculous sign that Yulisa Beatrice was meant to be our daughter.

With zero hesitation we accepted this referral, and Yulisa Beatrice was put into a foster home until the legal work was complete and we could go to Guatemala to get her. Our daughter—knit in her mother's womb in the hill country of Guatemala but created to be raised by us in a big white house in Hudsonville, Michigan, with her two brothers and one sister. Not to mention four loving grandparents, eleven adoring cousins, her own pink bedroom with two matching white lamps and floral curtains made by Grandma, an amazing church community, the best public school system in America, and a support system of friends that just doesn't end. Yes, that girl, this place, this family. It's exactly what God orchestrated.

Guatemala

Four months later, we were off to Guatemala to meet our new daughter. Although the adoption wasn't final and we wouldn't be able to take her home, we simply couldn't wait to hold her and let her little fingers curl around ours while whispering "I love you's" in her ear. We also wanted to express our love and gratitude to the foster mom as she stood in the gap for us. We didn't know if the legal process would take an additional two months or two years, but that uncertainty didn't stop us. Without much thought to cost, we brought ten-year-old Andy and eight-year-old Josiah along, while three-year-old Grace stayed in Michigan with Grandma.

Prior to this trip to Guatemala, our international traveling experience was minimal. In the early years of DeBoer and Goodyke, Paul and I traveled with the Goodykes to Puerto Vallarta, Mexico. We stayed in a luxury hotel built for foreigners and almost never left the grounds except to eat in high-end restaurants catering to luxury-seeking tourists. We sat around the pool all day, and Georgio, our sweet and over-zealous poolside bartender, would greet us every morning with "Buenos dias! Strawberry margarita, jes? How many?" And we proceeded to put a buzz on around 10:00 a.m. In a half-drunken stupor we would head out each evening and buy Mexican trinkets made in China from the overpriced shops along the main touristy road and then head to authentic Mexican restaurants where the chef prepared the food differently for weak-stomached American guests. We took a taxi everywhere and laughed loudly when the driver didn't understand our English or the maybe thirteen random words we remembered from seventh-grade Spanish. We would have seriously failed any cultural intelligence test.

Aside from that trip to Mexico, I was the only one in our family who had traveled outside the USA with my trip to Germany. However, because that trip had been so structured and controlled by well-meaning organizers who didn't want us to have to worry about a thing, we didn't really learn anything either. It's the hardships of travel that teach us the most.

So stepping off the plane in Guatemala City, we were extremely unwise and looked ever the part of naive gringo tourists. I had my big gold hair, big gold purse, big gold watch, and big gold diamond ring. We spoke no Spanish (save those thirteen words from seventh-grade Spanish, three of which, I believe, were swear words), and the only homework we did on Guatemala was to read Lonely Planet. Perhaps we reacted like every other American who doesn't have a clue what to expect when traveling to the developing world—we panicked. My fearful, overactive mind thought the armed military men scattered throughout the airport were angrily staring at us and contemplating shooting us right then and there. The place reeked of an entirely unfamiliar odor—one part sweat, two parts garbage, three parts tomalitos— which, when combined with the constant stream of Spanish all around us, left us a bit queasy and not able to think straight.

We had coordinated this entire trip ourselves. No travel agent, no tour guides, no drivers, no translators, no guidance whatsoever (not even an iPhone!). When we stepped out of the airport into the blinding, sun-soaked Guatemalan habitat and were assaulted with chaos akin to Black Friday at a big box store, we reeled in unbelief. Hundreds of sweaty, pushy, noisy Guatemalans crowded around the airport doors and yelled to us, insisting we needed their services or assistance. Many were pulling on our sleeves, pulling on our boys, or reaching for our luggage. Some in the crowd were beggars and used a gentler touch but still pulled on our arms and heartstrings simultaneously.

To leave the airport meant we had to pass through this crowd. There was no other way to exit. I looked down at my two young boys—all wide-eyed and vulnerable and trusting our leadership—and choked back the tears. I felt a strong urge to grab their hands, run back to that TACA flight and yell, "Hey, Mr. Pilot, we made a terrible mistake! Take us back to Houston immediately—where we last saw *normal* civilization of calm and quiet white people who stand in nice, neat lines awaiting their Starbucks and McDonalds while speaking English! Please Mr. Pilot, take us back!!"

We paused. We gave the moment a ten-second assessment. And we realized this: We were in a situation completely out of our control, with zero prior experience or cultural wisdom to lean on, no people around who could give us help, uncertain that even if we could find help that we could communicate with them, and we had our two little boys in tow. Paul and I agreed we'd never knowingly put them in dangerous situations, and this felt kind of dangerous. What was left for us to do? Only this: Pray. There was simply no other alternative in that moment. Upon my insistence, we retreated back into the relative quiet and safety of the airport, and with watchful military in earshot, Paul said a quick prayer that went something like this: *"Help. Please, God, help us. This is kind of scary—but you're not scared. We feel kind of stupid in this situation—but you're not stupid. Please, give us wisdom to handle things we know nothing about. Amen."* Then we made a plan.

It was a simple plan: Hold hands tightly and march right back out those big airport doors with a very confident air, then quickly and forcefully splice through the aggressive crowd acting as if we knew exactly where we were going. Once away from the mob and out in the open, we reasoned, we should be able to flag down a taxi.

Again, we were nearly mauled as we pushed through the crowd. Everyone wanted to "help" the helpless gringos dripping in gold. My fear abated a bit with our good plan, but in its place anger crept in. I had never experienced such disregard for personal space! To make matters worse, Josiah kept pulling on my sleeve trying to ask me some ridiculous question while I was already seriously multi-tasking: forging a path through the crowd, keeping an eye on our six pieces of luggage that kept falling off Paul's luggage cart, and maintaining a death grip on my purse and two little-boy hands. Finally, free from the crowd, I turned to Josiah and said, "Whaaaaaat?"—giving the monosyllabic word about four extra ones to let the kid know this better be good and I really didn't have time for his questions.

He asked, "What are all those signs that everybody was holding up back there?"

"What signs?"

"The signs that people in the mob were holding up with names written on them," he persisted.

"Oh, those! That is for people who are getting a ride from someone they don't know, like a chauffeur or a hotel shuttle, and they hold up the name of the people they are picking up so the travelers can identify them."

"Oh," was all he said. And we walked another hundred meters or so trying to escape the heavy airport traffic and trying to size up a taxi driver that we hoped wouldn't drive us to the mountains, rob us blind, and shoot us in the head (something I naively assumed Guatemalan taxi drivers often did) when Josiah finally offered this, "So why would there be a sign with our name on it if we didn't need a ride?"

Paul and I stopped in our tracks, looked at each other in disbelief, then spun around and headed straight back toward the crowd. Sure enough, the sweet hotel owners of the little two-star dive we had reserved took it upon themselves to send us a driver even though we hadn't asked for one. I think they knew just how lily white we were from our emails.

When we arrived at the hotel, our jaws dropped in unison because of its stunning beauty. Despite its ridiculously cheap prices, the place screamed "five-star resort." Palm trees graced the curved drive leading up to the arched, mahogany double door at the front, and gorgeous pink bougainvillea cascaded over the perimeter walls, creatively masking the coiled barbed wire that is a staple of Guatemalan City architecture. It was like a mini paradise. Not quite the posh resort we experienced in Puerta Vallarta, but it was very Eden-esque all the same. The hotel owners continued to pour out hospitality by preparing a hot meal for us and bringing out Coca-Cola for the boys. We didn't have a clue what was going on all around us in this foreign land, or how to relate to these different people, but they read our gringo minds and put us right at ease.

We spent three glorious days with Yulisa. We were able to keep her in the hotel with us, but we weren't allowed to leave the hotel premises at all because too many Guatemalans believed Americans came to buy children and used them for harvesting organs or to resell as slave labor. It makes me want to vomit knowing even the nastiest of rumors usually begin with a sliver of truth. Anyway, if we were seen with Yulisa in public without our legal adoption papers on us, it could create an issue. Issues were definitely something we were trying to avoid. Although three days is a long time for two school-aged boys to be locked up in a hotel with only Spanish television and no video games (it was 2001, pre-iPod and iPad days), Andy and Josiah made the most of it. They gushed over Yulisa and helped with her feedings and baths. They made friends with other kids in the hotel, rapidly learned some Spanish, and played imagination games out on the hotel's front balcony. I realized then that our kids had some extra chromosome or something that made them extremely adaptable, easily entertained, willing to eat strange food, and quite comfortable in foreign settings. That was an unexpected new discovery and something that would influence our future decisions.

After three days with Yulisa, her foster mom Yolanda came to pick her back up. She was a widowed woman of retirement age who fostered one child at a time and spoiled that child with unmitigated love. Yulisa was no exception, and her eyes brightened when she heard Yolanda's voice entering the lobby. Asking God for a wonderful, loving, and caring foster mom for our child wasn't even something we knew to ask for—God simply gave us far more than we could have hoped or imagined. This woman, in so many ways, gave Yulisa the essential foundation for future stability in our family by loving her those first few precious and formative months. All research indicates this is one of the keys to preventing severe attachment disorder, where the adopted child fails to attach to her new parents. Meeting Yolanda was a rare and sacred gift, one we did not take for granted.

Even though I felt incredible peace regarding Yolanda, I thought I might pass out as I handed our child back to her, not knowing when we'd see her angelic face again. My heart climbed right into that taxi with Yulisa and Yolanda, and it stayed there in Guatemala City for the next few months until we brought Yulisa home for good. But Paul and I and the boys had to press on. We had planned another six days in the country to try and soak up knowledge and wonder about our new daughter's homeland.

Less than an hour after kissing Yulisa goodbye, we were in our own taxi headed for the mountains.

We arrived at our hotel in the mountain town of Antigua super late at night. Everything was dimly lit with candles and we couldn't agree if the hotel was more like a barn, a monastery, or a cave. We decided to go with "spookily intriguing." The concierge, a smiley little ten-year-old boy with very white, crooked teeth greeted us with a hearty *Buenas tardes!* He needed a step stool to see over the top of his podium. He scanned the handwritten list of names for our reservation and smiled even broader when he found it. "*Si! Si!* Right this way!" and he led us to our room. The Don Rodrigo was not going to disappoint—even though they employed children. In the center of the building was a huge courtyard teeming with rose bushes, bougainvillea, and banana trees. Vibrant red, orange, and yellow hammocks were strung from palm tree to palm tree in all four corners of the courtyard. A fountain centered the space and the trickling sound of water immediately made us all sleepy.

Smiley turned the turn-of-the-century key in the door and nodded to us, letting us know we were to follow him in. The room was huge with twelve-foot ceilings and ten-foot doorways. The center of the room was anchored with a medieval-looking chandelier, but Smiley did not turn it on. Instead, he lit two candles, one next to each of the two beds. He proudly opened the bright hand-woven curtains and gave a Vanna White gesture to show off the view of the courtyard. He led us to the bathroom and pulled back the shower curtain to reveal how clean the shower was. He then led us back to the sleeping quarters and pulled back the sheets on both beds. That's when I finally noticed—two single beds for the four of us. We very politely asked him in our best

Spanish if he had a different room available with two double beds since there were, in fact, four of us. Turns out, our Spanish is about as good as Rachel Green's French. The kid didn't have a clue what we said. The hotel manager arrived a few minutes later. I think he was Smiley's older brother. He smiled even broader than his counterpart—clearly proud to be so accommodating for his demanding American patrons—as he handed us two additional pillows.

We hopped from city to city via a Turismo van—sometimes alone and sometimes with other tourists. I was extremely uneasy about it because the van did not have "Turismo" written on the side which Mr. Lonely Planet had explicitly said is essential to assure you've hired a legitimate company. Mr. Planet also mentioned there had been incidents of tourists robbed, raped, and murdered on certain desolate roads in the past—so, "be cautious," he said. As luck would have it, when we were high up in the mountains and far away from any civilization, our non-identifiable Turismo van was pulled over by armed militia-looking men.

I've never seen a bandit, but if I were to dress my kids up like one for Halloween, I'd copy these guys.

I told the boys to pray. We were in the back of the van, so I quickly sized up the situation and felt we were at good odds to not be harmed. Mr. Planet also said bandits typically act very quickly, rarely kill their targets unless they feel threatened, and really just want your cash and valuables. I thought about my purse, my wedding ring, and my watch—all the things the world calls valuable—and without a second thought I knew I'd relinquish it all if it meant staying safe. But there was one thing I would never hand over, the one thing of real value to me—the photos we had just taken of Yulisa during our three days spent together in Guatemala City. I emptied the camera of the film (gasp, I know, this was in the olden days before digital photography) and put the four rolls of film we had taken underneath my shirt, making me just slightly plumper than normal. Imperceptible.

Our boys saw me do this and I think that's when they realized the depth of my fear and how potentially dangerous this situation was. With two wide-eyed boys, I choked back the tears and the four of us huddled close in the back of that van, held shaking hands together, and quietly prayed.

Turns out, Guatemalan police looking for drug traffickers and your run-of-the-mill bandits look alarmingly similar. The gunmen and our van driver just shouted back and forth for a few minutes—then they waved us on.

I really don't know if it was because Mr. Planet had his head up his ass when writing his book, or if it was the fact we were using a 1997 edition in the year 2001, or if it was the supernatural powers of the Creator of the universe that turned those events around to be nothing more than a standard military checkpoint, but the fact remains, when we prayed over a situation, any disastrous might-have-beens will instead be remembered as divine intervention. And two young boys, ages ten and eight, were changed forever.

It was the first time I remember begging God to deliver us. I wondered how necessary it was to actually face "bandits" to know Him in this way, but it was effective.

On the plane ride home from Guatemala, the four of us were not able to get seats together. I sat with Josiah in the back of the plane, and Paul and Andy were together near the front.

Unbeknownst to the other, Paul and I both had a little debrief with our sons on the flight. The conversations went something like this:

"How many times did we experience miraculous answers to prayer this week?" I asked Josiah.

"More than I can count, Mom."

"Let's try." And we sat and tried to recall every time we prayed and something amazing happened—often beyond what we even knew to ask for. Over and over we recounted incidents where we experienced a reality bigger than our personal scope of ability, understanding, or comfort level. And now here we were, on the plane ride home, totally fine, and totally alive. In fact, we both agreed, never more alive. Never *more* alive.

I told Josiah, "I don't know what that was we just experienced in that country. I don't know what to call it or name it or even how to describe it. All I know is, I want more of it. I want to live like that all the time."

"So do I, Mom. So do I."

I choked up when Paul told me he had had the exact same conversation with Andy. Almost verbatim. Together, we were discovering what it means to truly need God. We recognized that the posture of surrender, dependency, and trust was powerful while we were in Guatemala, but we all wanted to know—how do we get more of that in Hudsonville? Why can't we depend on God like that no matter where we are? Why is it we try so hard to be self-sufficient, comfortable, and safe when, it seems, those things sometimes get in the way of experiencing God?

We didn't have any answers yet—only a growing list of questions.

Yulisa

August 20, 2001, we received the phone call that our adoption was complete—we could go get our daughter in Guatemala. We bought our plane tickets for October 1, 2001.

When the Twin Towers were hit in New York City on September 11, 2001, millions of people all around the globe had millions of different reactions. My reaction was a horrific, gut-wrenching fear, but not at all from a fear the world might be ending. I was afraid we wouldn't be able to fly to Guatemala in just three weeks to get Yulisa.

The ban on air travel was miraculously lifted in time for us to depart for Guatemala. Airport security was insane. Travelers were quiet, staring at each other and sizing up one another as they searched for potential terrorists. We were all racial profilers. People were rude and edgy, and there was little to none of that mindless plane chatter. The plane was only half full because most people had canceled their plans and were still afraid to fly. We weren't afraid, though. We had a child waiting for us—her parents!—to come and get her. *Get me on that plane now, Jesus!*

This time, our visit to Guatemala was short and uneventful. We had one of the smoothest adoption processes ever. But over that long weekend, we discovered a God who is bigger than this life, bigger than this universe, and bigger than my mind could handle.

Before our departure, our case manager, Kristen, gave us wise advice. She explained that we would not have the privilege of meeting Yulisa's birth mom, but the Guatemalan attorney handling our case had met her several times. Kristen urged us to ask the attorney as many questions as possible to learn everything we could about Yulisa's birth mom, as this would be Yulisa's only glimpse into her biological past. Such information, Kristen said, would be invaluable—especially during Yulisa's teenage years when she began forming her identity.

We met our attorney, a well-dressed, semi-English-speaking Guatemalan woman, in the hotel lobby early on our first morning. After going through the business details of our embassy visit and paperwork, the attorney stood to leave. I begged her to sit because we had more questions.

"We want to know anything and everything you can tell us about Yulisa's birth mom. You met with her several times, correct? What was she like? What can you tell us about her personality? Interests? Hobbies? Education? Employment? We just want to be able to tell Yulisa someday a little bit about her mother."

"Jes, jes, I meet her. I talk to her many times," the attorney said. "But I know not much. She very, very poor. She no hobbies or interests. She just very poor. She no education. None. She cleans house for money—but not much. No money for her children. She no money for Yulisa. She love Yulisa very, very much but no money. That's all I know."

"Really? There is nothing more you can tell us? Do you know anything about where she came from, or the story of this pregnancy, or why she chose adoption, or anything at all about her family? Anything—please, anything!" I begged her.

The attorney took a deep breath and said, "I tell you what I know. It's not much, but I tell you anyway. Maria marry very young, maybe twelve or thirteen, I don't know. She have two babies with her husband but then he die. She very, very poor but very beautiful. She is cleaning lady for rich family. She have, how you say—affair?—with man of that house who is important married man in her village. Not good. She was shamed. But Maria hide pregnancy and then give baby for adoption. She have no money and the married man no help her. But she keep cleaning for this family. Then, she get pregnant again from same man. She really have no money now and knows she cannot keep baby. She knows baby will starve. Lots and lots of babies starving in Guatemala. She so sad. She so ashamed. She says to me she has no choice, and must give baby for adoption or baby would die from hunger. She says to me she will never get pregnant again. She is very, very poor. That is Maria's story, and that is all I know."

Paul and I stared at her in total disbelief. I had never in my life felt my heart race the way it did in that moment. The whole universe seemed to fade away, and an alternate reality took over—because her words could not possibly have been more mind-blowing to us. Here's why:

A couple of months prior, in the midst of preparing our adoption dossier for the courts, Paul spent the day at the courthouse in Grand Haven, Michigan, obtaining proof of his own adoption. Somehow, neither we, nor his parents, had any copies of these important papers. While at the courthouse, the clerk asked Paul if he wanted to open up his own record because his adoption case had always been closed. To open it up would mean that if his birth mom ever wanted to find him, she could— and vice versa. So for sixty bucks, Paul opened the case. It was something he had previously never felt the need to do because, as he always said, "I know who my parents are" (meaning his adoptive parents). But now, going through the adoption process himself, he thought about his birth mom more and wondered if maybe, just maybe, she was out there searching for him and wondered if she craved the peace to know he was okay.

Several weeks later, we received a file of legal documents. They informed us his birth mom had not, in fact, ever opened up the case from her side, so there was still no way Paul could find her. However, there was now some information that could be shared with him. It was titled, "Non-Identifying Family Information for Adopted Children." The document told us a little about his family's health history and ethnicity. And then it included this short narrative of the situation surrounding his adoption: Paul's birth mom was not from Michigan, but from somewhere in the South. She married young and had two children soon after. Then her husband died. As a young, widowed woman, who was also very beautiful, she had an affair with a prominent man in the community. She found herself pregnant and ashamed and came to Michigan to give birth to a son, whom she gave up for adoption. A couple of years later, she became pregnant again by the same man, and again she came to Michigan and gave that child, a son, up for adoption as well. That son was Paul.

Did you catch that miracle? Paul and Yulisa have the exact same adoption story! Their mothers were both married young, widowed after two children, became pregnant in a scandalous situation and gave that child up for adoption. They both continued the affair and got pregnant a fourth time, choosing to give that child up for adoption as well. Both Paul and Yulisa are fourth-born children of widows who simply couldn't afford their children.

We have always told our kids that there's no such thing as a coincidence in the kingdom of heaven, so we don't really use that word. Stories like these are nothing short of miraculous, and only God could have written them.

Our ever-increasing desire to experience more of God's faithful, powerful, and demonstrative love for us propelled us forward on our faith walk, but time and time again, the seductive lure of a cushy and luxurious life would pull us back again.

My neck was starting to ache from all the spiritual whiplash.

CHAPTER 10

Bite Me, John Deere

"To believe in something and not live it is dishonest."

MAHATMA GANDHI

The first spring after Yulisa came home to us was one of the wettest on record. My weary and bleary eyes were afraid to look out the window each morning because it was always raining. Life was busier than I'd ever imagined it could be, and with these ridiculous rains and these rambunctious kids, the walls of the big white house seemed to be closing in on me.

So as soon as the skies parted and the rains stopped, I flung open the windows, tossed the kids their list of chores, and skipped outside to hop on my new shiny green lawn mower.

One of the many ways we had justified our big house was that it would be good for the kids to do chores, help with home maintenance and gardening, and develop a solid, country work ethic as they participated in the care of a large piece of property. What a joke. Our kids didn't learn squat about any of those things. For one, they were too little to do the big jobs; and two, the chores they could manage, they didn't do well enough to suit me. Their pathetic little efforts to help me clean all those toilets and the high ceilings and the cupboards and closets, the pool and yard, and the wood floors and windows were mostly met with my scrutiny and disapproval.

I believed big houses didn't look quite right unless they had big yards. So whenever there wasn't snow on the ground, our big yard required an all-too-frequent, four- or five-hour mowing and trim job. Since Paul worked such long hours, and because I enjoyed it, mowing became my jam. Plus, Paul mowed too fast, often missing wisps of grass on his turns, which annoyed me beyond reason. Because of this ridiculous lawn obsession, I literally cried (happy tears) the day Paul surprised me and brought home a shiny, new John Deere lawnmower. I told him it was the nicest gift he'd ever bought me. I guess lawnmower trumps tennis bracelet (more on that later).

Normal people would probably mow our lawn in less than the four hours it took me, but the remnants of my perfectionist past were a formidable force. I wanted perfect mower lines. Perfect! Even as our boys grew older, and could have easily navigated that John Deere for me, I would never have relinquished that chore. They could never have done it quite right. Every week, and sometimes even two or three times a week, I honored that very important rendezvous with Mr. John Deere.

I'd put Andy and Josiah in charge to keep an eye on their younger sisters on lawn mowing days. They were both so cautious and mature, I knew they could handle things. I'd tell them that if they had any problems to just come out on the way-too-big wraparound porch that we never slowed down enough to enjoy, and wave to me so that I would know they needed something. I didn't really have time for serious parenting on these days.

I'd get angry just seeing one of the kids out on the porch because it meant they couldn't work out their differences, and it meant slowing me down on creating my beautiful lawn. I'd roll my eyes, thrust the throttle into neutral so I could hear their complaints over the sound of the motor, and play Judge Judy for fifteen seconds before saying, "Oh for Pete's sake! Get over it! If you guys don't stop it, I'll spank you all when I get in there!"

As if a spanking, with seriously questionable effectiveness normally, would be worth anything at all delivered two hours after the crime. That is one reason—along with thousands more—why I will never write a book on parenting.

But on this long-awaited dry and sunny spring day, when everything outside smelled like lilacs and evaporating rain, our eleven-year-old Andy, a born leader whose deep chestnut eyes often betrayed his emotions, came out on the porch and just sat in the rocking chair, looking at me. He didn't wave. He wasn't asking me to come in. After all, he was the leader, and he was leading just fine. He simply stared at me with indignation and sadness. Without uttering a word, his eyes said it all: "Get off the damn lawnmower, Mom. We need a mom in here, and I'm sick of taking care of the other kids. I'm eleven years old and we're tired of nuking hot dogs and watching mindless TV and fighting through our differences so that you can have those stupid perfect lines in your stupid perfect lawn. Get off your damn lawnmower, Mom."

I've never heard Andy swear—ever. He's a young adult now and still not a single swear word. Ever. I don't think he even swears in his dreams or thought life. But I believe the visceral disgust I saw in his eyes that day—that he felt in his soul—toward my poor decision-making was expletive worthy. That's how mad it makes me now, anyway. I don't think he could ever swear at me, but in retrospect, I want to swear at me.

And then I made a terrible, awful mistake that I strongly advise all mothers to never do. I took my eyes off him for just a second, and Andy grew up in that second, and I can't get back those years I lost to lawn mowing for anything. So you can just bite me, John Deere. Because no matter how many times I click my ruby red slippers, I can't go back and regain the hours and hours and hours you stole from me—up and down, up and down, back and forth, back and forth, week after week, year after year. For what? To win the contest in this meaningless game of life called, "Nicest Lawn"? No thanks. Perhaps I won. But really, I lost.

We lost so many moments with our kids as we took care of things. We lost so many opportunities to invest in worthwhile activities—like playing Cats in the Cradle, or reading *Little Boy Blue*, or looking for the man in the moon. We lost rest and peace of mind as we strived to impress others. And we lost integrity as Christians as we said one thing about what we believed, yet lived very differently.

I am so ashamed. I'm so sorry Andy, Josiah, Grace, and Yulisa. I'm so sorry.

Even though we had started asking God and ourselves: "What if we lived what we say we believe?" the perplexity of that inner battle raged on. We wanted to continue to live our lives surrendered as we had throughout Yulisa's adoption, but we also wanted our nice house. And lawn. And cars. And cottage. And, and, and, and.

Mostly, we complained of exhaustion during these years of spiritual whiplash. It was a no-win and thoroughly impossible balancing act to take care of everything: the kids, the stuff, *and* the notion we were living surrendered to God. Something had to change, or we were going to crash and burn.

CHAPTER 11

When Yoda Speaks

"In a dark place we find ourselves,
and a little more knowledge lights our way."

YODA, *THE EMPIRE STRIKES BACK*

Without Yoda, Luke Skywalker would not be a Jedi. Without Gandalf, Frodo could not have completed his ring quest. Dorothy without Glinda would still be stuck in Oz. And Neo without Morpheus? I shudder at the thought.

Tiaras and Dirt Bikes

I roll over in bed and reach under the sheets to where my husband should be lying. The space is both empty and cool. I glance at the bedside alarm clock. Five o'clock. In the *morning*. Who goes to work (at a company they own, no less) at 5:00 a.m. on a Saturday? Only the most bizarre breed of humans who actually enjoy looking at numbers and making them make sense and have promised the government to learn ever-changing tax laws so they can help normal people pay said government. It's a career choice I'll never understand but am grateful for nonetheless, because my handsome husband enjoys it, and it pays all our bills nicely. It's just that during this time of year, tax season, I'm often at the end of my rope. Tax season widows are an actual thing.

I say a quick prayer asking God to let the kids sleep in.

Before I say amen, there's a delicate knock on our bedroom door and our four-year-old Gracie glides in wearing a toddler-size wedding gown, bright pink plastic heels, and a glittery tiara. She's ready to play and she's hungry. And here we go again.

I make the five of us breakfast. Alone. While the kids take in a Saturday morning PBS show, I check the laundry. There's still a load in the washing machine that now smells moldy. Sigh. I run it through the wash cycle a second time and chastise myself for inefficiency. I tell the kids they're watching too much TV even though I'm the one who turned it on for them. I tell them we're all headed outside hoping it will burn off some of their Saturday-morning energy. It's a typical gray and frigid March day in Michigan, and I count six complaints, three fights, two "I hate you's," and one frozen tiara stuck in curly brown hair before I say, "Forget it! You kids are driving me crazy out here! We're going back inside!"

It's 8:00 a.m.

This is gonna be a long-ass day.

I don't remember all the things that went wrong that day, but I know it was a doozy. Typical things that set me off back then were spilled colored beverages on our mostly white family room carpet (the carpet I chose fully cognizant of how often kids spill things), back talk, teasing of the younger girls followed by shrieks from the younger girls, slothfulness from an eleven-year-old boy, and begging. But mostly begging.

When Josiah came to me that afternoon, however, I do not now believe he was begging. I think he was a typical nine-year-old boy with a passion. And, on most days, we wanted to hear about that passion and discuss ways we could fuel that passion, and we loved to watch that kid get all lit up inside. This was not one of those days for me, and I immediately interpreted his request as begging. Poor kid.

"Hey, mom. I just talked to Eli on the phone and he wants to sell me his dirt bike. I know I don't need two, so I'll sell my old one. I just might have to put about $400 with it to buy his. It's just that—you know—I've always wanted a 250cc bike, and I've ridden his bike several times so I know I can handle it. I know I don't have enough money, but I promise I'll work and pay you back for it. Can I tell him yes? Can I call him back? He has another friend who wants it too, so I don't want to wait to tell him yes."

I lost it.

Who can say what it is exactly that makes mommas snap? Is it the sleeplessness? The hormones? The incessant crying from the littles? The lack of adult conversation? Or just lack of adult activities in general like dinner out, dancing, seeing a play, or having sex? Is it because we are just plain worn down? Or is it because, as several pious friends have pointed out to me, we may not be praying or reading our Bibles enough?

"Oh for heaven's sake, Josiah! No, we're not buying you another dirt bike!" (Did I hear anything he just said?) "You never even paid off your first one, and you just sit here all day picking on your sisters and watching TV and not helping out one bit around here while I'm running my ass off doing all the housework alone. Why would we keep buying you stuff? You kids are driving me crazy! I swear. You don't appreciate anything we do for you!"

On a normal day, the tragic, sad look in his crystal blue eyes would have destroyed me, and I'd immediately apologize (especially for the swears). But today, I am unfazed. Crushed, confused, and defeated, his shoulders droop a few inches as he sizes me up, wondering if he dares offer a rebuttal. I'm sure the fire in my eyes gave him his answer. He dared not. He walked away quietly and spent the rest of the day in his room.

By the time Paul returned from work later that afternoon, I had nearly forgotten the incident because there had been about ten more incidents involving the other kids, and my wits were just fried. I unloaded all the sins of our children onto Paul within minutes of him walking in the door—completely ignoring the fact that he had just put in a ten-hour day, on a Saturday, on top of already clocking around sixty-five hours Monday through Friday. He patiently listened to my rant.

Then, almost as an afterthought, I added, "And Josiah's been pouting in his room all day because he wants to buy Eli DenBesten's dirt bike, and I said no. Please back me up on this one, because it's ridiculous how our kids think we'll just buy them whatever they want."

Paul took his signature staccato breath that warns me he's about to say something I'm not going to like. "Maybe because we do."

Before launching into a tirade refuting his claim, I, uncharacteristically, paused to let his words sink in—which also gave me time to form my counter-argument. "The thing is, hon (always good to throw one of those in before a verbal bombardment), I don't truly have a problem with getting Josiah the dirt bike. I don't think it's wrong to buy our kids nice things, and I love to make them happy and watch them enjoy the stuff we buy them. I just wish they were more grateful. I wish they could understand how hard you work to pay for this stuff, and I wish they would pitch in around here more as an act of gratitude for all we do for them. I wish our kids were more like the Zimmermans."

"But the Zimmermans don't buy their kids everything they want. Their kids are grateful because they know what it's like to go without. What if we tried that for a while?"

The Zimmermans

We dubbed the Zimmerman family our Yoda's. Paul and I often looked to them for parenting wisdom. They were a family of seven—four boys and a girl—similar ages to our kids. Their home was exactly one mile due east of ours and separated only by thick woods and farmland. The parents had regular jobs, paid their bills, fed their children, and even took an occasional vacation. But try as they might, they struggled a bit financially. Our lives were on parallel train tracks, but we were on the fast bullet train and their little choo-choo just slowly chugged along. The world would have recognized Paul and me as the duo to emulate—the couple with the money, power, and prestige—but the world would have been wrong. Despite their modest incomes, the Zimmermans gave their children every good thing money cannot buy, and those kids were and still are some of the best kids we've ever met. They were so extravagantly generous, kind, and others-focused that their home was a magnet for anyone hurting, lost, or needing love.

I think every parent living in our town at that time wanted their kids to behave more like the Zimmerman kids.

Whenever their kids came over to play, they would gush with comments like, "Wow, this is just the best day ever!" or "I told my mom that coming to your house is like going on a vacation!" or "Man, Mr. and Mrs. DeBoer, you sure know how to make a guy happy!" I marveled at their manners, contented disposition, and willingness to help out whenever they came over.

Sometimes kids from wealthier families would hang out at our house and say things like: "Why don't you guys own a gaming system?" "What? You have a pool but no slide?" "How come you only have two ATV's?" I once had a little fella throw a mini-fit in the backseat of my car. He folded his arms, stared out the window, and gave me the silent treatment because he thought I should have been willing to go to multiple drive-thrus instead of just one to fulfill the various food orders of all five kids in the car.

There was a palpable difference with the Zimmerman kids. Paul and I desperately wanted kids who were more like them: selfless, generous, and grateful. But it was as if we couldn't put two and two together. We couldn't see how (lovingly) gifting our kids everything they wanted actually resulted in spoiled and entitled kids. We had never been willing to do less for them simply to help them become more.

Paul was right. Observing the Zimmermans made us realize if we wanted the same attributes in our kids, it would be necessary to first withhold some things from them. How do you teach someone gratitude unless they know what it's like to go without? It's entirely counterintuitive for well-off, well-intentioned, loving parents to let their kids go without something they can easily afford just to build character. Who chooses to make their children suffer?

Additionally, it seemed to completely escape us in those early years that the best way to get the kind of kids you want is to model for them how you want them to be. Maybe we needed to be more generous. Maybe we needed to say no to a lot of things we could afford even when we were able to say yes. Maybe we were not grateful for things because we had too much. Maybe we needed to give more and expect less. Could it be that if—if—we lived that way, our kids would too?

More Yoda's

In rapid-fire succession we began meeting a small army of Yoda's. We met a Catholic family who revolutionized our views on Catholicism (for the better!) and taught us so much about living beneath our means because they modeled it so well. We sat around a campfire with new neighbors who, after getting to know us a bit, said this, "You two have a lot of gifts to offer the world. Do you think it's possible you're holding them back? We challenge you to start asking God what are the great things he wants to do in your lives."

Next, we received a chance invitation to the home of a truly wealthy couple (their wealth made our wealth look like a child's piggy bank) who had sold their big house (their big house made our big house look like a dog house) and moved to the inner-city of Grand Rapids. They told us how they now lived a life of more intentionality and purpose as they served college kids and single moms in their neighborhood. They shared their tipping point that made them ready to make the move came after hosting an exchange student from Russia. While driving her to the airport to leave, she said she couldn't wait to return home adding, "All people do in America is shop and buy things and take care of their things. In Russia, we care more about people. In Russia, we spend our time with people, not things."

Ouch.

Paul and I were silent the night we drove home from their house. We were reading each other's minds.

We both wondered if the best way to get more out of this life is the antithesis of the American Dream. We both wondered if true fulfillment comes when we find a way to do with less. We both wondered if living like Jesus, who essentially had nothing, would make us the kind of people who produce offspring more like the Zimmermans. We both wondered if perhaps we walked away from our incessant pursuit of upward mobility and wealth accumulation, we'd find more meaning and purpose.

We drove in silence wondering if we should speak these thoughts into existence or bury them, deny them, and just keep them to ourselves.

That would have been safer, for sure.

Instead, we got home and started talking. And talking. And talking. And our safe, predictable world started unraveling. Unraveling. Unraveling.

CHAPTER 12

Vivre le France!

"There is no passion to be found in settling for a life
that is less than the one you are capable of living."

NELSON MANDELA

Our inaugural trip to Guatemala conceived something in us that just wouldn't stop growing. The alien inside us was the new knowledge of how uncomfortably most of the world lives. We had always lived our lives incredibly comfortably. So content in our safe America. So satisfied with three meals a day. So reassured by our great medical insurance. So cozy in our year-round seventy-two-degree home. So secure in our future with financial savings. So confident we would never know true need.

We had never been forced to ask ourselves one simple question: Why?

Why are we so comfortable and so many others in the world are not?

This new alien feeling, combined with all our Yoda influencers, created a nagging suspicion we were meant to live for so much more than paying bills, watching *American Idol*, and cleaning the garage. The band Switchfoot's newest song, "Meant to Live," seemed to be taunting us. I've long wondered if Jon Foreman (lead singer of Switchfoot) hid cameras in our home and secretly watched my life so he could write songs about us. It creeped me out sometimes to think of it. After returning from Guatemala, I'd use our incredible central sound system to pipe "Meant to Live" into every room several times a day. Then came Jon's next (personal) challenge to us via the song: "Dare You to Move."

While continuing to regularly experience relapses into our materialistic mindset, we still would often feel hunted—haunted even—and "Dare You to Move" yanked us right back into the discussion, *"Are we living what we say we believe?"*

The more we prayed that prayer, the more it felt as if someone was watching us and that the way we chose to spend our minutes, our hours, and our one wild and crazy life suddenly mattered. My whole life I've known God sees us, his children. Ever since preschool Sunday School and learning the song: "Oh be careful little eyes what you see (and ears, and feet, and hands . . .)" I've had no doubt that "the Father up above, he is looking down in love . . ." —so feeling watched was in no way a new revelation for us. But this just felt different. We begged God to make clear what He was telling us. Was He asking us to actually move? Or was it just Jon Foreman getting in our heads?

We talked to a few trusted friends whom we knew had experienced God in tangible ways in their own lives. They kept telling us to just keep taking the next step—to never find ourselves standing still. Just keep leaning in, they'd say. We decided to start every day with the simple question: "What, God, what?" And like a Polaroid picture, things slowly came into focus—almost as if we were truly opening our eyes for the first time.

Stacie

One of the first things our new eyes "saw" was a girl in Andy's class at school who kept insisting she lived in a hotel. After asking around a bit, we discovered it was true. Cassie, her toddler brother, and their single mom were homeless and were currently housed in the only hotel in Hudsonville. I was horrified to discover homelessness existed in Hudsonville. Who knew? Hudsonville had, in my opinion, successfully achieved its goal of being a beautiful bedroom community, nicely insulated from pain and suffering by keeping it about, oh, ten miles away in either direction.

So in an unprecedented move, we decided to reach out to this family. We knew of other Jesus-freak families who did this kind of thing, but this was not what the Paul DeBoer family did. We talked about the poor and needy, but never really intended to get to know them. This leaning in was a weird and uncomfortable step for us.

Initially, we gave this family rides to school, work, and appointments—their old car was rarely operational. Soon we were giving them money, as their income never seemed to make it to the end of the month. Eventually Paul hired Cassie's mom, Stacie, as receptionist for his firm because, try as she might, she just couldn't find a decent job to pay her enough to get her family out of that hotel. Stacie was sorely unqualified, but Paul hired her anyway because we were out of sustainable solutions to help this family. Soon, Stacie moved out of the hotel and back into the trailer park.

We tried not to scare Stacie with our Jesus talk. But at the same time we were on a bit of a spiritual high and couldn't contain our emotions and experiences. I'm not sure if Stacie felt obligated to join us in coming to church or if she was genuinely curious, but she eventually asked if she could come with us to Mars Hill. Soon, it became a weekly ritual. Then, one particular communion Sunday she announced, "I want to do that."

In my limited understanding of the Eucharist, I recoiled, thinking I would probably be committing some kind of mortal sin for letting a messed up sinner like Stacie participate in communion. After all, she had two illegitimate children from two different men and had just moved in with a man who had zero discretion as to when, where, and how often he jacked off to pornography. In my fundamentalist mind, Stacie was way into the red zone on the bad-girl spectrum: She showed way too much cleavage; she wore way too much make-up; and her way too tiny thong peaked above her way too tight jeans way too often. Stacie also had a potty mouth worse than my own. Since coming to Mars Hill, she would slap her cheek whenever she swore and say, "Pardon my French!" but I was pretty sure that wasn't the same as asking for forgiveness (which is how I handled that transgression). She hadn't even prayed the obligatory "sinner's prayer" yet! That, and because her sins seemed pretty bad, I was pretty sure she shouldn't be taking communion.

But she went forward with us and took the wafer and drank the wine. I didn't get struck down by lightening or anything, nor did she, but I sure felt uneasy.

Later that week I called the church and asked what their position was on non-members taking Communion. We had only been at Mars for about a year at that point, and although we were in a great house church, involved in serving at the church in several ways, we had yet to meet any of the pastors. It was a megachurch, after all, and we were just a number in the stackable gray chairs.

The switchboard lady, a staple for big churches, patched me into the office of Pastor Keith Sparzak. Neither of us could have imagined this would be the start of a lifelong friendship. Over the next several months Keith coached us frequently on the Stacie thing. He helped me process through one particular night when I went to see Stacie at the trailer park. Because she was acting so bizarre—uncontrollable crying that would ricochet into uncontrollable laughter—I asked if I could pray over her. When I did, she ran to the bathroom, vomited for several minutes, and returned an entirely different person—calm, collected, and normal. Keith said I had probably cast out a demon! Coming from the Reformed church tradition, I was most definitely new to demon casting. I wondered if I could cast out the demon that made me eat too much and just solve that little problem once and for all too. Keith said he doubted it.

We were in so far over our heads here engaging with the needy, the emotionally scarred, the manipulative, and all the "other" kinds of people Stacie represented. We had spent our entire lives up to this point effectively insulating ourselves from anyone different from us. We, those who lived in the country and the burbs, didn't say this part out loud, but the truth was, we didn't want the "others" around us because they might corrupt us.

Stacie consistently challenged us. She always needed something. She needed medical advice, child-rearing advice, and budgeting advice. She needed me to remove head lice from her kids' heads and porn films from her doublewide trailer. She needed a reality check when she tried to put a $3,000 professional-series refrigerator on payments. She needed a friend, a housekeeper, a babysitter, a mechanic, and a pest control expert, and she always looked to us to direct her to these people. And more than anything else, she really needed us to not give up on her because everyone else in her life did. She was appreciative of all our services, but all she could give us in return was an education in "othering." And it's easy for resentment and fatigue to set in with such a lopsided relationship. We either had to accept the reality of this serendipitous friendship and keep plodding on or let the weightiness consume us and give up. I can see why people eventually give up. It's exhausting caring for the needy.

Keith taught us much about walking with the poor. Stacie taught us even more. We learned that if you want to understand and help the poor, there is no substitute for getting to know them. We learned that although the neediness of some people may wear you down, it is never a reason to not do it.

Oh, and we learned it is perfectly acceptable to take communion at Mars Hill while still a sinner. In fact, we all do.

Un-missionaries?

Eventually, Keith made a professional move and transferred from Community Life Pastor to Global Outreach Pastor. At the time, we simply thought, "That's cool, Keith," because we didn't understand what the title change meant. But the more we hung out with Keith and his wife, Suzann, the more we learned about and were intrigued by this revolutionary idea of serving Jesus globally. We were hearing messages every Sunday on how we, the body of Christ, were really all missionaries—simply living out the gospel of Jesus wherever we are geographically. We had grown up thinking missionaries were boring, out-of-touch-with-reality individuals who were specifically trained to spread the gospel of Christ and yet always seemed to be incredibly poor at communicating. They were the no-make-up-skirt-ladies and the high-rise-pants-men, and when they came to speak at church, it was definitely a justifiable cause to skip a week.

Despite this confusing understanding of mission work, as well as our disdain for it, we still kind of felt something pulling us toward it. Tugging, really, and whispering to our souls to just let go of the lie we had bought—the pursuit of prosperity—and to take a risk trying to live for something more.

One night Paul confided something to me that was kind of shocking to hear from a professional accountant: "You know, I'm so sick and tired of helping rich people get richer. I know it pays the bills, but I've got to find a more meaningful way to spend my days on this planet." Likewise, although my days were full and fulfilling, loving and caring for our family, I knew I had been holding back. I knew there was something inside me lying dormant because we had bought the lie that says to stay safe and comfortable, and God will reward you richly for your successful avoidance. Again, our experience in Guatemala had given us a glimpse of a more purposeful, intentional way of being, and we longed for more of it. We just had no clue how that translated to life in the here and now.

Together, we agreed to give a whole month to a very specific prayer where we'd ask God: *"What in the freak* (even I know it's not good to swear while praying) *is happening here, God? What are you telling us? How now shall we live?"*

God refused to give us an answer via a message in the sky or a random note from a stranger appearing on our doorstep, so we had no choice but to take a leap. We had to just go forward into the unknown and trust that our restless spirits were indeed from God and that we needed to do something. Doing nothing just wasn't an option. With Guatemala still fresh on our minds and our little Guatemalan baby daily reminding us that some people in the world are so poor they need to give up their children, we decided we'd like to start by taking a couple of weeks in the summer to serve in that country. That sounded possible and doable to the two of us and we grew more excited about the possibility every day.

Yes! Two weeks in Guatemala serving the "least of these!" That must be what God's been trying to tell us!

Then Keith and Suzann invited us out to dinner.

Throughout the lively conversation about many global initiatives Mars Hill was involved in, Paul and I were both feeling our hearts racing. We were loving this stuff and felt even more compelled to bring up our idea of serving in Guatemala. On the way home, from the back seat of Keith's car, Paul took the first step and asked a question that forever changed our lives' paths. He asked Keith, "Realistically, Keith, what kinds of things could Cindy and I actually do globally? I mean, we've been talking about how it sounds great to go to Guatemala for maybe a couple of weeks this coming summer, but we are not missionaries, nor do we want to be. We have no Bible training or seminary background. I'm not a doctor or a dentist and I certainly can't build a darn thing, so what could a couple like us do? We're just an accountant and a nurse. That's all."

Keith's head tipped back slightly and he let out a little chuckle. He had us against the ropes and knew it.

"I'll tell you exactly what you could do. Just today I received an email from a guy named Henry Deneen. Henry lives in France, and just this morning he and his teammates were praying and asking God to find them a finance guy who could step into their work of business development in North Africa. You'd be like an un-missionary—where you simply do the work God created you to do. In your case, Paul, you just go do accounting. It's called Business As Missions—or BAM—and it's all the rage in Christian circles involved in global outreach. You just go live for Jesus in a location where not many others do. It's the new wave of missions, Paul."

Paul squeezed my hand. I think I leaked a little pee.

My heart picked up pace as I tried to imagine France from the pictures in the Madeline books I often read to Grace. I was incredibly naive, ignorant, and culturally dull, and I'm fairly sure I couldn't have located France on the kids' globe. *Would God really orchestrate a prayer meeting this very morning where folks are looking for an accountant and then here, now, over dinner with Keith, lead our conversation to this place of consideration? Could we really go to France for a few weeks, and Paul could pour his accounting/business expertise on this Henry fella, and soon Christian businesses would just start popping up all over North Africa? How cool would that be?*

I had no concept, really, of what Keith was proposing.

Then Keith dropped the proverbial bomb that would later blow up our world. "I think Henry is looking for about a year or two commitment. You guys would be perfect."

I never, ever, in my wildest dreams, imagined this moment, that invitation. Never once did we consider living anywhere but Hudsonville. People come from all over to move into our city, no one moves out.

Paul squeezed my hand again, but I didn't know if it was a "Wow, this is incredible" squeeze or a "Screw this idea. Two years? No way" squeeze. I tried to make sense of all the crazy thoughts and emotions swirling around in my head, and when I couldn't, I did what I always do: I wept. I didn't want Paul or

Keith or Suzann to know I was losing it so I wiped my tears with the sleeve of my white cardigan. When we got out of their car, I noticed Keith noticing my mascara-smudged sweater.

Paul and I had both been experiencing some kind of stirring, no doubt. And we wholeheartedly agreed we needed to redirect our lives, most notably our finances, to find a better purpose. But we never wanted to be missionaries. We never wanted to be pamphlet passers and Bible thumpers who go to school specifically to learn how to coerce others to join their gang. While we believe in the lifegiving, saving knowledge of accepting Jesus Christ as your Lord and Savior, we felt more compelled to just spread God's love and let the Holy Spirit do any coercing. And like Keith suggested, we just wanted to be Christians using our God-given talents to do something for Jesus in a foreign land. Un-missionaries. Like 7-Up. I liked that. We'd be the un-cola of Christian outreach.

This logic made sense to me. In our little town of Hudsonville, there is a gas station owned by a Pakistani family. They came to America simply for the business opportunity and a better life. They are Muslim and nobody expects otherwise from them. They live out their faith in all their day-to-day interactions, and I would suppose, at times, they are more than happy to share about their faith and religion with those who may be intrigued. We would be no different. This idea of simply working in your professional giftedness in a foreign country, yet still living missionally in our day-to-day walk with Jesus, wouldn't look any different whether we were in Hudsonville or Paris, Hong Kong or Paraguay. We are Christians. We believe in living our faith out loud. Is that a missionary? Not in the traditional sense, it isn't.

We were left with a colossal question: Was this France thing from God? Paul working in his giftedness, serving with an initiative to reach North Africa. . . . *That's pretty cool, isn't it? And you sometimes do cool things, right, God?* Keith was right. This opportunity in France was a good fit for us.

Uh-oh. Crap.

Perfect perhaps except for four rather significant things: (1) a boy named Andy, (2) a boy named Josiah, (3) a girl named Grace and (4) a girl named Yulisa. Oh wait, (5) an accounting firm Paul owned (perhaps it owned him, we were never sure). Oh wait, (6) grandparents who would never forgive us for taking their grandkids across the ocean. Oh wait, (7) a huge home mortgage. Oh, and another thing: Did Keith fail to mention there would be no pay for joining this initiative? Oh—and the follow up to the previous thing—we'd need to raise our own financial support, something we didn't believe in and scorned other Christians who did. What is that, now? About nine really logical and solid reasons to not even consider such a radical opportunity. It was absurd and out of the question.

Let's walk away now, Paul.

Tomorrow, I'm going to search the Internet for something we can do in Guatemala for two weeks this coming summer. Better fit for us. Safer. Shorter. Easier. Yes! Guatemala it is.

Simply as an act of honoring Keith, we agreed we'd follow up with this Henry character and would, indeed, commit the opportunity to prayer. But we knew there was no way we'd move overseas. We were just way too embedded in Hudsonville—in every conceivable way. My head kept speaking to my heart with rationalizations and justifications as to why this whole calling thing was messed up. *Certainly, this is not from God,* I told myself, *and certainly not intended for us.*

My head (and relatives) kept saying things like, "You'll ruin your kids for life! If you guys won't be traditional missionaries and raise support, it'll cost you a fortune and you'll never recover! You cannot leave your family and friends! You'll never find a community like the one you have here!" This one, constantly playing on repeat in my brain, may have hit home the hardest: "Certainly God doesn't ask families like ours to do stuff like this—those who are so rooted in the community, who recently built their dream home, who volunteer at their church and school, who teach Bible studies, who coach Little League, and who own their own business—families who are just so . . . so . . . so . . . comfortable."

And there it was. That word. That word that was beginning to feel a little prickly—like swallowing granola before chewing. *Comfortable.* And why? Why was that word starting to make me uncomfortable?

Why was *comfortable* starting to feel like a swear word?

STOP IT, GOD! Stop making me feel guilty for being comfortable—it's not a sin!

Even though some part of me was screaming, "Don't do this, Cindy, you idiot! Don't you dare uproot your family and move to France! Run for the hills!" my heart felt a very strange tugging forward.

What Happens When You Pray?

We prayed for clarity so we would know we were really wanted and needed in France. We still mistakenly believed that missionaries, or anyone who lived for Jesus overseas, could only be old people or college students and certainly not families with children. We still believed only evangelism geeks or rich doctors are called to do this kind of thing. We emailed Henry and told him so. We told him it probably wasn't going to work because we were just so, so . . . so average. We are just two ordinary, run-of-the-mill, nothing-special people: an accountant and a nurse. Neither of us has had any Bible training and—brace yourself, Henry—we even attended public schools! For goodness sakes, Henry, as a junior higher, I regularly copied Betsy Tacoma's Bible quiz answers at Wednesday night catechism class! Not to mention, Henry, we have four kids. Four! Nobody pulls up stakes and moves halfway around the world with four kids! And these aren't just any kids, Henry. Oh, no! These are extremely special and gifted kids who are most likely going to secure college scholarships in sports or academics or both and then probably go on to play professional sports, solve world hunger, and find a cure for cancer. These kids? These kids cannot possibly give up their travel teams, their special classes for gifted and talented children, and their blue star school which is going to guarantee them college admission to the university of their choice just so we can "follow God" to France. No, Henry, we are very sure our family is not what you were looking for.

Henry emailed back: "My wife and I have four kids too—nearly the same ages as yours. In fact, they have some of the same interests as your kids, and they're involved in those same activities here in France. I am a lawyer, also not an evangelist. My wife is a schoolteacher. We prayed specifically for an accountant to come join us and even more specifically asked God to send us a family with kids. You are exactly who we are looking for and exactly who we've been praying for."

When Paul and I read that email, we fell to our knees on our bedroom floor (this was before laptops and so our nearly two-ton computer resided on our solid walnut, nearly four-ton desk in our bedroom). We had this moment of quasi-praying and pleading with God: *What the heck is going on here, God? It feels like You're really telling us to do this thing! That's not really You, is it? You don't ask Your people to do hard things, do You?*

I looked at Paul, and he had this strange look on his face. It wasn't the look of fear I expected to see. He had a look of sad resignation—almost as if someone just burst his bubble. And, in a way, it was exactly that for him—the beginning of the deconstruction of his empire. He had poured his life into his work to build this imperial life we enjoyed. And it was as if, with each step closer to affirming a move to France, God was slowly tearing down the walls. The look on his face was freaking me out a little. I had never seen anything like it before.

I felt the air grow thin in the room, yet it was strangely fun and trippy, and perhaps I wanted more. The room was kind of spinning, but in a good way. I felt like I was floating away from life—all I had ever wanted and all we had worked so hard for—was slipping away and life was, at that moment, starting to redefine itself.

Yes, give me more . . . more of this trippy stuff . . .

I think taking a hit of marijuana might feel similar, but I can't be entirely sure. I only tried it once, in Ft. Lauderdale, spring break my freshman year of college. But I'm pretty sure, just like Bill Clinton, I didn't inhale.

After that email, we started to get a little more serious about praying. We prayed for a way that an owner of an accounting firm could leave for two years. *I mean, come on, God, that's not possible, is it? We'll lose the business, won't we? Then what? Won't our lives be ruined forever?*

What happens when you pray? This:

A serendipitous golf outing brought Randy, Paul's business partner, together with the guys' former employer, Scott VanPopering. Scott and his three business partners had taught Paul and Randy everything they knew about accounting. When Paul and Randy had branched out on their own with many of the firm's clients following them, they received blessings from Scott and his partners instead of an insolent brush-off—no small accounting miracle.

Out on the green, Scott happened to mention he was between jobs. The big thing he'd been a part of for the last few years was winding down and he just hadn't made his mind up on what he'd do next. Randy informed Scott our family was contemplating moving to France but the only way it would work for Paul was if someone could fill in for him for two years. On a whim, Randy asked Scott if he'd ever consider working at DeBoer and Goodyke. With barely any hesitation, Scott said yes. Yes, he would very much like to step in and manage Paul's clients, many who used to be his clients, for a couple of years.

Now, please hear me, friends. God alone could arrange for the one and only person who could seamlessly step into Paul's shoes as owner of a busy accounting firm—the very man who trained Paul and had previously done the accounting for many of these same clients—to be in a season of unknown and willing to pinch hit for two years. At this point, the hair on the backs of our necks stayed stuck in the air, because things were starting to get weird. Miracle-weird.

Still, we had that big darn house. No one in his or her right mind would pay us the rent we would need to cover our ridiculous mortgage. Besides, big houses on ten acres in the country just don't rent. We contemplated selling it. But how in the world could we sell that monster in just a few months, and didn't we want to return home to it in two years? Yes, we did. We couldn't sell it. We thought the big white house might be our albatross. But then, out of nowhere, my sister Diane called. They were in the process of selling their home and hoping to build their own dream home, but their plans took a twist when their current home sold much too quickly. They needed to move out very soon. Yet, they were at least a year away from having their new home built and completed, so they needed somewhere to stay for a minimum of a year, maybe longer.

We said, "Ha! That's actually very funny. Because, you see, we have a house. And we have a little inkling to move to France, so we need renters in said house. And truthfully, we still care too much about this place to have just anybody rent it. If we could choose from all God's people on all of God's green earth who we'd want to rent from us, it would be you guys. We need to talk!"

Things were moving faster and faster, including my heart!

But we still faced what we perceived to be the biggest barrier: our kids. If I'm honest, there was this little part of me that deep down believed our kids truly were the exceptional ones who were going to defy the odds and secure college athletic scholarships and maybe even carry on professionally. It sounds ridiculous as I type this, but isn't there a part in all of us parents that believes our kids are exceptional? I mean, our kids did have some natural athletic ability, but I had bought into the lie that the only way their skills could develop into something with a real pay-off is if we stayed in the American rat race, signed them up for pro lessons and travel teams, and sucked up to all their high school coaches. This is America, and it's just what we do here. And if I'm honest, I'm sure that somewhere deep down I wanted to redeem my mediocre athletic achievements by sending four kids through the same school district and watching them make all my dreams come true.

As I wrestled with those irrational thoughts, we came across a news article covering an interview with Sparky Anderson, the winningest coach of all times for the Detroit Tigers. The interviewer asked Sparky what advice he'd give parents who want to get their sons into the Major Leagues. Sparky told the reporter that a young man will make it to the Major Leagues *in spite* of anything his parents do for him. Sparky knew that if your son is Derek Jeter or Willy Mays, that even if you wanted to, there's not a darn thing you could do to keep them *out* of professional baseball. And the inverse is true as well—there's not a darn thing you can do to make a Major Leaguer out of a boy who doesn't have the total package. That level of talent and drive isn't something any amount of professional training, travel teams, or perfect parenting can create. When kids have both God-given talent and an "eye-of-the-tiger" spirit, nothing can stop them. You can't give your kids those gifts, nor can you take them away.

That revolutionary mindset suddenly released us from the death grip of children's sports craziness. Our kids would be fine if we moved to another country. If they were destined to greatness, in any capacity, they would continue toward that end no matter what country they lived in.

One click at a time God convinced us we needed at the very least to explore the France thing. Now we just needed the kids convinced of the same thing. We had not even shared with them the possibility of moving until it looked like all other roadblocks were removed. Finally, we decided it was time to get their input.

We took the boys out to dinner, and over burgers and fries we told them we thought maybe God was asking us to move to France.

"Why?" asked Andy, who was smarter than any sixth grader has a right to be. "Why would anyone do that?"

"Why not?" I asked him back. The four of us spent about an hour discussing all the "why nots." I had to admit, from a nine- and eleven-year-old boy's perspective, saying goodbye to your friends and family, Little League and golf lessons, the Disney Channel and the English language, summers at the lake and hanging out with awesome grandparents, all because God wanted you to move halfway around the world, sure makes God look like a bad guy. Neither boy shed a single tear over dinner, yet they were clearly united, saying they thought it was a bad idea. They were, however, willing to commit the idea to prayer.

We agreed that if after two weeks of committed prayer they were still dead set against the idea, we'd drop it. And we meant it. We repeatedly promised them we'd never take them to France kicking and screaming. Either we were all on board or none of us were. I guess we just overruled the feelings of Grace and Yulisa who were three and one at the time. (I do think the two of them just thought of France as being about as far from Hudsonville as, say, Chicago—just a long ride away. They never quite grasped the enormity of the decision.) Anyway, if after two weeks of prayer the boys were opening up to the idea, we would take them to France to visit the location, the families we'd be working with, and their potential schools. We'd all give France a fair shake before deciding this was a definite yes or no. We also threw the boys a bone. We promised to take them to the beaches of Normandy while in France. They were both history buffs and what red-blooded, pre-teen boy wouldn't want to see a real-live World War II German bunker on *the* Omaha beach?

They took the bone. Four weeks later we were on a plane to Paris.

Our Boys

Like Cinderella slipping her foot into the glass slipper, everything fit. I couldn't deny that this France opportunity felt custom-made for us. And as the reality crept in that a move might actually happen, I panicked and searched for problems, red flags, or personality conflicts that would stop the wheels on this bus. There were none.

I even baited the other American families in Aix-en-Provence (the city we'd call home should we accept the offer) with our hesitations so they could open up about how hard it was for them to live in France. At a gathering of English speakers who all attended the same church, I approached the Fishers—a couple wrapping up their two years in France and whom we'd be replacing—and said, "You know, I think we're probably going to pass on moving here. The idea is definitely intriguing to me and Paul, but we just can't do it to our kids. And maybe the problem lies with us. Maybe we're just not strong enough to watch them suffer. Even the thought of it makes me weepy. I don't know if we'd be disobeying God, but I don't think we can do it to our kids."

Paige Fisher's response nearly leveled me. She gently said, "You know, I've been reflecting back on these last two years here in France as we're preparing to go back to the states, and I can honestly say I can't think of a better gift we could have given our children. Our two years here have molded and shaped them in new and rich ways that I didn't even know were possible. They have grown so much in their faith and love for others that I truly think it's one of the best decisions we've ever made."

I was so not expecting that.

We were under no illusion that a move to France would be challenging in the same way a move to a place like Guatemala or Haiti or Burundi might be. France is France. In fact, if you *had* to move your family somewhere, many Americans might even choose France. For us, it wasn't the location so much that intimidated us (although, by this time, many well-intentioned people had warned us that France was notorious for eating expats alive), but it felt like pure lunacy to uproot our kids and move them so far away from normal. I had not considered that something so ridiculous could actually turn out to be a gift to our kids. I had been imagining the six of us squirming, straining, and suffering as we gutted out two years in France. I was only willing to consider doing it because God had clearly opened many doors. But when push came to shove, I was sure we'd still say "no, thank you," because the sacrifice and suffering would simply be too great.

With one fell swoop, Paige had turned that notion on its head.

And then the thing I never imagined could happen happened: In just one short week, both our boys fell in love with France, the American families we'd just met, and the whole idea of moving. They literally cornered me and Paul on our last night and said they were afraid we might be the ones to pull the plug. They wanted to make sure we were going to accept the invitation to move because they didn't want to say goodbye to their new friends forever. Isn't that hilarious? Our boys—our big fear—our biggest reason for thinking we shouldn't even consider an overseas option, were now the ones saying they wanted to do it, and they feared we would be the ones to change our minds!

I've come to believe that if we want to experience a wild, ridiculous, and completely impossible answer to prayer, we've got to start by asking God to do something wild, ridiculous, and completely impossible.

We had simply experienced too many miraculous events to deny God was calling us to France. At that point, anything else would have been pure disobedience. It was that clear to us.

So yes, our boys agreed to move to France.

Almost four months to the day from when Keith first told us about the opportunity in France, we were loading up our family, sixteen pieces of luggage, and a two-year supply of peanut butter and chocolate chips onto a British Airways flight out of Grand Rapids, Michigan. It felt surreal—with a big dose of exhilarating and a little dose of sexy—to be actually moving to France! We had almost zero expectations. How can you create expectations for something of which you have no understanding? And that turned out to be a good thing. If we had had grand expectations, we would have fallen harder.

CHAPTER 13

Number 1,264

"Never be afraid to trust an unknown future to a known God."

CORRIE TEN BOOM

For the first time in twenty-four hours, I successfully navigated the complicated locks on our apartment building with their eighteenth-century skeleton keys and finally got off the elevator on the correct floor—the ground floor. The European system calls the ground floor 0 instead of 1, which threw me at first. My spirits buoyed slightly by that tiny feat, I took in the warmth of the Provençal sunshine along with the unfamiliar sounds of an awakening city. The plane trees across the street with their signature look of leprosy-bark seemed to be saying, "Welcome, to France, Cindy." I felt a little surge of hope—maybe I could tackle this task, after all. I summoned my strength and courage and moved toward the sidewalk, promptly stepping into an enormous pile of *caca de chien*. There couldn't be a more apt depiction of how I felt our lives were going so far in our new home country.

We had just arrived the previous evening, and I was already going out alone. Most of our sixteen pieces of luggage were still unopened, the kid's toys were strewn all over our living room, and we'd lost Grace's comfort animal, Teddy, in all the chaos. We had unpacked the essentials the previous evening: toys, movies, and peanut butter, and I was anxious to get at the rest today and try to make our very ancient looking apartment feel more homey. But somewhere during the night, Paul became ill, and I had to pause my nesting instincts. He'd pushed himself so hard in the three months leading up to our move that now that we'd arrived, his body simply crashed and burned. It wasn't just the "little sick" some men exaggerate to extract some rare sympathies from their wives—he was "BIG sick." I heard it. There was no way he was exaggerating. *It* was coming from everywhere. And it was evident he needed medication for *it*. Fast.

Unfortunately, the only provisions we had in our little two-bedroom, fourth-floor apartment were the things we'd taken from the States along with some starter groceries supplied by our friends, the Deneens. Neither of us had thought of medicine. Those fifteen jars of peanut butter were of no use in this scenario. Rescuing this dying man was entirely up to me—his only hope. I had no choice but to leave our safe apartment and venture out alone into our new hometown: Aix-en-Provence.

My task was to find an ATM to retrieve some Euros (I also didn't think of exchanging dollars for Euros before we left. I mean, seriously? I remembered to pack plastic applicator tampons and chocolate cake mixes because Fodor's Travel Book told me France had neither, but I never thought of getting the correct currency!), and then I'd need to find a pharmacy and figure out how to communicate Paul's needs. It sounds so easy and ridiculous now. I can do those things in my sleep all these years later. But at the time it felt like stepping out of my lunar lander and going to find alien life forms on a foreign planet.

My heart raced and the backs of my eyeballs were on fire. But I was also determined to stay the ever positive and confident wife who may have been slightly more certain of God's call to move here than her counterpart. I spent the morning frantically trying to memorize the French words for "fever," "vomiting," "diarrhea," "stupid American," "husband," and "just moved here" before heading out the door.

As it was years before the iPhone or before anyone had even heard of GPS, I reached into my purse and grabbed a piece of paper to take notes on the route I'd be taking. The last thing I wanted to do was get lost and need to ask someone (in English, no less) how to get back to my apartment (of which I didn't even know the address). My notetaking turned out to be genius. The cobbled labyrinth of streets in Aix-en-Provence (pronounced "ex-ahn-Pro-vahnss") is a challenge to every newcomer, and I would have been hopelessly lost without playing my version of Hansel and Gretel.

Within a few blocks I found an ATM. Little did I know at the time, but many months later accepted as commonplace, that the ATMs in Europe are kind of a crapshoot. Sometimes they work. Sometimes they don't. Sometimes they have cash. Sometimes they don't. Sometimes they eat your card. Sometimes the bank actually cares.

I had seriously handicapped myself by not writing down the French words for "under repair," "account balance," "withdrawal," "service fee," and "receipt." It may be improving around Europe these days, but these ATMs offered no English options. You either learned French quickly or just guessed a lot. That morning,

I made a lot of lousy guesses. I went through four ATMs before finding one to cough up some Euros.

With my entire face now on fire, I felt an all-out meltdown encroaching. But just a few blocks further, I scored on finding a pharmacy. All the French cramming I had done that morning evaporated from my stressed-out brain, and I couldn't even come up with "Bonjour." Instead, I smiled a lot, and I think that softened the team of people who had gathered to come to my assistance. I had two pharmacists, a clerk, and a customer all huddled around me trying to decipher my gestures, hand motions, and English. In the end, I walked out of that place with 42 Euros of medicine, four new friends, and zero pride.

Aix-en-Provence

Paul felt better a few days later, and I found my adventurous nature returning with him at my side. We walked all over Aix— identifying the closest grocer, the best bakery, the cheapest flower market, and the quaintest coffee shops. Aix is something out of a fairy tale. Its fabled main street, the Cours Mirabeau, is lined with chic restaurants and coffee shops whose canopied tables spill over onto the sun-soaked sidewalks creating a sea of well-dressed humanity. All the chairs are positioned to face the street so patrons can be fully engrossed in people-watching while political debating and fine-wine drinking. It feels like walking into the movie set of *Chocolat* or *Les Misérables*.

But we didn't have much time to sightsee or even soak up any culture. We were not on vacation. We lived here now. My heart skipped a beat just at the thought of it. I felt a little cloud of anxiety return. We had a huge to-do list. Get cell phones. Find a pediatrician. Open a bank account. Find the big box stores for things like a TV and microwave. Find a church. Get our computer working. Secure internet. Enroll our kids in school.

There. That one. Holy freaking-out moment: Get our kids enrolled in school! The whole France experience thus far, four days since arrival, had me unhinged from all the differentness: different words, different foods, different money, different smells, different toilets, different toilet paper, different products for everything, different outlets, different home—different life. But to watch my kids—my flesh and blood and adopted blood— suffer through some of that same fear as they experienced all this differentness was just too much. Taking Andy to the large public middle school around the corner from our apartment turned out to be one of the hardest things I've ever done in my life.

As soon as we officially decided to move to France, we began praying about where our kids would go to school. The other American families we were joining in Aix sent their kids to a lovely, small, Christian school called La Nouvelle Alliance. The school battled low enrollment and never knew from year to year if it would remain open, but it turned out to be the perfect solution for Josiah and Grace. However, the school only offered kindergarten through fifth grade and Andy would be entering the sixth grade. So we prayed and prayed some more about where Andy should attend.

Again we looked to the wisdom of other families who explained our options were few, and none too great. They had chosen a large public middle school for their older kids called College Mignet (pronounced "cull-ledge" and translates as "middle school") and found it to be decent. The school was unique in that it had an international section for expatriate kids. This program placed qualified international kids on a fast-paced course toward French fluency so they could be mainstreamed as quickly as possible. It sounded like the only viable option for Andy. And then it sounded impossible—because there were only twenty spots in the international section for each grade and nineteen spots were already taken as early as July. We weren't going to arrive in Aix until October. We prayed and prayed for Andy to receive that one remaining spot. So again, it was nothing short of a miracle that when we landed in France, College Mignet still had an opening for Andy.

The night before he was to begin classes, Andy's chocolate brown eyes betrayed the terror he was so bravely trying to mask. Like any overbearing mom, I repeatedly asked him if he was okay, but he refused to answer. Andy is typically the epitome of kindness and respect. Shunning a direct question was so uncharacteristic. He silently watched us move around our too-small rental apartment and with those huge brown eyes steadily growing bigger, he was beseeching us for an answer. An answer to that unanswerable question, "Why are you doing this to me?" Although Andy had agreed we had somehow, supernaturally, felt God telling us to move to France, and had even pleaded with us to say yes when we were hesitant, I don't think he had ever processed all that a move to a foreign country would entail. He hadn't anticipated what an enormous challenge starting a new school, in a foreign language, in a foreign country would be. How would any kid be able to comprehend it?

We had worn out that pithy, empty phrase long ago of "God told us to." When you are an eleven-year-old ripped away from all that is safe, familiar, fun, and easy in the world and then dragged halfway around the globe to France to be plopped in a French-speaking international school where you don't speak the language and there is no one you know, well, at that moment, you don't particularly care much about the stupid voice of God. In fact, the incredible, painful look of sadness in his eyes made me think we hadn't heard from God at all. I mean, we hadn't really heard an audible voice, had we? So could it be this was our idea and that our ideas had run amok? Were we the bad guys inflicting this pain on our sweet firstborn? Or was God the bad guy inflicting this pain? Either way, for an eleven-year-old, the people (or entity) you were supposed to trust were causing you pain. How in the world can an eleven-year-old reconcile such crap? I imagined he was thinking: *Why is God so mean to tell my mom and dad to do this to me? Is God actually evil—wanting to watch His children suffer? Why would He ask this of me?*

Imagine was all I could do—because he said not a word.

One Friend

We put him to bed that night and prayed with him like we've done with all four of our kids every night of their lives. We prayed for many things that night—including a request we had been praying for the last month leading up to this monumental step. We prayed for just one friend. One true friend. We've always told the kids it's not really necessary to have a whole posse of friends, as long as you have one good and trusted friend who has your back and truly loves you. One true friend can make all the difference between a good and a bad school year. So again, that night, we asked God to bring Andy just one good friend at College Mignet, Aix-en-Provence, France, come the morning. Paul prayed and I could only listen. It wasn't just that I had a tennis ball stuck in my throat—it had also been dunked in gasoline and set to fire. I was a hot mess. Paul too, choked his way through that prayer, and then we retreated to the too-small living room.

I felt doubt creep in. I despised France at that moment. I despised this smoke-drenched, backward, bureaucratic society. I despised this sing-songy language I knew I'd never conquer. I despised this too-small apartment. I despised the Deneens for asking us to come. I despised that my son had to share a room with his three younger siblings and on this, the eve of his first day at a new school in a foreign country that he never asked to attend, cried himself to sleep while his siblings listened. Honestly, I despised God at that moment and I doubted he truly ever calls anyone anywhere. And so I did the only thing I could think of at that moment (besides run to the computer and order the first six flights I could find from Paris to Grand Rapids, Michigan). I flipped open my Bible.

I had no inspiration. I had no idea where to turn to for help at a time like this. So I did what I've heard they do in the Apostolic church—they just kind of toss their Bible up (reverently) and let it fall open randomly to whatever page God wills. The passage their eyes first land on is their message from God. My Bible opened up to this passage: "Listen to my words, LORD, consider my lament. Hear my cry for help, my King and my God, for to you I pray. In the morning, LORD, you hear my voice; in the morning I lay my requests before you and wait expectantly" (Psalm 5:1–3 NIV).

Can you even freakin' believe that? My Bible has 1,278 pages and 783,137 words. But out of all that, God leads me to the verse reminding us He'll be with us *in the morning*!

I rushed back into Andy's room hoping I'd catch him still awake (he wasn't going to sleep at all that night, who was I kidding?), and I shared with him that Scripture. I told him I believed, with all my heart, that God was going to reveal Himself enormously through all this. I believed that because Andy was putting himself out there to be tried and tested through this extra suffering, God was going to meet him in that need and so he (and all of us) would never be the same because of it. He cried. I cried. Paul cried in the hallway. I tried to sound so brave with Andy, but when Paul and I retreated to our room, we held each other and cried ourselves to sleep. This was our firstborn—our leader of the pack who led the other three brilliantly. We had spent his whole life sheltering him from pain and doing everything within our power to keep him from any suffering—of any kind. We would both willingly lay down our lives for this young man if the need arose. In fact, there's not a thing we wouldn't do for that boy to keep him from harm. So how in the world did we find ourselves in this position of having to choose between trusting God and protecting Andy? Is there any possible way this was how Abraham felt? Is it possible the purpose of the story of Abraham and Isaac is to give us strength when we must watch our children suffer?

Morning was brutal. Again, he spoke not a word. Like a lamb being led to the slaughter, he didn't make a sound. I felt as if I should be struck dead by lightning or called into Child Protective Services for this kind of parenting malpractice. Although we somehow survived breakfast, the worst was yet to come.

Andy and I walked the short distance to College Mignet and the Provincial bright sunshine tried to make us smile. Andy was having none of it. About a dozen elderly men wearing woolen plaid knickers and berets were playing boules in the park next to the school, and for a split second I thought about taking a picture. Then I heard Andy sniffle and was catapulted back into reality: *We are not on vacation here, Cindy.*

Our friend Celia greeted us at the entrance of the fortified school. Celia would be our translator as I enrolled Andy. We were able to get right in to see the principal, Monsieur Constantine, a surly looking Frenchy-French man with a handle-bar mustache and a cheap-looking navy suit. He shook my hand and said a quick, "Bonjour, madame" but that was the last of our contact. He sat with his back to me and only talked to Celia—about me and about Andy—and completely disregarded the two of us as if we were not worth his time or energy. After all, we don't speak French, so we must be stupid, right?

Monsieur Constantine told Celia he didn't believe Andy would succeed at his school. He said Andy was too old to be thrown into a language immersion program and have any level of success. He said normally eight years old is considered the cut-off age for joining a school in a foreign language. He said without French-speaking parents at home, Andy would most definitely fail at French as well as fall behind in his other subjects. He said it just couldn't be done. He said the French schools are not like American schools. The staff here don't babysit, coddle, and nurture the students—they simply teach. He said that if a student succeeds in France, it's because he or she made it happen, not the teachers. He said in France, students are just a number. And then, for the first time, he looked at Andy, whose brown eyes were melting down his cheeks, and said (now in perfect English!) "And you are number 1,264. Now grab your cry rag and kiss your momma goodbye."

My vision went blurry, and the room started spinning, and I can't remember if Celia carried me out on her back, in a cart, or just rolled me out like a log on the floor, but I'm quite certain my noodle legs were not functional. Celia kept telling me, "It's fine. He'll do fine. Really, Cindy, trust me, he'll do fine!"

Andy's big brown eyes begged to differ. But somehow, we exited the office and turned left, and Andy and the nasty mustache man turned right. And I left that building thinking to myself that that moment hurt worse to me than the day I birthed that kid with no anesthetic in twenty hours of labor, all nine pounds six ounces of him (nine pounds of that being his big head). Yes, this moment hurt even worse.

I'll deliver a dozen more nine pound six ounce babies right here on this sidewalk if someone would just go rescue my eleven-year-old boy from the nasty mustache man in that jail-like school-wannabe building!

I was furious with God. I mean, really, what kind of no-good, nasty God would pluck an eleven-year-old out of the Shire-esque town of Hudsonville where there's a church on every street corner and where they still pray in their public schools and plop that kid in a big ol' public school in France with no language, friends, or support and with a wicked principal who thrives on making foreigners feel ignorant and stupid? A mean, heartless God is what I thought. A God who doesn't know what's best for an eleven-year-old.

Back at the apartment, I told Paul to drop what he was doing and clear the day of any appointments or hopes of accomplishing anything. These were my orders: "We are going to spend this day in prayer and we are going to give God ONE CHANCE to fix this. If Andy doesn't have a great day—not just a good day, but a great day—I want to start looking for tickets back to Michigan. I mean it, Paul. This is bullshit. I can't stand watching my kid suffer like this. What were we thinking? What was God thinking?"

Paul lets me rant like this often. So he obliged me. But he knew all along we weren't going to pack the family back up and move back to our white house, kick Diane and Bryan out, and start back at the accounting firm after just one week of trying out this "France thing." But he did agree to pray. And pray we did. All day.

I also cleaned that apartment like a freakin' Merry Maid on meth. To my horror and disgust, I discovered the black grout between the kitchen floor tiles was originally white and so I scrubbed those filthy floors till my fingers nearly bled, cursing the dirty French people and ancient apartment buildings built before Columbus (or whoever!) had even discovered my beautiful America. But I did pray fervently while I scrubbed.

At exactly 4:45 p.m. we left our apartment to pick Andy up outside the College Mignet building. French schools have extremely long days because they factor in a two-hour lunch break where many of the staff and students go home for lunch. I noticed, over time, many staff head out to restaurants and return just a wee bit intoxicated. After all, second to their lovely language, the lovely French do love their lovely wine. And third place goes to their lovely food.

So it was approaching 5:00 p.m. as Paul and I waited on the sidewalk outside this monstrous brick building probably built mid-nineteenth century. The bell rang. The kids spilled out of the ginormous double doors—many of them dressed in black (a French trademark of good style), many of them somewhat Gothic (a French experiment among middle school students to separate themselves from their overachieving parents), many of them smoking (wow, do the French love their cigs), and many of them with a darker complexion and darker hair than our Andy. When his bushy blonde hair peeked around the corner, I spotted him immediately. He paused ever so briefly at the top of the giant steps that led up to the front doors, and he scanned the crowd of parents to try to find us. With incredible tenacity, speed, and accuracy, my mommy radar kicked in—the one God gave to mothers that gives us unbelievable perception of our children's emotions by reading barely perceptible nuances on their faces. Moms, you know what I'm talking about. I looked for anything from his countenance to give me a window into his heart. Glossy eyes? Furrowed eyebrows? A quivering lip? Twinkling eyes? A flash of confidence? Despair? Rejection? Joy? Something . . . anything . . . give me *something*, Andy!

And then our eyes met. He found me in the crowd. What happened next is etched in my memory forever, and it was one of the holiest moments I've known—because God showed up. Goosebumps on my arms, chills down my spine, and dizzy from awe, He showed up. The corner of Andy's mouth curled upward—not even enough to be called a grin—but just a slight curvature. I knew that look as if it were a part of my own being—like looking at my own hand or knee—and it spoke at least a thousand words. He had had a good day. I knew it, and I was barely containing my tears or myself as he approached. After a hug and a kiss, he broke right in with this, "I met a friend. His name is Tom. He's Israeli, and he doesn't speak French either, so we're both in beginner French class. And he didn't arrive at the start of the year either, so he knows exactly what I'm going through." Then he smiled broader. I hugged him again and said, "One friend, Andy." And he echoed, "One good friend."

And that Tom kid made all the difference for Andy's experience in the international program at a French middle school, in Aix-en-Provence, France, for the years 2003 and 2004. The two were inseparable. Mr. Mustache Man never apologized to us, but we felt vindicated just the same when Andy not only survived College Mignet, he thrived. He sailed through the entry-level French classes and was speaking fluent French in no time. Within three months he was mainstreamed. He finished his seventh-grade year as the top international student and in the top ten of his class overall.

I looked at Andy on that first day of school on the sidewalk in front of College Mignet, beaming with self-confidence, with a new Jewish-Israeli friend, with a God bigger than life itself, and a promise in his pocket that God never leaves or forsakes us. I can hardly think of a better gift to give one's child. And we'd do it all over again in a heartbeat.

Just like childbirth.

CHAPTER 14

The Angel Two Floors Down

"Then you will call, and the LORD will answer.
You will cry for help and he will say: Here I am."

ISAIAH 58:9 (NIV)

Soon after surviving his first couple of weeks at College Mignet, Andy started vomiting. Not just once. Not just twice. Not just three or four or five times. He vomited for two days solid. On day three, he couldn't walk straight and bumped into the walls when he raced to the bathroom to puke. On the third night, he said he couldn't get off the couch and asked if he could just sleep in the living room. The next day he barely moved and lay motionless on the couch. He wouldn't turn his head or open his eyes because every time he did, he would throw up again. He had easily vomited (now, well into dry heaves) over twenty times by this point. Whenever he attempted to take a drink, he'd vomit—so he stopped putting in the effort, and I knew he was dehydrated. He stopped talking to us too. It was as if it just took too much energy to say words. He also developed nystagmus, when the pupils rapidly dart back and forth making it impossible to focus. When he should have been turning a corner toward improvement, Andy was getting sicker. My nursing instinct told me something was seriously wrong.

I called our pediatrician, Dr. Hoppe, a wonderful German man who spoke English (thank God for Europeans who learn many languages). He said we needed to bring Andy to the ER to be seen immediately. Looking back, I feel as if I should have moved sooner and should have known to bring him in, but my nursing background has over and over proved to be more detrimental than beneficial to my own family. I know just enough to be dangerous, but not enough to normally be helpful.

We told Andy we were bringing him to the hospital. He didn't move. We tried to sit him up. He threw up. We helped him to stand. He threw up. We talked about calling an ambulance, but we knew we'd never be able to say all the right words in French. So Paul picked up that kid, who was about five feet five inches tall and 120 pounds by then, and carried him down four flights of stairs, across the street, and down to the basement level of the car park where our car was located. I carried the bucket to catch Andy's frothy saliva when he dry heaved.

At the hospital, it felt like we'd stepped into a scene from the movie *Halloween*, where Jamie Lee Curtis keeps choosing to walk down abandoned hospital corridors as Jason lies in wait for her. *Are you stupid, Jamie? Don't go down that dark hallway. Choose the one on the right that is all lit up and people are milling around! You're an idiot, Jamie!*

Again, Paul hoisted Andy over his shoulder while I maintained the puke bucket directly beneath his bobbing head and we strode across the dark, eerie parking lot. No one came out to meet us like they do at our favorite hospital in Michigan. Utterly alone at the dimly lit Emergency Bay entrance, we channeled our Jamie Lee Curtis courage and entered the ivy-covered, centuries-old, brick French building. We were greeted with the stench of something like fish and asparagus—not at all the latex-gloves-and-hand-sanitizer smell of American hospitals. The reception area was abandoned, and the one small flickering fluorescent ceiling light was no match for the long dark corridor in front of us. We saw no indications of human life whatsoever. In a hospital. In a decent-sized city. No one. No one but Jamie Lee Curtis and Jason lurking somewhere in the shadows.

We wondered if sometimes hospitals in France just decide to close for no apparent reason—kind of like their gas stations and restaurants and schools. Paul picked up his pace and headed straight down the corridor looking for humans to help us. He walked too fast for me and I couldn't keep the puke bucket under Andy's head. Andy retched and the frothy saliva ran down Paul's back instead.

We finally found the staff and although they spoke not a word of English, we were able to convey that Andy had been sick for four days with *beaucoup, beaucoup de vomis.* They understood and brought us to a dark cubicle to sit and wait for the doctor. Six hours later, with nothing more than an X-ray of his stomach and some blood tests performed, the doctor said we could take Andy home. I asked him, in terrible, broken French, why Andy could be discharged when he was still so gravely ill.

With long pauses, and great deliberation, he mustered up his best English to impress his monolingual Americans and told us this: "The . . . film . . . finds Andy . . . with . . . hhhhair in his stomach. Hhhhe goes hhhhome now." The French don't pronounce the letter *h* like we do—it is almost always silent, as in "hors d'oeuvres"—and as a result you will often hear French people who are trying to learn English insert extra h's where h's don't belong simply because they are overcompensating. The doctor meant to say Andy's x-ray showed "air" in his stomach and that, being nothing at all, meant he could go home. However, air in the stomach clearly does not cause days of endless vomiting. We were so mad, we couldn't even laugh at his language *faux pas* (a French word, by the way).

We carried Andy back to the car while he wretched. We couldn't believe they were sending us home. I started to cry. I knew there was something more going on with Andy than "h-air in his stomach." That doctor was an idiot. Paul knew it too. But Paul always looks to me to make the medical decisions for our kids. I'm not blaming him for that. I look to him to do our tax returns and to make all monetary decisions. Thank God! We'd be in financial ruin if it were up to me. But Paul should know better by now—if the medical question isn't ICU related, such as a post-quadruple-cardiac-bypass patient with a pacemaker and on a ventilator, I was pretty much useless. However, we both knew we had to do something more. By the time we got home, the sun was beginning to rise.

We called Dr. Hoppe's office but got the answering machine. We left an urgent message for him.

Paul and I slumped down in the two chairs opposite Andy on the couch, both of us breathless and exhausted—Paul from carrying Andy up four flights of stairs and me from all the crying. For several hopeless minutes, we simply stared at our son. We watched his limp, weakened frame take slow, shallow breaths. His pale skin was taking on a grayish hue and some weird blue veins had appeared around his eyes. His cheekbones were much too prominent. I suddenly had a terrifying thought: *He's getting worse every hour now and I don't think he can keep going like this for too much longer.* Yet we were in a stupid foreign country where we didn't know their stupid systems, the ins and outs of their stupid healthcare, or even their stupid language. For the first time that evening, and for the first time in my life, a horrific thought crossed my mind—*Could we actually be losing him here? Is this the panic one feels before losing a child?*

I turned to God in a fit of rage, *"I'll tell you what, God . . . You listen here and you listen close . . . I will never, EVER, forgive you if you take my son."*

Almost as quickly as that prayer left my lips, the irony hit me. There could never be another being who would understand this moment—or understand my emotions—better than God our Father who surrendered his very own son. Not only did God surrender His son, He did it for me, so that in this very moment of panic, I would have a Savior to whom I could cry out to and who would understand suffering like no other.

House Call

Finally, after a few hour-long minutes, the phone rang. We told Dr. Hoppe the whole story of our night at the hospital. He was furious. He couldn't believe that "blankety-blank" hospital and their "blankety-blank" good-for-nothing doctors. He swore in German (which is a fun way to make expletives even more potent) and barely hesitated before telling us we needed to bring Andy into his office immediately. I told him I didn't think he could make it there. I explained how he puked with even the tiniest movement and how he just wouldn't (couldn't?) walk anymore. I said that although his body was now quite limp, he still was a very heavy boy and Paul just couldn't carry him back down the stairs and out across the street to our car again.

With very little deliberation, Dr. Hoppe agreed to make a house call and showed up at our apartment within half an hour. Only later did I find out how incredibly rare it is to have a doctor make a house call in France. I guess that's probably true in America too. Dr. Hoppe quickly realized how seriously sick Andy was and said we needed to have him seen by a neurological specialist right away. He said this was definitely a neurological illness and something very wrong was going on in Andy's brain. The hospital had completely missed it (or perhaps it had gotten worse as the night went on), but he said we needed a specialist now because it was such a bizarre presentation. He left to go back to his office and said he would call us within the hour to give us the name of a neuro specialist and that he would personally set up the appointment.

Paul and I were frantically praying at this point and I was on the verge of screaming. There was no way we could move Andy to take him to an appointment! We needed an ambulance and a hospital and an IV to restore his fluids and a competent doctor and a diagnosis, and ideally, we needed medical professionals who spoke some freakin' English! I couldn't keep my anger with God at bay. I felt my sanity slipping.

Then the phone rang, and it is truly unbelievable what Dr. Hoppe said. He gave us the name of the specialist and said her address was 1247 Rue Anatole.

I asked him to repeat the address. He did.

"Are you sure, Dr. Hoppe?"

He said, "Yes."

"Because, Dr. Hoppe, do you know that that is our address? You just read me our own address!"

He said, "Well, perhaps the office is near your home."

"Yes, perhaps Dr. Hoppe, but that is exactly our address! You must have made a mistake! You must be looking at our paperwork or something, not the doctor's information."

"Hmmmm, I did not make a mistake," he said. "I think this specialist might be in your building. Do you have doctors' offices in your apartment building?"

I said we might have—on the first couple of floors, but I wasn't sure who they were or what their specialties were. We had only lived here a few short weeks, and I never saw people coming and going. I supposed there could be doctors in our building, but what were the chances that this particular doctor was?

Please hear this: There is a God in heaven! We had to carry Andy down two flights of stairs—but yes, that neurological specialist was in our building! Who but the creator of zebras and armadillos, Mother Teresa and The Hulk, the galaxies and ocean flora could have come up with that? In a city of several hundred thousand people and many hundreds of apartment buildings, who but God would have us live in the exact building where a neurological specialist has offices so that when our son was too sick to be transported, we could just take the elevator down two floors? Only God. Only God.

Angel

That specialist cleared her schedule in a blink to see Andy. She spent several hours running all kinds of neurological tests and in the end, determined that Andy had an infection of the eighth cranial nerve. She prescribed numerous medications to reverse the condition and gave him several meds right there. That specialist was prepared to start an IV if we couldn't get Andy to start drinking with the medicine. That specialist didn't let us leave the office until many hours later when she had Andy at least able to be propped up and sipping water and her personal cell phone number in our hands. That specialist said we were better off in her hands than if we returned to the hospital. That specialist said to rest assured, she was only steps away from our home and she would gladly come to our assistance in a matter of minutes. And best of all, that specialist told us all this in English!

That specialist probably doesn't even exist in the here and now. She was probably an angel sent by God, plopped in our apartment building for the day, because God knew we needed a miracle and nothing else would do. God wanted to give us an angel so we would have an angel story bigger than life. The angel was wrong about one thing, however. She said that for the rest of his life, Andy was likely to have a weakened eighth cranial nerve making it susceptible to infection whenever he became ill. To date, he still has not had any recurrence of that illness. I guess angels aren't perfect.

God the Great Physician—we know Him by that name now too. But only because we were desperate for a Great Physician while living in a foreign country and in a situation completely out of our control.

All six of us were changed to the core by our experiences abroad, but Andy, being the oldest child, truly took the brunt of the razor-edged learning curve.

Risking greatly (which some judgey Christian people sweetly suggested was analogous to abuse) with our kids turned out to be one of the greatest ways we all discovered a bigger God. It was transformative to the degree that I don't think could have been achieved in any other way.

Almost Fearless

A couple of years post-France, Andy and I were discussing the possibility of him flying alone for the first time. He was fifteen years old. Our family was returning to Guatemala for a week to work with our favorite ministry, and Andy wanted to stay on for two additional weeks for intensive language study. We had made arrangements for him to stay with a Guatemalan family who lived on the outskirts of Antigua so he could take classes every day in the city. This meant Andy would have to take public transportation every day—or, as they are affectionately known in Guatemala: chicken buses. Guatemala resurrects old, discarded American school buses, paints them shocking, bright colors and complicated patterns, and then adorns them with house-appropriate decorations like crushed velvet curtains before putting them back out on the streets. They are always packed (hence, their name) and are widely known for the fast, wild, and reckless ride. Not exactly a comforting scene for me to imagine my fifteen-year-old in. Andy was culturally savvy and seasoned at this point, to say the least, but we were still concerned that all of this might be a bit too much for him.

"You know Andy, if you're not up to flying alone, I could stay back in Guatemala with you. I could find a hotel in Antigua and just hang out and explore the area for the two weeks you are living with the Flores family—you know, just to be nearby."

He tipped his head slightly to the side and then a tiny grin formed on just the left side of his face. Without even picking his head up from his homework he said, "Actually, mom, I can't wait to try to do this all on my own. I've been thinking a lot about time alone in Guatemala and even other experiences I might want to have someday. I really can't think of anything I'd be afraid to do.

France taught me that. I know this sounds arrogant, but I almost feel fearless."

I wanted him to think I was as nonchalant as he was in the moment, so I didn't look up from peeling the potatoes either. My head was reeling with thoughts and how best to respond to a fifteen-year-old who says he feels fearless. What I really wanted to say was this: *Oh baby, you have no idea. You have no idea what those words mean to me. I have felt guilty for yanking you out of Hudsonville, for denying you Little League and travel baseball and golf lessons knowing we've robbed you of a future in sports. You gave up piano and guitar lessons and said goodbye to your best friends, your grandparents, and your comfortable Hudsonville life so we could haul you across the globe. We've lost sleep wondering if we've asked too much of you kids by taking you to hard places and teaching you about hard things. I've worried about silly things I know you'll never have because of the choices we're making today—a decent car, resort vacations, an inheritance. Dad and I struggled enormously with every single one of those choices. You know that, don't you? Do you know the price you've paid in exchange for that kind of courage, Andy? Do you know? Oh, how badly I want to know if you'll use that courage someday to go change the world. Will you, son? Will you?*

Instead, I nonchalantly said, "I don't think that's arrogant, Andy. I just think because of your experiences you know a really big God. And you know He can be trusted. I also think you're very courageous. You're totally ready to do Guatemala on your own."

CHAPTER 15

Toddler Babble

"It may be hard for an egg to turn into a bird; it would be a jolly sight harder for it to learn to fly while remaining an egg. We are like eggs at present. And you cannot go on indefinitely being just an ordinary, decent egg. We must be hatched or go bad."

C. S. LEWIS, *MERE CHRISTIANITY*

What grown person, given the choice, would choose to sound like a toddler when they talk—using the wrong tense of a verb, lacking basic vocabulary, and mispronouncing words in every utterance?

I'm inclined to think it is only those of us who enjoy pain.

I've seen wicked smart millionaire corporate executives reduced to caveman-like grunting when attempting to speak a foreign language. I've seen high school valedictorians who have taken six years of French clam up and forget even their *bonjour's* and *merci's* the second they open their mouths. I've witnessed an accomplished accountant employ the translation services of his twelve-year-old son to do business. I even know an extremely talkative nurse who was rendered mute an uncomfortable amount of times for fear of sounding stupid . . .

※))))

Every semester, new international students would descend on Aix-en-Provence for the ever-popular semester abroad. I made it my mission to be a surrogate mom of sorts to many of these students. Paul and I spent numerous evenings sharing dinner with students, and often joked that our little blue van knew its way to the airport independent of a driver from all the airport runs we made for students. We loved serving in this small way. For me, one of the best parts of playing temp-mom was taking a newcomer out for lunch. Rebecca had been in town just a few weeks when we arranged for a lunch date together.

I took her to a restaurant I'd been wanting to try, but knew it wasn't likely anyone could or would speak English there since it wasn't a typical spot for tourists. I had finally reached a point in learning French that I felt confident enough to try out this new place—plus I assumed Rebecca could help me too. She had completed six years of French in junior high and high school, but as soon as the tightest-pants-ever-maître d asked us if we wanted to sit inside or outside, she nervously deferred to me with this look of terror. I knew the look well—because that had been *my* signature look thus far living in France. It was the look of "What the hell did he just say?"

Fortunately for Rebecca, I did understand his question and I requested a table *dehors*, outside, and he nodded understandingly. (To this day, even after years of studying French, I still find it mind-blowing that I can put together bizarre sounds that to my ear sound like, "Gobble-de-gook-de-gobble-dee-dee," yet someone will nod their head, understand me, and follow my commands. It's like having magical powers.) But when Tight-

Pants returned to our table to take our order, I knew we were in trouble.

I had rehearsed our order in my head and confidently ordered: "*Nous voudrions le petit coq avec la pomme de terre, s'il vous plaît.*" It was so simple. "We would like the little rooster with potatoes, please." Nothing weird about it. But Tight-Pants just stared at me blankly. I repeated the phrase, adding an extra firm "*s'il vous plaît.*" More staring. Finally, I said, "*D'accord?*" which was bad because that was informal and we were in a formal setting, but I only had a very limited vocabulary at this point, and it was the best I could do. I was simply asking him, "Okay?"

Tight-Pants proceeded to go off on a rant, speaking some wicked-fast French, leaving me in the wake of his *le's* and *la's* and *les*, and all I could pick up were a few words like "difficult" and "American" and "accent." I couldn't be sure, because he talked faster than Sophia Vergara, and I only picked up about one out of five words, but I thought he told me he couldn't understand my French. I asked him if he had trouble understanding me. This time I understood exactly his reply: "It is not *I* who have troubles. It is *you*! *You* need to learn to speak better French." I dug deep and pulled out every language tip Madame Prudhomme, our tutor, had taught me, and I repeated our order again. I kept my tongue flat in my mouth and swallowed my consonants and added a little more sing-songy intonation.

Again, he simply stared back at me. I repeated our order a third time and channeled my best tourist impersonation as I pointed to someone else eating the little rooster and held up two fingers, and adding, "*Deux. S'il vous plaît.*" Did he understand? He shook his head no, picked up our menus, and walked away. I couldn't believe it. I told Rebecca I think he was refusing to serve us because I just slaughtered French. She kind of chuckled but also still had that terrified look on her face. We sat there for at least another fifteen minutes, but as I tried to call him back it was clear he was ignoring us. We were refused service in this swanky little French diner because I couldn't pronounce "little rooster" well enough!

We were so hungry by this time, Rebecca and I surrendered and left. We grabbed a chicken sandwich at Quick Burger, which is, believe it or not, a worse version of McDonalds. I was disgusted with myself. Aix-en-Provence is a veritable cuisine mecca, and we were forced to eat at a sticky-floored, fast-food, fries-n-burgers joint!

That evening, our friends, Henry and Celia, stopped over, and I vented: "I'll never learn that devil-language! Today made me think I hate France. All of it: the French people, their stupid food, expensive cheese, and ridiculous wine. Also, how insane is it that I must dress up wherever I go? Doesn't anyone in this country wear hoodies and tennis shoes? How many decades before I can speak enough French to order in a stupid restaurant? I'll never fit in here! I think I'm just not a fit for this fancy country, and it was a mistake that we came."

Celia, having years of experience in this stuff, knew exactly what to do. She leaned in and looked me squarely in the eyes and in her sweet, South Carolinian southern-belle sort of way told me, "Cindeee, this is what you need to do to get over this bump. You need to go right back out there tomorrow and go out for lunch again. Pick another restaurant and order in French and succeed. You need a win so you get your confidence back. You cannot let yourself feel defeated. Believe that you can do it, and just go right back out there and do it. I know you can."

Going out the next day was the last thing I felt like doing, but she was so right. Whenever I wallowed in my language failures, my inclination was to stay home, avoid any need to speak French, and eat my weight in chocolate chip cookie dough.

I did have a successful trip to the grocery store the following day as defined by the meat counter guy understanding my order and me understanding the cashier when she asked if I brought my own bags. The definition of success is so nebulous. Later that day I also found solace from the language grind by a hilarious language *faux pas* of Paul's.

Lost in Translation

Thankfully, we only had to live in our two-bedroom, too-small apartment in the heart of Aix for a few months. Per usual in this unusual story of ours, God had the most perfect home waiting for us on the outskirts of Aix-en-Provence. It had not always been a home—in its former life, it had been a horse stable. It sat high on a bluff overlooking the city and Mount St. Victoire, a mountain made famous by French artist Paul Cezanne who brilliantly captured its ever changing mood. It didn't entirely smell like horses anymore, so we thought we'd give it a go. The property had been part of a large estate, which included a pretty decent castle. A young couple had bought the castle and parceled out the rest of the property. Our landlord bought the stables and converted it into a home for rental income. It was a quaint, low-roof structure with a long, interesting layout. Where there had been four stable doors, now existed four sets of French doors (duh!) facing the garden area and overlooking the city. Except for the sewer regularly flooding our backyard, insufficient and often failing electric heat, and the occasional scorpion hiding unsuspectingly in our shoes, we loved that house. Oh, and the mice. They weren't much fun either.

Our castle-dwelling neighbors were young, rich, and wildly hospitable. Even though we didn't share a common language, they kept inviting us over for goûter (pronounced goo-tay)—otherwise known as afternoon snack or the French's excuse to get drunk in the middle of the day. We'd drink whiskey and wine together for hours while barely speaking a word! (This was after we overcame our little "alcohol problem"—more on that later). They loved us.

The rich neighbors had several poorly behaving horses that escaped regularly, and we'd try not to laugh as the couple chased after them, running painfully slow due to their way-too-tight jeans.

One warm spring morning while preparing the kids' school lunches, I heard a loud "swish, swish, swish" as if someone were outside sweeping down the walls of our home. I went to the girls' bedroom located at the back of the house to see where the sound was coming from. At about six or seven feet tall, stood one of the neighbor's Percheron horses, forcefully swishing his mighty gray tail back and forth across the girls' window like the powerful brushes of a car wash. Upon further inspection, we discovered all four of the neighbors' Percherons were in our backyard—one enjoying a little goûter of our clean laundry on the clothesline.

The neighbors weren't home. We panicked realizing we'd need to call them. It's so much harder to speak a second language via phone. Face-to-face allows use of hand gestures, facial expressions, and body language. In person, you can pause and think, and you can rephrase something if your listener appears confused. On the phone, you get none of that extra help. Since

I'm the bigger wimp, Paul called the neighbors and told the husband this: "*Tes cheveux sont dans mon derrière.*"

The last thing you want to hear when you deliver a message in a foreign language that you diligently practiced beforehand is laughter.

Paul's statement brought wild and hysterical laughter from our young hip Frenchy neighbor.

Paul knew immediately he said something wrong and his cheeks were crimson before he even knew what it was. Pierre could barely catch his breath, but eventually he repeated the phrase just to clarify he understood what Paul was really trying to say, "*Mes chevaux sont dans votre jardin?*" And Paul understood this enough to respond with, "*Oui! Oui!*" Yes! Yes! Your horses are in my backyard! Immediately after hanging up, we sat down at the desk and reconstructed Paul's first statement on paper and suddenly realized, in horror, what he had originally told the neighbor that elicited such wild laughter: "Your hairs are up my butt." In French, *horses* and *hair* are similar words, as are *backyard* and *butt*.

Now it was our turn to laugh! If it weren't for laughter and a beckoning sense of humor, I believe learning the French language would have provoked me to grab the butane gas tank we used for the oven and play a quick game of Sylvia Plath.

New Language

I nestled up next to Paul in bed that night and said, "Living here has been one of the hardest things I've ever done in my life, but doing it with you and with the kids, makes it a riotous adventure. I wouldn't trade these experiences for a thousand fully funded Target shopping sprees."

After talking a bit longer about how the kids have both excelled and struggled, I shared this: "Just today, when I arrived at the school, I decided to watch Grace a bit before going into her classroom. She was playing house with her classmates and they were all speaking to each other in French. '*Viens, viens!*' '*Toc, toc!*' '*Ouvrez la porte, s'il vous plaît!*' '*J'ai besoin d'un rendez-vous chez nous!*' All that cute playhouse talk. On the way home, curious to hear what Grace thought about her new language skills, I asked her, 'What were you saying to your friends back there, Grace?' She told me she didn't know what she was saying! I asked her how that could be because the other little girls were understanding her completely and responding appropriately. She said, 'I'm telling you, Mom, I don't know. I only know it in French. I don't know it in English.'"

And that's how our four-year-old Gracie picked up French—in an entirely different lobe of her brain. She twirled and danced around the house singing "*Dieu est si bon. Dieu est si bon. Dieu est si bon. Il est bon avec moi,*" ("God is so good. God is so good. God is so good. He is good to me.") She expressed her stubbornness with, "*Non maman!*" And, sadly, when she was upset, I'd sometimes hear her say under her breath, "*Merde,*" (a little gem of a swear word she learned from her older brothers). After just a year in France, Grace was fluent, for all practical purposes, but useless as my translator when I needed one because she just couldn't reconcile the two languages. She had a near perfect French accent, and the rest of us were fairly jealous that our little preschooler sounded the most French of all of us.

As the three older kids soared in language acquisition (as a two-year old, Yulisa poured her energies into grasping English!), Paul and I embarrassingly fumbled behind them.

While climbing aboard a packed train, someone reached into my backpack-style purse and snatched my wallet. Paul had to go to the police station in person to report the theft. He's a bright, accomplished accountant, but knowing his level of French wasn't strong enough for this important task, he took Andy along as translator. With words he wouldn't even normally use in English, Andy explained the entire theft incident to the police, and to his monolingual father he explained the process for filling out a police inquiry, an affidavit of theft, and an asset recovery identification form. After a couple hours of wading through typical French bureaucracy, the duo walked home together, which Paul described like this, "Cindy, I'd swear that kid grew an inch during our time at the police station. When we walked out of there, he held his head a little higher, walked a little straighter, and even talked more maturely. That experience, where my lack of skills required my twelve-year-old child to step in for me, gave him a confidence unparalleled to any experience he could have had in America."

Josiah quietly and subversively conquered French. Attending a very small Christian school where several other kids in his three-grade-combined classroom spoke English made it too easy for Josiah to stay in his first language. His teacher, however, only ever spoke to Josiah in French and never doubted for a moment that Josiah would eventually be fluent. His friend, Francois, a kind, shy boy from South Africa with a solid grasp of French, was positioned right beside Josiah to serve as his translator. Josiah never complained about school and never fell behind even though that first year had to be exceedingly challenging for him. Josiah has an uncanny ability to make everything in life fun and his life-of-the-party personality brought so much joy into that one-room upper-elementary school.

I don't know when exactly it happened, but since I volunteered at the kids' school several times a week, I had numerous opportunities to spy on the kids. One day I took a step into Josiah's classroom and saw him with his desk scooched up close to a new kid's desk—a round, gentle boy from Korea—as Josiah was now the translator. I backed out through the door before Josiah could see me and basked in the miracle before me. Our jovial, ever smiling second-born had not opened up to us much about challenges or victories at school. He just dutifully went to school every day and quietly picked up a second language, made many friends from several different countries, and warmed the heart of his teacher who was certain God had called Josiah for great things. That day, as I watched him animatedly describe a history lesson to his new Korean friend and as his French teacher approvingly nodded and smiled back at him, I understood what Paul had experienced that day at the police station. Josiah looked taller, more confident, and more complete than ever before. The gift that Paige Fisher had described to me months earlier now made sense to me.

Americans can live just fine in France, or anywhere else in the world, without learning their host country's language. People do it all the time. But, oh, what a woefully hollow experience we would have had if we never put in the blood, sweat, and tears of language acquisition and had only made friends with other English speakers. I think we would have missed a huge part of the culture and probably a huge part of God's lessons for us.

I remember moments in France where I'd think to myself, *What if the people back home could see me now? They'd be so impressed.* My head would swell as I drove around town in our maimed and rusty manual transmission minivan we swore was demon-possessed (the door locks randomly clicked up and down like fifty times in a row with the van in motion) simply because I knew my way around a European town. My pride inflated watching Paul successfully navigate a bank transaction or communicate with a teacher while speaking a foreign language. Or when the kids would get the highest score in their class on a test *in French*! Even buying groceries made me feel like some kind of superhero human because the huge French market was daunting—but I, the great Cindy, had mastered it. I just felt like people should be so stinkin' impressed with me. But the fact is, the French were anything but impressed. They mostly looked down their noses at us—frustrated that we brought a slice of America to their beautiful France and dismayed by our slow language acquisition. And no one back home in Hudsonville cared one tiny bit that I just discovered cheese is called *fromage* but *formage* is when something is formed.

Swinging the Bat

But a miracle happened amid all that learning and growing: After a lifetime of doubting my worth, my self-confidence soared in France. Mastering new challenges and nurturing neglected parts of myself ignited a surge of self-love, and I watched the same thing unfold in every one of our family members. And as our self-love grew, so did our love for God and others. In France, I finally grasped what it means to love your neighbor as yourself, because it's impossible to love others well if you don't first love yourself well.

Paul and I once read that life should be like taking an "at bat" in a baseball game. Anyone who's ever played even an inning of baseball will tell you that if you want to get a hit, you're gonna have to swing the bat. The best players know that if you're gonna strike out, you want to go down swinging. You don't ever want to find yourself standing there watching the ball whizz by you three times. That type of offense will never—no matter how you cut it—result in a hit. And hits are really the only way to win a game. And if there's one analogy I understand, it's baseball/softball. My dad would go nuts and kick the dusty dugout ground if we girls just stood at the plate and watched pitch after pitch zoom past us. "Swing the damn bat!" he'd say.

Swinging hard makes you feel so much more alive than just standing there.

For Paul and me, France felt like taking a solid, give-it-all-you-got kind of swing. Even if we ended up striking out, we knew we'd at least go down swinging.

CHAPTER 16

"Your Brassiere, Madame"

*"I hate it when I'm an idiot and don't know it.
I like being aware of my idiocy."*

LORELEI GILMORE

Paul and I were told we'd need to secure a *carte de séjour*, or resident visa, if we wanted to live in France. Without one, long-stay visitors may only stay in the country on a tourist or student visa, which requires you to cross the border every three months and get your passport stamped by another country to prove you are "transient." Essentially the French government doesn't want you in their country for prolonged periods if you are draining necessary resources or taking employment away from its own citizens. The French (and basically every country) are more than happy to have you stay in their country if you're dumping money from your home country into theirs.

Since we didn't have gainful employment, there was no way we were drainers. The frequency with which we pulled cash from the States to cover our costs in France made us obvious dumpers. Once the government determines you are not a spy, a terrorist, or a mooch, they will grant you a *carte de séjour*. Something we learned in France that we'd never heard in history/geography class is that the French are definitely not stupid. I feel like Americans often denigrate them unfairly.

One of the requirements necessary to obtain a *carte de séjour* is a French-certified health physical. Coincidentally, the government offices offer these for just a *petit* fee. Our friend Celia made our appointment, but Paul and I decided to tackle the task without a translator even though we had probably mastered only twenty French words at that point, none of them useful.

So when the incredibly young and attractive nurse called our names, right off the bat we were thrown. Did she say both our names? Or did we confuse that? Could it be that *Monsieur* and *Madame* sound curiously similar when impossibly gorgeous French nurses say them quickly? Did she really intend for both of us to come at once? We had a brief exchange in the waiting area already arguing over our French deciphering skills and then decided to just go in together. *Weird, but, whatever.*

She doesn't smile, but gives us a quick "*Bonjour*" (ah, we know that word!) and leads us to a massive, very white, and very antiseptic room. It was about the size of an elementary school gymnasium. At one end of the room were two metal folding chairs facing a large folding table that served as the desk for two, even more gorgeous French women—both dressed to the nines in stunning skintight dresses and high heels topped with the obligatory, professional looking, white lab coat. Their perfectly coiffed French-dos, and those long, lean legs that silently proclaim: "We walk everywhere, you fat Americans," and their I-never-eat-a-French-fry tiny waists, just screamed Parisian models to me. *These svelte French goddesses cannot be physicians, can they? Are we sure we've found the medical office, not a modeling agency?* They looked about sixteen years old, but I suppose they must have been in their upper-twenties. It's all that damn olive oil and fish they eat. Oh, and that year-round Mediterranean sun that gives their skin an ethereal glow.

I quickly examined the room and noticed on the far side, opposite the desk, there was a small trifold fabric room divider that was failing miserably to live up to its name. Behind the room divider was a small examining table. A very flat and ancient looking examining table that King Louis himself probably brought with him from England. Paul and I could have run laps or played a volleyball game in the massive expanse between the two furniture groupings. On the upside, the room was extremely clean, and it had decent lighting. But it was entirely eerie to walk into that cavernous, cold space, to sit opposite these two hotties and know we were completely at their mercy for what came next.

They didn't ask us if we spoke French, nor did they try to speak any English. They just started talking—a lot—sometimes to us, but mostly to each other. Even though they weren't laughing or even smiling, I think they were having the time of their lives. Or possibly they were bored to death of these mundane physicals and were talking about the wine they just had at lunch.

They told us to undress. I shot Paul a quick sideways glance—panicking—hoping he was doing better than I was at understanding their French. I expected we would have a little "convo" first, you know, the kind of get-to-know-ya banter physicians like to race through before the exam normally starts. I had hoped for a little bit of something—anything!—before, "Take your clothes off."

"Did they just tell us to undress? Right now? Right here? Both of us?" I asked him quietly.

"Uh huh. At least, I think so," he whispered back. "That's not normal, is it?" Again, because I'm the nurse, the numbers man (wrongly) assumes I know what's going on in every medical scene.

"Yeah, I'm pretty sure they don't mean both of us. That wouldn't make any sense," I whispered. "I see clothing hooks over on that far wall. They can't possibly mean for us to undress right here and hang our clothes up way over there, can they? I mean, there's nowhere else to go privately. This is so bizarre. Let's just wait. I don't think we heard them right."

A few seconds later the alpha doc, now somewhat exasperated, repeated her request: "Please, now, remove your clothing."

"Paul, she's not kidding! Oh. My. Gosh. Right here! She wants us to get undressed *right here*! This is crazy! I hate this stupid country. Why don't I just go first? I'll just undress by those hooks over there and then go right to the examining table."

I was halfway across the wide expanse toward the wall with the hooks when the ladies saw I was alone. They jumped up to tell Paul he needed to go too. He choked out a few French words that made him sound like a toddler: "Moi? Aller? Aussi?" ("Me? Go? Too?"). And they nodded enthusiastically, "Oui! Oui!"

So together, we traipsed across the mini-gymnasium, approached the hooks, and sheepishly undressed in front of each other—in full view of our hottie French doctors. We were trying to decide who should head toward Napolean's examining table first when they waived us both back over to the folding chairs. *Seriously? This is insanity.* In nothing but our socks and underwear, we walked back across the massive room and slunk down in our cold metal chairs.

This is when the ladies noticed I still had my bra on. I couldn't understand anything they were saying, but there was no mistaking there was something about my bra that was upsetting them. My look must have conveyed my confusion when alpha doc finally said, in English, "Your brassiere, Madame." And her hand motions were very clear: Remove. It. I walked back to the hooks, removed my bra, shivered, and gave a few seconds thought to breaking down crying. But instead, I walked back ever so slowly to give myself time for a micro daydream of all things American: Target and Trader Joes, Jif peanut butter and chocolate chips, grandparents and cousins, fall football games and Fourth of July fireworks, Panera Bread and Steakhouses, English-speaking physicians and pharmacists. I shook my head to bring myself back to reality and took my place beside my nearly naked husband. If you've ever lived in a foreign country, you know what I mean by those micro dreams. They come out of nowhere and carry you away for a brief, beautiful, breathy second to the homeland flowing with milk and honey.

How the French Do It

Our abnormally attractive physicians chatted for a bit before they engaged us while we shivered in the cold in our socks and underwear. I think they were telling jokes about our middle-aged bodies and were doing their best not to bust a gut at the fact that they got me to take my bra off. I truly do hope, and it's the only way this story is redeemable, that they are writing a book too, called, *The Ridiculous Things We Were Able to Get Foreigners to Do*.

The only thing that made me feel somewhat comforted at the moment was that I had heard—multiple times, in fact—that our experience was quite commonplace in the French medical system. Bras must be shed for all examinations. We worked with a sweet, young American while in France named Annalise. Annalise spoke flawless French so the following situation can't be chalked up to miscommunication. Thinking she needed a new eyeglass prescription, Annalise went to get her eyes checked. Before the ophthalmologist began the eye exam, he told Annalise to take off her shirt and bra. She questioned him on this, and he said, yes, of course he meant it. She endured the whole eye exam topless, as well as a little walk down the hallway where he guided her to another examining room with different eye machinery. Then he led her back to the first exam room, told her to put her top back on, and wrote out her prescription for eyeglasses. I'm not making this up. This is France—where every fifth or sixth billboard shamelessly flashes bare breasts, and where I was in the minority at the beach because I chose to keep my top half covered. The French just have no hang-ups with boobs.

One at a time, our hottie doctors gave us our physical examinations. First Paul. I felt a little uneasy as I sat topless and looked down at my figure which screamed "Mom of four!" while the two goddesses simultaneously checked out my husband. But truthfully, I wanted out of there so bad, I didn't even care what they did to him. I heard a lot of French. I thought it sounded something like: "This man is so smokin' hot. What is he doing with that ol' bag?" Or it might possibly have been, "Normal, healthy, forty-year-old male, no signs or symptoms of illness or deformity." I couldn't be sure. And I just didn't care anymore.

Then it was my turn. The dynamic duo looked me over good too, but they didn't seem to be enjoying it as much as their examination of Paul. I kind of slipped back into my American Dream anyway, and the three-minute physical was over quickly. The two doctors went back behind their table-desk and told us to get dressed. So we headed back to the hooks and got dressed, together, in full view of both of them once again.

How on God's green earth the French government felt that two idiots like ourselves were worthy of receiving a *carte d'sejour*, suggesting we had any chance at all to survive life in France, or furthermore that we could contribute anything of value to their beloved country, I'll never understand. But they did grant us residency. And somewhere in France are two physicians who have the best "Idiot Americans" story ever.

If you seek humility and want to take a backseat to humanity and observe a true, level playing field where all are God's children, created in His image, where no power or intelligence or wealth or passport color separates one another, go live in a foreign culture for a while. It taught us a whole new way of defining intelligence, power, dominance, control, and belonging, and it forced us to ask ourselves: *How do I portray myself when all these things have been stripped from me?*

That, and my clothes.

CHAPTER 17

Imbibing With the Dancing Pastor

"There came a time when the risk to remain tight in the bud was more painful than the risk it took to blossom."

ANAIS NIN

When Andy was only two years old and barely forming sentences, Paul took him along to pick up a few things at a quick mart. Before exiting the car, Andy asked, "You buyin' beer, dad?"

As new parents, that moment catapulted us into new conversations. Do we really want one of our toddlers first words to be "beer"? How about "tipsy" or "sloshed"? Is it our hope and dream that our children will grow up to love alcohol and regularly partake? Or would we prefer they didn't? Are we okay if they observe us drinking? Are we okay if they don't? What if we only drank when they weren't around? What if we stopped drinking entirely? Can we?

Gah. If you're a new parent, and especially if you were raised in a conservative Christian community with black and white rules, you can probably relate.

With the motive to protect our kids, and because choosing a binary system is easier, we decided to be a teetotaling family. We thought it might just be better if the kids weren't around alcohol at all. Our hope was they'd grow up with no need for the stuff whatsoever. And, as every good parenting book will tell you, if you know what you want to see in your kids, model it for them. So we stopped drinking entirely. I'm not bragging here, but making this change in our home was actually very easy. We just didn't miss it. We didn't think that choice mattered to anyone except our kids.

Until France.

It's funny how we often don't recognize the bubbles that surround us until they begin to leak air.

Dry City

In our small village of Forest Grove, everyone knew all the "Thou Shalt Nots." An important one God forgot to put on the stone tablet he gave to Moses, was Thou Shalt Not Drink Alcohol. I don't remember hearing sermons about the evils of drinking or ever receiving any lectures about it from my parents. It was just one of those things we all inherently knew was a sin. And by *all*, I mean the Reformers AND the Christian Reformers—the only two church denominations in our Dutch-drenched city.

Our church was one mile away from our home and right across the street from our elementary school. We all went to that church. We, that is, as in everybody I knew. Forest Grove was small—population maybe 500 or 600—but even so, we were definitely big enough to support two churches. Our family attended the Reformed Church. Seven doors down on the right hand side of Perry Street was the *Christian* Reformed Church.

Rarely can one little word make such a critical difference. I didn't know much about those Christian Reformers. But what I knew for sure, because Betsy Tacoma told me it was truth, was that they literally interpreted the commandment: "Thou shalt have no graven image before me." To them, that meant they could not hang pictures of Jesus in their Sunday school rooms. We Reformers had Jesus pictures everywhere in our church— sometimes a white skinned, brown-haired, feminine-looking Jesus, and sometimes a white skinned, blonde and muscular Jesus.

The CRCs (their given acronym) all sent their kids to the Christian schools and those of us in the RCA (our given acronym) never did. When we had to ride the same school buses, the Christian school kids always sat in the front, and we public school kids always sat in the back and wondered why having pictures of Jesus in our Sunday School made them afraid of us. We called them "Post-Toasties," referencing a cereal from our parents' generation that had the slogan, "A little better than all the rest." I never saw the commercial, never ate the cereal, and never even saw it at the grocery store. But the adults in our community made sure we understood those Christian Reformers thought of themselves as "a little better than all the rest" and that we were thoroughly disgusted by that. In terms of American demographics, we could not have been more similar—us Reformers and those Christian Reformers—but in the community and on the bus and especially on the way to church, we were as segregated as the blacks and whites of the deep South in the sixties.

But the one thing both denominations easily agreed upon: Drinking is bad. If you drank, you were a sinner—no doubt about it. More honestly, if you drank and got caught, you were a sinner. I now know that the majority of us drank alcohol in secret because I guess Jesus can't see through doors.

Hudsonville, the closest city to our village of Forest Grove, was a "dry" city—meaning, no alcohol was served at any restaurants and not a single store sold it. The brave drinkers in our city had to drive to the neighboring heathen city of Jenison to buy alcohol. Paul's parents pretended they never drank, but all three DeBoer children knew where the Mogan David was stashed way back behind the wicker baskets in the cabinet above the refrigerator. My parents were more open about it. My dad liked a cold beer after mowing the lawn on Saturdays. But oddly, because my dad kind of looked and acted like a guy from a Bud Light commercial, a six-pack of beer would last him all summer. Sometimes, but not often, when my parents had friends over, they would make mixed drinks like Brandy slushes or Rum and Coke. A couple of times Mom let us girls take a sip of her drink. I thought it tasted like toilet water, and even after just a sip, felt obligated to confess my sin to God hoping I could still escape hellfire and damnation.

All these things contributed to the perplexities of alcohol consumption in the Paul DeBoer home, and as it turns out, living in France with alcohol perplexities is like living near the ocean without a bathing suit.

Beverage Options

In a poetic, Jesus-y kind of way, our first alcohol obstacle was brought to us by the letter C, which, in case you didn't know, always stands for church.

We had trouble finding a church in Aix.

Not only were there no Reformed churches in Aix, there also weren't any Christian Reformed, Baptist, Methodist, or

Presbyterian—the only Protestant denominations Paul and I even knew existed. There were a couple Catholic cathedrals, but as was typical throughout Europe, they were frequented more often by mice than parishioners. We ended up at a nondenominational charismatic church that met in an old storefront. Paul and I didn't know a lot about the Pentecostal movement, but we liked the part about a church gathering in a dilapidated old storefront. We have always longed to be a part of a community that would rather spend its money on people in need than on big fancy buildings.

We understood about 10 percent of what the pastor said, so the services turned out to primarily be a lesson in French. My sermon notes were simply two columns: one for the words I recognized, one for words I didn't. We bought a French/English Bible so we could follow along with the scripture reading. But after the reading, I became increasingly antsy, and Paul became increasingly annoyed. Charismatics like long services, and they won't stop worshipping until the spirit says stop—which could be late into the afternoon. When one-year-old Yulisa could take it no longer, I'd immediately offer to walk out with her just to get a break from all the French. Fortunately, the older three kids weren't as restless as me and they suffered for Jesus better than I did. I always came back at the end of the service in time for the Eucharist. Other than drinking real wine from a common glass, the practice was basically the same as in our Michigan church, and I loved being a part of that universal spiritual experience in a foreign country. We eventually got used to the speaking in tongues and the pastor dancing in the aisles and emphatically concluded we loved our little church in Aix-en-Provence.

Within a few months the pastor and his wife invited us to their home. They lived in a storybook French château made of weathered white stucco, enveloped in vines, and sitting at the end of a gravel path that meandered through a vineyard. I felt like Peter Mayle driving up their driveway.

The Weiner (pronounced "Vine-er") family of four, plus the church secretary, lived in this small home together. They also kept one bedroom empty as a place for any needy person to crash for a while. They were minimalists before it became a thing, and they lived extravagantly generously. I had little understanding of just how great an impact this family would eventually have on ours.

We sat on their back patio—drenched in the glorious, piercing sunshine of the south of France. It was noon. After *bisous* (a kiss on both cheeks) all the way around the table, Marie-Pierre, the pastor's wife, offered us drinks. She rattled off our options in French, and the only one I heard was *biere* (beer). Which, of course, we were too good of Christians to partake, so I asked her to repeat the other options. I couldn't understand anything she was saying. Surprisingly, at this early stage in our French experience, my ear for deciphering French was the best in our family. So if I couldn't get it, probably no one else would either.

Finally, Jacques, our pastor, stepped in. He had acquired some choppy English over the years and so he repeated our beverage options in our embarrassingly lonely single language. "We have beer, wine, Pastis, or Panache." I had read about Pastis before we left America. It's a wickedly strong before-dinner drink and tastes like black licorice. Even the thought made me throw up in my mouth a little. Panache is a light beer/lemonade blend that I saw en masse everywhere I shopped. The French drank it like Kool-Aid. Jacques looked at me for my order, then back at Paul. We stared back blankly. He didn't even offer water. Impatiently, the pastor turned his questioning to our kids, "What would you like? Beer? Wine? Pastis? Panache?"

I searched his face for a smirk.

He's making a joke, right? Oh God! He's not making a joke— there is no evidence of a smirk whatsoever. . . . He just offered our extremely under-aged children alcoholic beverages! What do we do now, smarty-teetotaling-pants?

Pastor Jacques was definitely not joking. He wanted to take alcoholic drink orders. From *all* of us. Now. At noon. And we were either going to embarrass ourselves significantly by refusing their drinks, or we were going to burn in hell forever. It was a tough choice.

Paul shot me a glance and I knew what he was thinking: "Sweeeet! We get to drink beer with the pastor!" He politely requested one. I had a split second to make what I felt was a monumental, life-altering decision, but the phrase "When in Rome . . ." jumped into my mind and I blurted out, "I'd love a glass of wine."

Our kids look terrified and betrayed. Their wee minds must have been whirling with questions, doubts, thoughts of treason, and hell-damnation. Andy asked for a glass of water, but Josiah, with a gleam in his eyes, said, "I'll take a Panache!" And, of course, the pastor's wife brought out juice for Grace and Yulisa.

When I saw both teenage Weiner sons slowly sipping on their Panaches, I realized we were going to have some interesting conversations that night about right and wrong, black and white, Jesus and that wedding miracle, and probably something about ten-year-olds drinking their first beer with their French pastor!

CHAPTER 18

An Aix-cellent Christmas

"It is no measure of health to be well-adjusted
in a profoundly sick society."

JIDDU KRISHNAMUTI

Life in France broke us, but also built us. Everything we thought we were or thought we believed in chipped away like a bad paint job on an antique armoire. Our bare, exposed wood left vulnerable and without protection from the assaults of the world meant we had to reestablish and redefine ourselves.

Our first Christmas in France was one of those major paint-stripping events.

Since I had never lived abroad before, I was clueless as to the difference between important and unimportant things to bring over from the States. Some things I brought with us but didn't really need were sheets, chocolate chips, and cake mixes. But there were several things I wish I would have packed but didn't know how much I'd need or miss them: books in English (!), framed family photos, a muffin tin, and Christmas decorations.

Certainly, Christmas decorations seemed frivolous when we were packing. But as our first Christmas rolled around, we realized in a hurry it was going to be a real challenge to make our house feel festive. We had zero decorations and basically no budget to go buy some.

We had told the kids to lower their expectations for Christmas. We told them things were going to look very different on this side of the Atlantic. Our France Christmas wasn't going to include multiple family gatherings. There would be no snow or ski outings. There would be no mall visits for massive Christmas shopping sprees. And there would be no trips to rich suburbs to look at Christmas lights. In fact, because our funds were so stretched in France, we told the kids we were going to entirely forego giving each other presents that year. We told them to look forward to a simpler Christmas where we'd just focus on the real meaning of the season and not have all the distractions of a culture run amok.

Surprisingly, they didn't give us much pushback on the simple Christmas announcement. Perhaps they'd become so accustomed to things not being like "back home in Michigan" that the news wasn't even all that jarring.

From Presents to Presence

Then one day, little crafty Grace decided all on her own to start making paper chains. We didn't have any colored paper, so she just made one extremely long chain with white computer paper. On her request, much to my chagrin, I hung that chain across the long expanse of our living/dining room. It looked pathetic and like a four-year-old had made it—because one had.

Back in Michigan, I would have spent hundreds and hundreds of dollars decorating our home for Christmas. I'd buy multiple poinsettias in every imaginable color and set them out in every room (even the bathrooms). I'd hang lighted garland on the stairway, the mantel, and anywhere else there was a level surface. We had about a dozen large storage totes full of Christmas decorations; it often took me weeks to get the house fully decorated.

Here in France, Christmas was two weeks away, and so far we had one lonely white paper chain to announce the biggest Christian holiday was coming soon. But I swallowed my Christmas pride and told Grace we needed several more paper chains to complete the look. She let me cut the strips of paper so the rest of the chains weren't quite as abstract. By the time we were done, the whole family/dining room had a white paper chain canopy overhead and it looked kind of, well, wintery. It may also have looked like a third-grade classroom in a poor inner-city school district, but hey, at least we had decor.

The next night, we set out to find a Christmas tree. We couldn't find a tree farm to save our provincial butts, but we did locate a nursery which was selling potted evergreens. So we bought a little four-foot potted Scotch pine and plopped it on an end table in the corner of our living room. I almost cried at how pathetic the poor thing looked. Even Charlie Brown would have been sad for us.

However, we still had that stack of white computer paper so I sat little Gracie down with a stack of thin strips of white paper and she made a Christmas tree garland of paper chains. That evening, we popped popcorn and strung it together with thread to make a popcorn garland. The white-on-white garland almost looked elegant, in a cheap Pinterest way. The following day a family who was moving back to the States stopped over with a box of things they couldn't fit in their luggage. At the bottom of the box were two strings of white lights. Grace and I immediately hung them on the tree.

Next, I showed the kids how to make paper snowflakes. They each made several varieties of snowflakes in all imaginable sizes. We taped them up all over the four sets of French doors that faced our patio and on the window in our kitchen. The effect was stunning.

I could tell the kids' excitement was mounting because the house was starting to look like Christmas. Even though the season didn't particularly feel like Michigan Christmases, at least the house had a new, festive look.

Amazingly, our kids seemed okay with this new look and feel to our Christmas in France.

You can call these things what you'd like, but I've got to call them miracles, because miraculously, within a day of each other, we received three very significant packages—like gold, frankincense, and myrrh.

The first was a small box in the mail from our friend Kurt who does a lot of traveling for work. While in Paris, he thought of us and put together a box of Christmas decorations he bought at a high-end boutique. There were twelve small white angel ornaments for our tree, a wooden nativity scene, and a lovely, rustic holiday table runner. When I added all those touches to our already very white and wooden living area, the final look was Pinterest perfect. I am the original Joanna Gaines. I had successfully pulled off the white-on-white-on-white with rustic wooden accents way before she even dreamed of her first fixer-upper.

The second package we received was a box of gifts from my family. They had bought all the kids a present and had them wrapped and ready to put under the tree. There would be gifts on Christmas morning after all!

The third package was a suitcase hand delivered by a friend of a friend recently returning from the States. She had visited our church while in Michigan and when our church staff heard she was headed to France, they packed a huge suitcase full of surprises for our family: two small gifts for each child, cologne for Paul, perfume for me, wrapping supplies, cookie cutters, frosting, sprinkles, Christmas candles—and even six white wooden tree ornaments!

On Christmas Day, we started the day with pancakes (because, as long as you have flour, eggs, milk, and baking soda, they taste the same on every continent), followed by a reading of the Christmas story—slowly this year—with lots and lots of time spent discussing it afterward. When there aren't a lot of gifts beckoning from the tree, other components must make a greater impact and thus take on greater meaning.

Next, we opened our gifts—again, much slower than Christmases past—in an effort to make the meager pile last a little longer. That afternoon we met with another family, and together we all filled over a hundred small bags with Christmas candy and a little piece of Scripture that shared the good news that Jesus was born and still lives today! We climbed into our beat-up old van and drove into the town of Aix—the kids giddy with excitement to do Halloween in reverse. Our combined tribe of ten spent the whole afternoon passing out candy bags to passers-by. The younger ones, especially, had a true knack for bringing out smiles in everyone—even those who looked tired and lonely and sad. This, this act of kindness that we never would have had time for on a busy stateside Christmas Day—this was truly the spreading of Christmas cheer. Afterward, we went back to our friends' apartment and shared hot chocolate as well as all the stories of the amazing encounters that had happened throughout the afternoon. We capped off the evening with pizza.

A Christmas to Remember

It's common for families to reminisce about past holidays. Sometimes, even throughout the rest of the calendar year, family members are asked to recall special memories from holidays gone by. Without fail, time after time, and for all four of our children, whenever they are asked about their favorite Christmas, they will share about their Christmas in France.

A simple Christmas, with homemade, colorless decor, with barely any gifts and no special gatherings or parties but a focus on the birth of the Christ-child and sharing that good news, is the celebration our kids pick as their favorite.

The best things we can give our kids are usually not things at all.

CHAPTER 19

Aragorn, Ranger
of the North

"My life is my message."

MAHATMA GHANDI

When I initially presented the whole France-thing to my mom, not surprisingly, she tried to talk us out of it. The two of us were very close and she didn't want me to leave. And she really didn't like the thought of us dragging four of her grandchildren halfway around the world for who-knows-how-long and thrusting them into who-knows-what-environment. She feared we would scar them for life. She barely even had a chance to get to know Yulisa, who was only eighteen months old at the time, and she also treasured the vital role she had in nurturing our other three kids. She didn't really want to hear about all the ways we had "heard from God" or how we believed He was "calling us to France." Mom is absolutely a follower of Jesus and has countless stories of her own of following God; she just didn't want *us* to follow Him to *France*. Probably more than anyone else, Mom knew how much this was going to hurt.

She had good reason. I get it.

One of her arguments was this: "You know, you're probably raising kids who will move away from you when they grow up. They might grow up thinking this is normal and then you won't be able to keep them close to you."

"Yep. I know."

I didn't say it, but I thought, *I've got to trust the reward will be greater than the pain.* I knew that thought would not help her in the moment. But I had to cling to that belief because it was, of course, extremely painful to pluck those four kids from their lovely American life and from their adoring grandparents— especially this one—and drag them to Europe.

I found trusting God with my own life so much easier than trusting Him with my kids' lives. There were many doubt-filled days as we prepared for France, and I prayed a lot of doubt-filled prayers.

You better not screw this up, God. We have trusted you with our kids here! You better not let us down!

In the City

One thing that was new and unfamiliar, and truly stretched us in France, was being city dwellers. Even though the house we rented was just outside the city limits of Aix-en-Provence, all of our activities surrounding school, church, and community were centered in the quaint cobblestone streets of the historic city of Aix. And although Aix had a small population of only 200,000, we still, for the first time in our lives, were really able to experience city life. And we decided we loved it. Street performers, café-lined streets, public transportation, large parking ramps, twice-weekly produce markets, endless shops, and narrow alleys were staples of our daily life. Quite a change for a couple of country kids.

As neo city dwellers, the most glaring challenge initially came from the constant presence of beggars. Our kids had so rarely in their lives encountered beggars and never on a daily basis. And so for us, to see the same faces every day, in the same places, holding up their signs of desperate pleas, brought a whole new set of questions to our family dinner table: *Where do those people live? Why don't they just buy a home? Why can't they find a job? Why can't we go buy them a home? Well then why don't they just come stay with us? Why can't we just give them money? How do you* know *they will spend it on cigarettes, drugs, or alcohol? Why doesn't anyone ever stop to talk to them?*

If you're like me, you have a polished set of answers to all those questions, and it's a pretty efficient way of numbing ourselves to the poverty around us as it nicely builds a little wall of insulation. A wall called denial. Keeping that wall up allows us to justify our reaction of ignoring these people, who are so much more than a term—*beggar.* But if we don't really know them, we don't really have to care, right? Well, our kids didn't give up on me so easily, and the questions persisted.

There were two movie theaters in Aix, and it was a glorious day, perhaps two or three times a year, when a film would come to the theater and be shown in *Version Originale*—in other words, English! When that happened, all the Americans would fill the theaters, setting aside movie preferences and watch any ol' stupid movie just to sit in the theater, eat the popcorn, and imagine we weren't in France for two hours.

We lived in France in the Lord of the Rings (LOTR) era and sometimes when I'd rattle off our kids' names to get their attention, Sam and Frodo worked best. Then a holy thing descended on the little town of Aix—either the sun, moon, and stars all aligned, or our son's prayers were heard—but the first movie of LOTR came to our theater, and we all shot arrows into the air to celebrate! Our boys counted down the days until the premiere like you would a wedding day, or a trip around the world. On the day of the movie release, accompanied with every other boy in their schools, they went and beheld the genius of J.R.R. Tolkien. Looking back, we should have never let Josiah go, however, because he was only ten and for several months after viewing the movie he'd wake us from a deep sleep and say, "I'm scared. I hear the Black Riders coming."

Parents of the year? I think not.

Aragorn

Andy, however, soaked in every word, every metaphorical scene, and every nuance of this dark film, and he became engrossed in all things LOTR and J.R.R. Tolkien. He was ferociously reading the books, his room was papered with LOTR posters, and he was forging bows and arrows out of every stick and string he could get his hands on. Then one day at school he heard that a local store had just received the mother lode of shipments from the States, and it was selling LOTR figurines. It's utterly shocking to me how hard it is to find the typical Target fare in any other country but America. Target simply takes all the work out of shopping—it has everything you ever need, for everyone in the family, all the time. Period. I've never seen it work like that anywhere else in the world. If you haven't done so recently, kneel where you are and genuinely thank the good Lord for your local Target store. I mean it.

After hearing about the figurine shipment, Andy started dreaming about purchasing Aragorn. His whole life would be fulfilled and complete if only he could have an Aragorn figurine living on his bedside stand. The only thing between that boy and his Aragorn was €20. He was so desperate he even asked to do chores, anything at all, to please earn him €20!

The stars aligned again, and Andy's grandma sent him a birthday card that arrived three months after his birthday, but right on time for Aragorn, for in the card, per normal, she had tucked $25, which at the time equaled exactly €20. That money burned in Andy's pocket for about six or seven days until we could find the time to go into town and visit the mother lode store. I thought Andy might burst as he was forced to put his patience to the test.

The public parking lot on our town's edge was a half-finished excavation site—dusty, chaotic, and seemingly abandoned due to funding or indecision. It sat twenty feet below street level, requiring a climb up urine-scented steps. Human urine, specifically—a distinction I've unfortunately mastered.

Most days, an eclectic gaggle of loiterers hung around those steps—bald men, in leather vests chain-smoking beside drooling pit bulls, or haggard figures begging for handouts. Today, there was just one old woman, disheveled and hunched, her face deeply creased with the toll of a hard life. She could have been sixty or eighty. We marched past her, as always.

Prior to living in France, our family motto was to never pass by a beggar without offering something. It was an easy motto to live by in Hudsonville because we rarely encountered beggars. Mere weeks after moving to Aix we decided we needed to alter that motto, simply because we couldn't keep up. With panhandlers at nearly every significant intersection, we just found it impossible to always have cash on hand or time to run and get more. Sadly, sometimes we walked past the panhandlers because we were simply weary of the rigmarole. Out of necessity we adopted a new motto, "I'll just pray for you, beggar person. I simply cannot handle the responsibility to give to you every time, so my prayers will have to suffice. I'm sorry, beggar person." So instead, we lived with the guilt that comes when ignoring the needy.

This time was no different. We said nothing as we passed by the old, nameless woman, but I hope—because my memory fails me—that I at least prayed for her. We climbed the steps, walked about three hundred meters, crossing several intersections of busy traffic, and just when I expected Andy to break into a run to get to the mother lode store, his pace slowed. Finally, he stopped in his tracks and said, "I'll be right back." Before I could question him, he pivoted and took off running in the wrong direction, back to the parking lot. Less than two minutes later he returned and said, "You know what, Mom? I've decided we don't need to go to the store anymore. I'm good without Aragorn."

It suddenly hit me. He had given his €20 to the woman on the steps! Andy, a twelve-year-old boy, having stared into the eyes of poverty every day, could take it no longer. All the justifications that most of us adults like to use to appease our guilty consciences for non-engagement don't mean jack-shit when you are twelve, and you have €20 in your pocket, and you see a woman with virtually nothing, looking like death warmed over, sitting on some pissy steps in the cold.

I'm sure Andy didn't worry if the woman might go spend the money on alcohol. I'm sure he didn't check out her fingers to see if they were brown from marijuana juice. I'm sure he didn't look at her antecubital vein to see if there were track marks. I doubt he contemplated her potential life circumstances to determine whether they really warranted his handout. I doubt he cared about any of that because I think he felt it just didn't matter. I think he realized there's no way to ever truly know why someone is begging, and so the only real question we should be asking ourselves is this: "What is God prompting me to do?" Andy knew beyond a shadow of a doubt what he needed to do—and he slept better that night than if he had lined his room with a hundred Aragorn figurines.

When we returned home, I told Paul the whole story of Andy's gift. With watery eyes, he took my face in his hands, kissed me on the forehead and said, "You know what? I want to always live in a place where our kids are daily confronted with need and poverty. I want them to always wrestle with the enormous responsibility that comes from having privilege."

Our kids may have sacrificed some of the finer things many of our peers were giving their kids throughout those same years, and they certainly exchanged a safe, comfortable, and known existence in Hudsonville for two years in a prickly country that was not exactly thrilled to host us. However, I realize the definition of sacrifice will vary drastically depending on the socioeconomic status of the definer. We never lost sight of the fact that although our kids gave up a few things, they still led lives of privilege. But that doesn't diminish the fact that what our kids received in exchange for the material things they never got, is something we'd give to them a million times over: eyes to see that God loves all people everywhere.

For me and Paul, a longing to travel was born out of a longing to learn, which was born out of discovering just how little we knew and understood about the world. Subsequently, our kids were the lucky beneficiaries of curiosity and wonder toward the people, places, and issues that Americans are sometimes oblivious to. And, indeed, their faith grew as they discovered God exists outside of America.

However—please hear me—I don't believe for a second that travel is a prerequisite for a charitable view of humanity. Globalization has brought the world to America as is evident in every decent sized city. No matter where we live, we're all just a short drive away from people very much unlike ourselves and a life-changing lesson in anthropology. With a bus pass, a library card, and a determination to not stay in our cultural bubbles, that gift of curiosity and wonder, I believe, is accessible to everyone.

CHAPTER 20

Au Revoir, Mes Amis!

"Whatever you do will be insignificant,
but it is very important that you do it."

MAHATMA GANDHI

I'm acutely aware of the bounce in my step. I catch a glimpse of my reflection in the window of the corner *patisserie* shop, and there, between the macarons and the crème brûlée, I see a brighter, fresher, thinner version of myself. I smile inside. Living in the city and walking everywhere plus eating a Mediterranean diet (not because I chose to, but because I live in the *freakin' Mediterranean!*) has trimmed off a good fifteen pounds. My hair is killing it too, with the latest chic French cut and blonde highlights, compliments of my gorgeous *coiffeur*, who now calls me "*Mon Cherie.*" My outfit is head-to-toe black because that's how the French women dress, therefore, now I do too.

I feel more accomplished today than if I had won the Nobel Peace Prize. I feel more powerful, intelligent, and significant than ever before in my life. This incredible feeling is not from looking like I now fit in or being able to communicate quite effectively in

French, and it's certainly not from pulling up roots and moving to a foreign country—especially a developed country as easy to live in as France (we never lost sight of the fact that God could have called us to places that would have been much harder to adjust to). I feel *alive* and *well* and *on fire* simply because I feel like I'm doing something with my life that matters. It's the growing, learning, changing, and becoming that makes me feel on top of the world today.

And then I realize the most beautiful, important, affirming fact that Paul and I can never forget: This on fire feeling is how our kids feel too. All four of them are now more confident, more compassionate, more whole, more aware of the needs of others, more interested in world affairs, and, as a by-product, more interesting humans themselves. They have never been more alive, and as we discussed this later that night, both Paul and I recognized there's not a single thing in the world that we would trade for the people we've become.

We were probably at the peak of our experience in Aix-en-Provence. But in the frustrating, mystical way of Jesus, this was also about the time when we started to wonder if it was time to leave.

Coming to Terms

Paul, especially, was questioning if there was any compelling reason for us to stay on. Although experiencing a new closeness to God in France, he struggled professionally. He just didn't feel his accounting skills were being utilized much, and the guy doesn't do so great sitting idle. We started wondering if his restlessness was God's way of nudging us to move on. We had been invited to join our France team so Paul could give business and accounting advice to the new Christian-owned businesses opening up in

North Africa. It just turned out that these folks didn't need much business advice from Paul. It certainly didn't help that we were living on the opposite side of the Mediterranean.

Other than a weekly meeting with our team leader, Henry, and a few hours each week of remote accounting work for the firm back in Michigan, Paul experienced precious few moments using his business expertise. I was quite busy volunteering at the kids' school and taking language classes, so Paul spent a good amount of time hanging with Yulisa, playing Candy Land, reading Mercer Meyer books, and taking long walks with the Red Flyer wagon. He'd get all fired up when the school would ask him to mow the kids' playground simply because it made him feel useful. But for a guy whose typical workweek is fifty to sixty hours of accounting nerdery and who reads the Kiplinger Letter just for fun, those random weekly activities simply didn't feel productive enough for Paul. It didn't help that we had made the classic rookie expatriate mistake of expecting the same level of production that we appreciated back in the States. In the States, I can easily accomplish ten tasks in a day. In France, if I made it to the bakery for a baguette and successfully paid our electric bill, that day was a very good, *tres bien*, productive day.

In an effort to make more friends, Paul tried to meet new French acquaintances for coffee as often as possible, but this too, wasn't how Paul was wired. Traditional missionaries call this relationship building, and they get a real kick out of it. Churches happily pay these folks a comfortable yearly wage so they can hang out in a foreign country, meet lots of friends at the coffee shop, and essentially do the same amount of nothing Paul was doing. That's why we knew we could never be traditional missionaries. We truly loved the French people and made many friends no different than if we were living in Fort Worth, Frankfort, or Florence. We just also believed we could have been working a full forty-hour work week while simultaneously hanging out with friends. I mean, that's how it works back in America.

Anger set in, and because we needed someone to blame (good Christians would never blame God and proud Christians never admit their mistakes . . .), we took our anger out on the Deneens. Our previously solid friendship became strained.

Oh, how I wish there was an app on our phones called "Hindsight." I'd use it all the time. I can now see how the Deneens had felt a clear call to serve God in France—a location they chose for the sake of their children's education and its proximity to North Africa. They had simply invited us to be a part of this initiative, believing there was a need for us to be there, but also knowing even if we didn't particularly feel useful, God would still, as always, be working in us. They already knew what we couldn't see or understand. We were blind to the fact God is always on the move even when we don't feel it. We were feeling useless, unproductive, and worse, like we weren't changing the world enough. (Gah!) But, most importantly, hindsight taught me: God changes the world one person at a time.

In France, God was changing the world by shaping and changing us.

All the while, our bank account was groaning due to the weakening dollar, the soaring cost of living in Europe, and the fact that we were paying rent in France as well as half our mortgage in the States. Paul had just turned forty, I was still in my thirties, and as two professionals with several letters behind our names, we were keenly aware of our earning potential while we sat in France going backward.

Our friends in the States were moving up their corporate ladders and socking away hundreds of thousands of dollars for things like retirement and their kids' college funds, but because we had that little hang-up with asking for financial support, we were draining those same funds—which was clearly unsustainable.

Paul had set out a fairly strict budget for us, which he believed could carry us for two years in France, but the rapidly changing economy and declining dollar meant that after just a year and a half we were over budget. Somewhere in the range of $40,000 over budget. Paul and I had never been the kind of couple who fought over money. Up to this time we had always had plenty, so what is there to fight about? But in France, we started bickering about money, and I learned a whole new empathy toward those who struggle financially.

A Tearful *Au Revoir*

I think Paul experienced an entirely new feeling: fear. And that made me afraid too. And it *was* scary. It's scary to lose the power and self-sufficiency that having money in the bank provides— especially, when that's all you've ever known. It's scary to trust God, whom your two perfectly functional eyes cannot see, with your hemorrhaging bank account that your two perfectly functioning eyes can see all too well.

We plodded along for several more months, pleading, *What are you doing with us here, God? Do you want us to stay? What's the point? Should we consider leaving? It took this long to learn the language and make friends! It feels like we're just starting to hit our groove. But it makes no sense that you would have us sit around here doing nothing. What's up with that, God? Why God, why? S'il vous plaît?*

In the end, without a compelling reason to stay, we simply decided it was time to go because of the financial strain. Our inability to afford staying was our simple answer to prayer. Perhaps God does speak through dollars or lack of them.

We cried and cried the day we left France. A large group had assembled at the airport to send us off in love. Love in the form of grown men crying like babies, women making snorting noises and smearing mascara all over each other's shoulders, and kids refusing to let go. We had to pry Andy and Josiah away from the arms of their friends to get them through security. All six of us climbed aboard that Air France flight with red and puffy eyes and brick-heavy hearts. I couldn't believe how much France stole our hearts. Well, actually, how much her people stole our hearts. The best words we have found to describe our time in our beloved France is the motto of the Peace Corp: "The toughest job you'll ever love."

A few weeks after returning to Hudsonville, we got a letter in the mail from our local bank. Before we moved away, Paul had had the privilege of serving on their board for a few years. Board members did not receive payment for their services, but instead they each received a little stock in the company. A total surprise to us, the letter explained that the bank had just been bought out, and that Paul was now receiving payment for his shares in the stock. This part is almost unbelievable: The check was for $40,000.

I wondered how many times in my life I had missed the miraculous because I was afraid of being afraid.

CHAPTER 21

Filthy Rags

Since 1986, Christianity in France declined from 82 percent to approximately 46 percent. Close to 50 percent of the population claim no religious affiliation at all and most of the country's exquisite cathedrals see more tourists than parishioners. France is sometimes dubbed the graveyard for Christian missionaries because her people, in general, are quite simply done with that nonsense and have moved on to find more tolerant and cerebral answers to the meaning of life.

Our French friends who pastored churches and taught in the Christian schools met an enormous amount of resistance as they did their best to share the gospel with people who just didn't want to hear it anymore. No one left a bigger impact on us than Ludovic Alcaraz, Josiah's teacher for two years. Ludo taught fifteen kids in his classroom of three combined grades: third, fourth, and fifth. Not exactly the stuff that headlines you in *Christianity Today*, but Ludo was a modern-day hero of ours. He strongly believed in Christian education and he fought hard to bring a softer, dare I say, more American approach to education where each child is valued and seen as a unique and brilliant creation of God, not just a number. Both Ludo and his wife, also a teacher, probably donated around three-fourths of their time to our little Christian school and received about a one-fourth wage.

This teacher duo lived in a third-floor apartment with two bedrooms and a tiny bath. They used public transportation most of their married life until they scored on a jalopy from some departing missionaries. The kitchen in their apartment was closet-sized and had no room for a table—only their daughter's high-chair. We shared several dinners with Ludo and Stephanie and sat around the only table in their home: the coffee table in the living area. This room was so small, however, that once you squeezed into your spot around the table, you were set for the night—there was simply no space whatsoever to move around the people seated at the table. If someone needed to go to the bathroom on the other side of the room, we all had to stand up and let the bathroom-goer pass by.

We'd talk for hours about how the French education system needs reform and all of Ludo's well thought out ideas on how to make it happen. He was brilliant, passionate, and felt called by God to this mission in life. The two things Ludo lacked, and it seemed to be essential to launch any of his dreams, were finances and expertise in business development. Two things, ironically, we could offer.

Now, settled back in Hudsonville, I can't stop thinking about how huge our house is compared to Ludo and Steph's little apartment. I think about how desperately they just need some seed funding and how much disposable income we spend on *stuff.* That gnawing suspicion we should sell this big white house returned with a vengeance.

I can't shake the question, "How much more could we give away if we didn't have so much tied into this house?" Paul often explained to me that the percentage we tithe and give away is already greater than the 10 percent that most Christians deem sufficient. He explained that we don't keep much beyond what we need. This makes sense to me, and I do trust his accounting acumen. However, the whopping problem with that common justification of a lifestyle is this: What is it that we actually need? I mean, realistically, how many square feet of living space does one human being need? How many acres are needed for a family of six? How many toilets does a family need? How much heat is needed to keep a family warm?

Stupid Ceilings

"I thought I just paid this bill!" I cried after opening yet another propane gas bill.

"Yeah, I know," said Paul. Walking away from me as if he didn't want to talk about it anymore, he dropped this: "One tank of propane doesn't go very far in our coldest winter months."

I normally have no clue who we pay for what, how much we pay them, and how often it gets done. I simply stink at all things financial and since Paul's uber-gifted in that arena, I figure I don't need to pay heed to any of it. But Paul recently insisted I understand our finances a bit better and suggested I pay the bills for a while.

I followed Paul down the hall and continued my lament, "But Paul, how in the world can this be right? I paid this guy over $900[5] just a month ago! It simply can't cost that much to heat this house!"

He didn't even acknowledge my rant. Of course he knew. I suppose he'd known all along how expensive it was to maintain all aspects of that house. I think he had numbed himself to the reality of our bills.

My eyes drifted upward. Heat rises. We were heating a lot of space above our heads that was not warming a single human being. My spirits nosedived as I thought about all the money we poured into heating unused space. A few days passed and I was full-on perseverating about our high ceilings. Those "stupid ceilings" sucking up our heat and money and yet giving absolutely nothing in return. I mean, there was no way you could enjoy that useless expanse apart from looking at it. Other than the extremely rare and rogue indoor volleyball game, it was entirely useless. After several days of focusing on our high ceilings, I concluded the only reason we have them—including those two lofty, gorgeous open dormers with large circle-top windows that made the architect wince and the builder cuss—was to be impressive. *There can be no other explanation. No one really needs high ceilings, do they God?*

As we poured money into heating those high ceilings every month simply to impress, I constantly thought of Ludo and Stephanie laboring in France, struggling to pay their bills, as they worked to bring Christ's kingdom come through a struggling Christian school. They were just two people out of millions stretched all over God's green earth who were living a surrendered life requiring financial support, yet we felt it was more important to spend money on ceiling spaces out of selfish ambition.

I was nearly choked by this paradox, so Paul came up with a solution to pacify my agony. He wanted to send Ludo a check, and when he told me how much he wanted to send, I piped down with my rhetoric for a while. In my lifetime thus far, I've yet to meet someone as unimpressed with money as Paul. It's that posture that allows him to part with it so easily.

A month passed, and we had yet to hear from Ludo. I was quite frustrated that he hadn't sent a thank you or even given us a call. On Sunday, I think the pastor singled me out of the crowd as he preached on integrity. Integrity, he said, is the stuff we do when no one is looking.

It's just doing the right thing—no matter what. I wanted to get up and walk out of church, but I stayed. God was rattling me good with this message. The pastor nearly flattened me with this: "God says, 'If you are good and kind and generous so that others may see it and be impressed, that is nothing to Me! Those are filthy rags to Me! You must give out of selflessness. Give because I've asked you to give and because it blesses Me. Give because it is the right thing to do. Period. And maybe it will always stay just between you and Me. And that's okay.'"

I hear you, God. I get it. Perhaps my need to be impressive isn't just with our big house. I'd like to be impressive with even the noble things of life—like generosity. I've taken pride in our benevolence! I am the worst of hypocrites. On the one hand, I'm against impressive high ceilings because they only serve to be impressive—but on the other hand, I want to be recognized for our generosity because that feels like righteous impressiveness. I must admit, not hearing from Ludo regarding our generosity has made me feel resentful.

How sick am I, God?

I'm reminded of one of my favorite artists of all time—Rich Mullins. I never met the man, but I still feel like it's okay to say I loved him. His music—both the songs he wrote and performed—came to me at a point in my life where they washed over my soul and transformed me. But not only was his music transformative, the man, Rich Mullins, left an indelible impression upon me. Rich was well known for never keeping any of his proceeds from his platinum record sales. He lived on an Indian Reservation in New Mexico and spent his days loving on those overlooked and oppressed by society. He wore threadbare t-shirts and holey jeans. One year, when Rich won a Dove Award, at the post-award reception, he put on the same aprons as the servers and walked around serving all the famous Christian artists their champagne. No one knew it was Rich Mullins behind the facade because no famous person would ever think of doing such a thing. Classic servanthood. The book, *An Arrow Pointing to Heaven*, the posthumous autobiography of Rich Mullins, as told by his friend, James Bryan Smith, tells the story that shortly before Rich died, he started to question his simplistic lifestyle. He started to feel that maybe he was taking pride in the fact that he lived on nothing, and he wondered if that, in some way, was as bad if not worse than enjoying the fruits of the work God had called him to do. Rich was wrestling with his prosperity in a world full of desperate financial need.

Rich taught me that even noble, Christlike actions can be sinful when you take pride in them. Like living abroad, or adopting a child, or living a simpler life.

I fell on my knees that Sunday after the sermon on integrity and repented. I told God I was a selfish, self-centered, self-seeker and that He and I needed to wipe that out of my life. I realized how much I was struggling with the same thing as Rich. I wanted to be humble and generous, but I wanted to be recognized for that humility and generosity, which is filthy-rag ridiculousness. The person I wanted to be, the person who gives just because giving is good and right and doesn't look for any personal acclaim, was my husband. I realized it was never I who was a selfless giver, but it was Paul all along. He just genuinely likes to give. It sincerely makes him joyful to bless others. Paul hadn't given it a second thought that we didn't get a thank you from Ludo.

About a month later, the check to Ludo cleared the bank.

Within a day, the phone rang at 6:00 a.m. on a Saturday. That was usually the first clue we'd get that it was a phone call from someone in a different time zone. It was Ludo. He was mortified, embarrassed, and extremely apologetic. Apparently, when he first looked at the check amount, he had missed one of the zeros. In France, the numerical nomenclature puts commas where we put periods, and puts periods where we put commas. If you saw a refrigerator for sale that cost $1,145.95, the French price tag would read: €1.145,95, so it was not uncommon for Americans to misread the price of something. This is also the case for French people reading American numbers. Ludo looked at our check written the American way and interpreted it with his French mind. It wasn't until he deposited the check that he came to understand the full amount!

He was speechless with appreciation, tearful even, and I was so incredibly ashamed of my second-guessing him. But I had learned a priceless lesson, that with or without Ludo's recognition of our gift, giving to him was simply the right thing to do. So you just do it. It matters not if anyone ever sees it, recognizes it, or thanks you. You just do the next right thing.

A Plain Building

For the next many months, I tried to convince Paul it was time to sell the white house. It wasn't just the heat bill that was eating me. It was the electric bill (equally hard to cool a big house in the summer), the property taxes, the power washer bill (hard to keep a white house white), the landscaping bill, the pool supplies, etc., etc., etc. I became more and more aware of how much money we were dumping into a thing we simply didn't need. It was just so dang impressive, and it's hard to give up on impressing others.

But just because we could afford it didn't make it right.

There were times during my relentless nagging that Paul would get angry with me. He simply couldn't fathom that I was the same woman who wanted this house more than life just seven years prior. He couldn't figure out who this schizo, fickle, nut-job was that he married. He couldn't believe I had done such a major about-face on him. So to shut me up, he kept giving more and more and more—with rather reckless abandon, if you ask me.

One time he gave away our perfectly good and newish car to a single mom who couldn't afford one. A whole dang car. He anonymously gave to our schools, our church, and our neighbors. To be honest, I wanted to sell the house, but I wasn't much on board with Paul's extravagant generosity in all areas of our life. I thought he was taking it all a little too far. But we would often prod each other with this question, "What is too far?"

And as the leader of our pack gave extravagantly, so did his tribe.

Two thousand and four was the year we had earmarked to take the kids to Disneyland. We had promised the boys for years that when Andy was fifteen, Josiah thirteen, and the girls had turned eight and five, it would be the year to finally go. We waited until they were all old enough to remember such a trip yet young enough to fully enjoy it. Our boys were sure we were the only family in Hudsonville who had never been to Disney, and they were probably right about that.

However, earlier that spring we went to Guatemala on a family missions trip where we built homes for widows and observed several feeding programs for impoverished children. The organization, Pray America, was trying to expand its feeding program into another nearby village but had run out of money halfway into the project.

As our family stood at the site of the new feeding program's half-built building, Paul asked us all if we wanted to consider reallocating our Disneyland money. We could go to Disney, for sure, or we could use that money to help finish this simple, plain building in the hills of Guatemala where hundreds of children who are on the brink of starvation would come to be fed every week. And as we looked at this man, the leader of our tribe, who has always modeled extravagant giving, we knew in a heartbeat what he would do if the decision were his. I said a quick prayer—and I really meant it—that if our kids decided to forego Disney, it would come from their hearts as a sincere act of selfless generosity. I wanted it to be their decision—not one influenced by us. Four for four. It was a quintessential no-brainer as our kids didn't even pause to think. "Give it to Pray America," they all agreed.

In our kitchen, on a side wall near our dinette set, sits an odd, amateur photo of that simple, plain building in Guatemala. No caption, no explanation, no engraving. To our family, the picture is the story. Yes, our kids may be the weirdest kids in Hudsonville because they've never been to Disney, but that picture serves as a reminder to us all to never forget that life is made up of endless choices. Sometimes you choose to forego one thing to give to another.

It's funny, as our kids got older, they stopped asking to go to Disney altogether. They did, however, keep asking to go back to Guatemala.

CHAPTER 22

They're Raping
My Daughter

"You may choose to look the other way,
but you can never again say that you did not know."

WILLIAM WILBERFORCE

My dad talked to me only once the entire time we lived in
France. Whenever I called home, I talked to Mom. Dad was
furious with me for moving away, so I got the silent treatment
for two years. The day we moved back to Michigan, he rushed
to me in the airport arrival hall, grabbed me by the shoulders
and shook me like a naughty toddler and said, "Don't you ever
do that again!" If I felt fallen out of favor with my dad before,
moving away sealed the deal. We were unable to connect in
nearly every aspect now, and the distance between us grew
from uncomfortable to abysmal. The crazy thing about that
strained relationship, though, is the miraculous way it taught
me beautiful new things about grace. Standing there in the
airport with our sixteen black travel trunks loaded down with

our French delicacies of Herbs de Provence and Nutella (which wasn't available in America back then), it suddenly hit me. There never was, and never would be a way for me to win my father over. He loved me. I knew that. But if I couldn't find a way to unleash extravagant grace upon him and simply accept him as is, I would inevitably carry my generational anger to my grave as well as this feeling of not being enough. There in the airport—my dad's firm grip still on my shoulders—I looked into his steely blue eyes and felt deep love and compassion for him. He was a broken man simply doing the best he knew how to do. And even if he'd never be able to tell me so, I knew in that moment that I was enough.

That was the moment I decided to accept Dad's efforts of loving me, no matter how poorly executed.

And that's also how I learned perhaps the most important lesson God tried to teach me in France. I suddenly realized I had merely been substituting the pursuit of God's approval for my father's. Two years in France taught me that God didn't love me even one ounce more afterward than before. Two years in France taught me that there was nothing I could ever do to earn God's favor either—His gift of salvation is free, no work of our own. And unlike my father, in God's case, it was perfectly executed.

In much the same way that Dad and I had locked eyes that day in the airport, I felt God look into my steely blue eyes too, and pour compassion out on me. I felt God acknowledge me for the broken person I am, just doing the best I know how to do, and graciously accept my efforts—no matter how poorly executed. And I felt God's tender love letting me know that I am enough. Just as I am.

Faith and Works

A lifetime of Sunday school plants a lot of scriptures in your brain—many of them helpful, but some that are confusing. I've got to believe there are many Christians who, like me, get tripped up on the faith and works issue. As far back as I can remember, I've always known this passage by heart: "For by grace you have been saved through faith. And this is not your own doing; it is the gift of God, not a result of works, so that no one may boast" (Ephesians 2:8–9). But as I got older, I didn't like this verse so much because it felt like a free pass for Christians who choose an entertainment-anesthetized life and just hang out till Jesus comes rather than participate in bringing Christ's kingdom come while living here on earth.

But like everything in the Bible, where you choose to focus can make a world of difference. Because Sunday school also taught me this one: "Faith without works is dead" (James 2:26).

France stands as our family's testimony that we became more alive when we surrendered security and instead chose to join God in His work here on earth. If faith without works is dead (and I'm shooting for as undead as possible), I've decided I have absolutely no choice but to get busy! I don't want to be breathing—alive, for all practical purposes—yet living like a dead person. I want to live all in for all my days. So for me, there's no question that I will do for God all that I am able, for as long as I am able, and as best as I am able.[6] I don't ever want to return to the passive participant I once was who was merely killing time waiting for Jesus to return.

Deconstructionism

One day, at a sporting event at our all-white suburban middle school, while everyone stood right-hand-over-heart passionately belting out "Oh say can you see," I stood quiet—indignant even—

with my hands in my pockets. A well-intentioned friend leaned over and whispered, "You're still not over it, are you Cindy? At some point you've got to get back to living a normal life."

Over it? What exactly do I need to get over? And "normal"? What exactly is normal?

I didn't want to "get over" the life-changing lessons we had learned while living abroad and traveling to developing countries. I didn't want to be normal like a good, white, suburban, Christian momma who quietly lives out her days in pursuit of safety and comfort. I didn't want to be normal like all my pro-life and faith-over-fear friends scrambling to buy guns while gun violence cripples our nation and remains the leading cause of death for already born children. I didn't want to be normal and return to the frenetic, panic-inducing, family-destroying pace of America. I didn't want a life that in any way looked like my former normal self: an energizer-shopping-bunny hopping from mall to mall with a Bible and a Beth Moore Bible study riding shotgun in my car (don't get me wrong, I love me some Beth Moore! Not my point here). I didn't want any kind of normal that consisted of competing with others for the nicest and biggest pile of stuff. I just couldn't—wouldn't—go back to that. And I certainly didn't want to be normal like many around us whose favorite topic of conversation was how much money they had, how they're currently spending it, and how much they need to save to finally feel "peace."

". . . o'er the land of the free, and the home of the brave."

Stupid song. Clearly, we're free here in America, but brave? Are we brave or are we just rich? How hard is it, truly, to be brave when you're the richest, most powerful nation on the planet? Similarly, how hard is it to be a brave American citizen when you've got enough money to never know powerlessness?

I was a mess. Coming back to America after living abroad, and especially in our small town of Hudsonville, was like returning to junior high school in the fall after the summer puberty hits—although you're still the same you, everything inside of you feels different, everyone looks at you differently, and you look at them differently. Our eyes had been opened to a bigger world laden with bigger problems than what we had ever known before. And we had met the God who cares about those problems just as much as our American problems. Our family, now interwoven with people from all across the globe, felt like global citizens, not just American citizens.

Back then, there wasn't a word for what I was experiencing, but the cool people today call it deconstructionism. When the theology, the paradigms, and the image of God that originally carried you in life no longer work, you've got to find a new way to make sense of the world. I had no inclinations to burn it all down. God had proven himself far too faithful over the years for that. For me, it was coming to terms with the fact that after Paul and I specifically prayed for our lives to reflect what we said we believed, we'd made some fairly radical changes. The thought of returning to the religious status quo made me nauseous, but any acknowledgment of that made me feel unloving and uncharitable to those who didn't feel the same. I begged God to grant me more grace. More and more and more, *please*, as I fought to push down the brewing frustration. Then, as the status quo tightened its grip on conservative ideology, my freefall from the American church accelerated. Many of the building blocks of my faith were crumbling now and slipping through the cracks in my fingers. And as I watched the rubble accumulate around my feet, it felt freeing. Not scary in the least. In that rubble, I recognized those controversial parts that no longer worked for me—the parts that felt too self-serving. What I had previously defended as our strong Dutch work ethic that provided Paul and I with many "hard-earned and deserved" blessings, now felt to me like a justification for selfishness. Reflecting back on that former belief system, I knew that no matter what I had said with my words (I follow Jesus! I love others! I believe we are to care for the least of these!), my actions still represented egocentrism if I advocated for things like: lowering taxes for *me* so *my* life will be easier regardless of whose life gets harder, passing laws that endorse *my* brand of faith but discriminate against that of others, getting rid of (or just make life harder for) those who might challenge *my* brand of faith or *my* perceived need of safety, and encouraging *my* country to become bigger, richer and more powerful so *I* can feel *more* safe and secure even if it means others will feel less so.

Those views just no longer worked with the way I now viewed Jesus as the Savior for the *world*.

In my season of deconstruction, I clung to the Lord's Prayer like a lifeline. For nearly a year, it was the only prayer I had left in me. But that prayer centered me daily as I repeated over and over and over the phrase, "Thy kingdom come, thy will be done" and realized that to surrender to the advancement of the kingdom of heaven, also required a surrendering of my will. *Thy will be done, Lord Jesus. If the bottom falls out on all else I used to believe, may I always return to this prayer, Lord Jesus, and be a part of bringing Your kingdom come.*

Returning from France, I could hardly set foot in a church—and not because I didn't want to. I desperately needed a loving, believing, and gracious church to come around me and listen to the stuff I was grappling with. Instead, my encroaching cynicism left me wandering alone outside of church circles. Paul was much more gracious than me, and faithfully plodded forth trying to find our place as new creatures in Jesus living in old spaces. All I could see were the many, many beautiful and enormous churches in our area seemingly focused on themselves—always growing, improving, expanding—while people just up the street were sleeping in tents by the river and mixing ketchup packets in hot water to make "tomato soup" for dinner. Anything even remotely resembling big production music and lights, elaborate rehearsed services, fancy Bible studies, and church bookstores housing coffee shops made me run in the opposite direction. For me, our pre-France consumeristic way of living and practicing faith felt unbearably heavy and I just didn't want to carry that load anymore. Any of it.

America, to me, felt like an arrogant and ridiculously rich uncle who lives in a mansion with a thousand bedrooms. He tells his family all the time how blessed by God he is, but as his family members lay their heads down each night on the street's cold, hard pavement, stomachs aching with hunger, lice crawling in their hair, and pulling their children in close, they wonder why God gave the uncle all this wealth when he's unwilling to help others with it. The uncle knows he has parents, grandparents, siblings, cousins, and many more distant relatives, actually, who aren't okay, and sometimes he'll give them a little help here and there. But the uncle is so afraid of losing his status as the richest and most powerful man in the family, that he only gives to them out of his abundance. He never feels the pinch. And, quite honestly, he worships comfort so much, he makes sure his actions keep him safely in the pinch-free zone and tells his family members to not come over—he doesn't want the uncomfortableness they bring with all their needs. When his family starts talking ill of him, even to the point of turning against him, he doesn't understand why.

Just like the rich young ruler from the Gospels, America, too, likes to proudly announce we're following God's commandments and insist we're a Christian nation. But when Jesus asks the rich young ruler to sell all his possessions and give to the poor, the ruler walks away sad. Are we Americans the rich young ruler? Are we only willing to take this Jesus-thing just so far?

We'll follow You, Jesus. Just don't mess with our money.

Who Are My Neighbors?

For me, the reverberating notion of selling the big white house was the only response that made any sense. I thought constantly about living more simply and adjusting our lifestyle to enable more generosity. At this point, I didn't feel we had a choice anymore—that walking away from the idea would have been disobedience. Paul still waffled back and forth on the idea a bit. He agreed we needed to make some changes but wasn't as quick to jump on the "sell the house" bandwagon. In a very vulnerable and honest moment, he admitted that since a home is often the most obvious way to gauge someone's wealth or position, he struggled a bit to sell ours and go smaller because some people might think less of him or wonder if he wasn't as successful as before. He was concerned some might think that he, a financial guy, had mismanaged our finances.

Paul, who never worries about what other people think of him, was suddenly afraid of what other people would think of him.

All our peers were moving up—bigger houses, bigger cars, buying second homes. We were at that stage of life where our kids, their toys, their junk, and their friends were all taking up more and more space. If you can afford it, logic says "go bigger." When most people our age were talking about needing more space for their families, we were talking about choosing less. The pit in our stomachs grew with every attempt we made to turn our back on what God was trying to tell us.

Then God jacked up the volume.

One Sunday, we walked into Mars Hill completely unprepared for the imminent assault on our psyche. When something messes you up so profoundly that you're never the same again, an assault is all I know to call it. We had a guest speaker that day whom Paul and I had never heard of: Gary Haugen, the founder of International Justice Mission (IJM). Gary started IJM in 1997 in response to the epidemic of sex trafficking in Asia. He was incredibly knowledgeable on the subject as he had extensively traveled and researched the cause and causation of this atrocity. As an attorney, Gary leveraged his law degree to take legal actions against corrupt governments who tended to look the other way when it came to the lucrative business of the sex trade. Gary shared story after true story of young girls, some as young as five years old, being kidnapped, stolen, or tricked into joining the business, then sold across national borders and taken to a place where they knew no one, had no friends, no family, no language, and no understanding whatsoever as to why they would be stripped naked, chained to a bed, and raped by strange men sometimes as often as twenty times a day.

I wondered why the leaders at Mars had not thought of passing out barf bags that day. Repeatedly throughout Gary's presentation I swallowed back vomit.

I kept thinking of our own precious five-year-old, Grace Evelyn, presently bouncing around in the children's ministry room wearing her new jean jumper trimmed in purple flowers and her white tights and brown buckle shoes. Although she wasn't at my side, I could see her brown curls, brown eyes, and olive skin as if it were my own. A five-year-old is one of God's sweetest gifts to the world. A five-year-old sings and dances and laughs and learns new things seemingly every minute. Five-year-old girls twirl in their dresses for their daddies and help their mommies bake cookies. They color new pictures every twenty minutes and tape them to the refrigerator and the walls of their room. They tell fantastic long stories of things they did at Grandma's house and take great liberties with embellishments as their brown eyes grow bigger and bigger with every detail.

Five-year-old girls and rape should never be in the same sentence. Never. But, in one of the most horrific moments of my life, because of Gary's words and my overactive mind, I immediately experienced imagery of our precious Grace chained to a bed, being raped by a strange man—brown curls tangled in a mess of blood, tears, and sweat and stuck to the mattress, body limp, bruised, bloody, almost lifeless as if she'd given up. Somehow, in a millisecond with that despicable imagery—as I panicked to chase it out of my mind—her gigantic brown eyes met mine and they spoke a million pleading words, all with the same message: *Why don't you do something, Mom? Stop him! Mom. Stop him.*

In that moment I suddenly felt something new about my Christian faith and responsibility to God's creation. I felt like every five-year-old girl in the world was my own five-year-old girl. As sick as I felt in my stomach, I realized I loved even the children I'd never met, who live tens of thousands of miles away, who don't speak my language or share my religion. It just doesn't matter. I love this little girl in Cambodia. I saw her eyes and they clearly messaged me: *Why don't you do something? Stop him!*

I knew something profound was happening in me. I would never be the same again. My head was pounding; my heart was racing; I was shaking all over. I was horrified by what Gary described. Before today I didn't know it existed. But now I do. And I instinctively knew this knowledge, on this day, in this place, would leave a mark on me forever.

Nowadays, people throw around the word "sex-trafficking" like they do "micro-finance" and "sustainable development"—all those tidy buzz words that are so popular in caring circles and NGOs. Recently the city of Grand Rapids held a Sex-Trafficking Expo, and the organizers had placed those little wire yard signs all along the highways, at intersections, and in neighborhoods: "Sex-Trafficking Expo! Don't miss it!" advertising it the same way as "Circus in town!" or "Need new windows? Call Hansen's!" It infuriated me that those barbaric words—sex-trafficking—were so flippantly plastered all over town. The words had lost their diabolical weight. But when I first heard Gary Haugen speak, sex-trafficking was a new term for me, as well as for most Christians, and the knowledge of what was happening around the world as well as right here in America and in my city, was rocking our comfortable Christian bubble. My bubble sprung a major leak that morning. I silently (well, sort of) wept in my seat for my little "daughters" all over the globe who were suffering this unspeakable abuse.

Gary concluded his message with this final blow: "Often, when I go around speaking, people will come up to me afterward and plead, 'What can I do? There must be something I can do!' And this is what I tell them—I really only need private investigators willing to enter these brothel hellholes and identify the criminals, therapists specializing in severe PTSD for counseling rescued girls, and lawyers willing to fight for justice and expose corruption at the governmental level—if you are not from one of those professions, then we probably cannot use you. Doctors, nurses, engineers, teachers, accountants—we just don't have a place for your skill set. But honestly, it takes a lot of money to rescue even one person who's been trafficked, and we are committed to this cause for each and every girl and boy—as well as rescuing any oppressed person suffering under the tyranny of injustice—and, quite frankly, we just need your money. You would better serve us by working in your giftedness or profession and sending money than by coming along on a mission."

And there was Gary's punch in my gut. He had read my mind. Of course, I'd been sitting there in my gray chair thinking I needed to hop the next plane to Cambodia. I imagined myself standing outside a brothel and having little girls run to me, arms open wide, and showering them with love as they recovered from life's worst nightmares. *Please, God! Let me go to Cambodia! Let me do something!* But Gary was dead serious— he even mentioned nurses and accountants (us!) as the types of professionals he couldn't use. No, Gary needed brave Christians from three distinct professions, and beyond that, he needed our money. He called it straight up.

As we drove up our winding driveway to our big white house, I was blasted by a series of rhetorical questions: *Who are my neighbors? Who are my daughters? Could our neighbors include even those we've only heard of, but never met? Is it possible that the children of the world are* my *children? And if so, when Jesus said I needed to love my neighbors, my children, as myself, what does that love look like for little girls being raped in Cambodia (or anywhere)? If they are my neighbors, my daughters, how can I receive this information from Gary and do nothing? Do we really need this much home more than Gary needs our money? Do we need a gourmet kitchen? Do we need five bedrooms? Do we need a sunroom, a pool, an in-home theater, all surrounded by our own ten acres of land?*

It's painful to pause long enough from this crazy consumption life and try to define need. But my questioning led me to this profound truth: It doesn't matter how other people define the word—what matters is how Paul and I do.

How could we possibly sleep at night with such excess, knowing that right now, in many places in the world, very young girls are repeatedly violated throughout the day and night and could potentially be rescued if IJM simply had more funding? I knew the answer for me: I would not, could not, sleep.

I tossed and turned all night long. I gave myself a headache, or maybe it was a self-induced internal concussion from two sparring realities throwing punches inside my brain. It sounded like this:

"There's nothing wrong with a nice house. It's not a sin in and of itself."

Sure, but—right this minute, there are five-year-old girls tied up and repeatedly raped in Cambodia.

"We already give away a lot of money—far more than 10 percent. Surely, it's sufficient."

Yeah, but—right this minute, there are five-year-old girls tied up and repeatedly raped in Cambodia.

"We built this house as an act of worship. We have always planned to use it to bless others." (Ah—a favorite justification for excessive homes from Christians.)

Sure, but—right this minute, there are five-year-old girls tied up and repeatedly raped in Cambodia.

"Without this house, no one will know we are actually very successful."

Yeah, but—right this minute, there are five-year-old girls tied up and repeatedly raped in Cambodia.

"God blessed us with this house. We prayed for it. It's a gift."

Sure, but—right this minute there are five-year-old girls tied up and repeatedly raped in Cambodia.

In the morning, seeing the bags under my eyes and sensing my sleepless night, Paul mused, "It looks like you slept about as much as I did."

"Really? You didn't sleep well either?"

"Terrible," he replied. "I can't stop thinking about little five-year-old girls being raped repeatedly in Cambodia. I feel sick to my stomach."

"Oh my gosh! Me too!" I cried. "I keep looking at Grace. Thinking of girls her age kidnapped, trafficked for sex, and raped every day for years on end. I just wanna run and scream and rage against this! I tossed and turned all night because I couldn't stop wondering what our part in this is? What can we do, realistically? Because, hon, for me, I simply cannot do nothing."

"I think we need to sell the house."

And there it was. He said it. I didn't have to. And, truthfully, there was no rush of adrenaline or surge of excitement. We both knew selling our house wasn't a big deal. It's not like we're Oprah or Justin Timberlake. People at our income level wouldn't even make a ripple toward righting the world's wrongs by simply donating more. But it was the one thing we could think of to do that just felt right. It just felt in alignment with the only thing we knew for sure anymore: We are called by Jesus to love others and treat them the way we would want to be treated.

For years we'd preach this to our kids: "With knowledge comes responsibility." After hearing Gary Haugen speak, we had new knowledge. So now we had to ask ourselves, "How will we respond responsibly to this new knowledge?"

We called the realtor later that week.

Although it felt like the timing was finally right, there was still one thing that needed to happen, apparently, before I'd take the leap. I needed to lay down the diamond bracelet once and for all.

CHAPTER 23

Diamonds Will Be the Death of Me (or a Small Boy in Sierra Leone)

"Then I saw that all toil and all skill in work come from a man's envy of his neighbor. This also is vanity and a striving after the wind."

ECCLESIASTES 4:4

The diamond bracelet story requires I take us on a journey back to the spring of 1991. It had been a year since Paul and his buddy Randy first began dreaming of their own accounting firm and only days after baby Andy entered the world when the two guys birthed DeBoer and Goodyke, PC, CPA. The two starry-eyed twenty-eight-year-olds launched the company with only a few years of experience, no savings in the bank, and with only two things in common: the love of laughter and Friday beers.

The guys borrowed the capital, rented office tables from our church, bought two adding machines and one filing cabinet, and opened shop in the basement of our home. Their two desktop computers (which were about as big as dorm room refrigerators), would get so hot they kept tabletop fans blowing on them. Every morning, Randy—already a father himself yet oddly uncomfortable with breastfeeding—entered our home and, with eyes awkwardly glued to the floor, darted past me on the couch as I nursed Andy. He'd squeeze his sack lunch into our refrigerator between the bottled breast milk and eggs and proceed down to our lower level to begin the workday. All day long I heard those two goofballs talk and laugh and fart and compete in push-ups contests and I'd think, "This thing is never going to work." While Andy slept, I'd comb the help wanted ads for a new nursing job that paid enough to support us.

However, in no time, without a dime spent on advertising, the guys were so busy they started turning clients away. I believe, as does Randy's wife, Brenda, it also probably didn't hurt any that neither of them looks like your typical nerdy accountant. They don't wear pocket protectors, hiked-up khakis, and Dwight Schrute glasses. I've got to believe most clients find that refreshing. And I probably need to remind you here that Paul is incredibly handsome. Randy's okay too, if you're into tall, athletic, blue-eyed blonde guys. I just know if it were me, it would help to ease the pain of taxes if my accountant wasn't an eyesore. Whatever it was, they didn't stay in our basement long, let's put it that way.

One day, mere months after the business launched, Paul came home from work acting very odd. He walked funny, knees bent a little—as if he were creeping up on me, but walking toward me in plain sight—and wearing a very sheepish grin.

On this otherwise very typical Wednesday, things felt atypical. The "I'm home" kiss lingered. Lingered some more— like he wanted sex. But it was the middle of the day and Andy, maybe only six or seven months old, sat staring at us in disbelief, seemingly aware of a pre-sex kiss. I remember thinking . . . *What's up with this, cowboy? Here? In the middle of the day? While Andy's awake? Who is this maniacal man? This is just not normal accountant behavior.*

Then Paul reached into his sportscoat pocket and pulled out a jewelry-sized long rectangular box. *Ahhhh! He doesn't want sex. He has a gift for me!*

His cute speech seemed well-rehearsed like a marriage or prom-posal: "With our new company's first real profit, I wanted to buy you a gift, Cindy. You and I are in this thing together. It's not just me suddenly doing well—you've put up with so much to help me get here. I know these long days are hard on you. So more than anything, right now, I just need you to know—I recognize that I'm here because of you."

With shaking hands, I slowly opened the box, even though I wanted to rip into it like a Snickers. Inside was the sparkliest, most stunning diamond bracelet I had ever seen (possibly because it was the only one I'd ever seen up to that point). Even though my love language is meaningful shared moments—like dinner dates, day trips, or walks on the beach—I instantly knew I'd treasure this piece of jewelry forever. I couldn't imagine that any *thing*—any tangible thing—would ever mean more to me than that beautiful bracelet. It was more than just a piece of jewelry to me; it was a symbol of Paul's selflessness. He could have taken a weeklong golf trip to Georgia and played at Augusta National (his dream). He could have upgraded his car (come on, should successful accountants drive an eight-year-old Camry?), or bought a new boat, a snowmobile, or fancier golf clubs. But, as his new accounting firm made its first profits, he spent it on me.

The Prayer That Worked

I became ever-so-slightly obsessed with the tennis bracelet. I was afraid someone would break into our home and steal it so I got all Nancy Drew-like and tried to think of a place where a thief would never think to look. I chose to keep the bracelet in a safety lockbox, high up above our kitchen cupboards in the peak of our cathedral ceiling. The only way I could retrieve the hidden treasure was to pull a dining room chair to the kitchen, climb up on the counter, and by standing tiptoe I could just barely stretch enough to reach through the sea of fake ivy that was all the rage in the early nineties and grab the box. *Ta-da!* I had outsmarted the most thievery-thieves! The only problem, however, was that it took so darn long to retrieve the dumb thing, I almost never wore it.

Then a jeweler friend of mine told me a secret about fine jewelry. She said people inevitably fall into one of two categories: They either wear it all the time, or they never wear it. There's generally no in-between. After that, I pivoted and decided to wear it all the time.

I wore that thing five years solid through the addition of Josiah and Grace and all their toddler years. I didn't remove it for showers, kids' baths, dishes, weeding the garden or swimming in slimy lakes. Diamond bracelet and I became one.

That is, until I lost it.

I didn't even notice it falling off, but suddenly one moment while folding laundry, I simply realized it wasn't on my wrist anymore. We searched the house high and low. Nothing. Despair set in as I called the different places I'd been over the last several days and repeatedly heard the same reply: no bracelet. I unraveled like a frayed cheap carpet caught in a vacuum cleaner. I cried like

I had lost a child. Paul tried to comfort me, telling me we had insurance on the thing and we could just go buy a new one. I didn't want a new one—I wanted *my* diamond bracelet!

After about a week of acting ridiculously unhinged, God made a breakthrough with me. I don't know how, and I don't know why. This all happened while I was still deep in the throes of materialism, and I never looked to God for direction back then. But I woke up one day with this epiphany. "That stupid little bracelet is just that: a stupid little bracelet." It's only a thing. It doesn't matter if it cost $200, $2,000 or $20,000—it's only a thing—and things should never have power to dictate our joy. I suddenly realized that Paul's love for me, of which the bracelet was only a symbol, would never change with or without a bracelet. That may have been the first time I realized that things do not make us who we are, give us our worth, or add even one second to our lives and shouldn't usurp our time from human beings. So that morning, while still in bed, I decided to give the whole bracelet matter to God.

In repentance, I prayed, "Lord, I have made a mockery of you. I think maybe I've made an idol out of my bracelet. I think I care too much about things and perhaps that's what you're trying to show me. I'm so sorry. Lord, if I have given this thing position over You or others, then I want You to keep it. Just keep it. I do not want that thing in my life if it's become too important to me. Please, God, teach me to always love people more than things."

That afternoon Grace found my stupid tennis bracelet under the seat of my big SUV as she dove for a piece of rolling candy.

I wholeheartedly believed I had learned my lesson and felt deep in my soul I would never let materialism creep in again. So I continued to wear that stupid bracelet 24/7, not worried in the least because I told myself, "I just don't care anymore." But I am God's most stubborn case, and my lessons were far from over.

I continued to lose that bracelet over and over and over. Every stinkin' time I'd repeat the exact same prayer of repentance, and then, *voilà*! Lo and behold, I'd find the bracelet yet again! It was like I knew a magic trick and my prayer served as my "Abracadabra!" It was uncanny how frequently this little drama played out.

I lost the bracelet several times in France. The first was at a picnic where we met twenty or so friends high up on a bluff overlooking the Mediterranean in the nearby city of Marseille. We all played softball then shared a delicious lunch of French baguettes, salami, and cheeses. I didn't notice the bracelet missing until we were almost back home, a forty-five minute drive north. Although he wasn't thrilled about it (huge understatement), Paul agreed to drive all the way back to the coast, and he and Josiah hiked back to the picnic spot. I stayed in the car and enlisted the other kids to pray my Abracadabra prayer with me. "Lord, you know the routine. Do I really need to repeat this silly prayer? You already know I love the bracelet, and you also know I don't want it back if it's beginning to mean too much to me again. If this *thing* is getting in the way of me loving people, then I don't want it back."

About an hour later, Paul and Josiah returned with my bracelet. They found it somewhere around second base and almost entirely obscured by matted grass.

Two months later I lost it again. *What kind of joker is God anyway?*

This time it was in our hometown of Aix-en-Provence, and I was convinced Diamond Bracelet had sung her swan song. I had had an exhaustingly full day walking all over the city center of Aix. On this rare day of snow and ice in southern France, I had parked in a city-parking ramp on the outskirts of town and walked about six city blocks to the apartment of my French tutor, Madame Prudhomme. She lived on the fifth floor, no elevator. Afterward, I walked another six city blocks to a little grocer and combed every single aisle to find raisins and cream cheese. I then walked back to the parking ramp, drove to another parking ramp on the other side of town, walked five more city blocks in the snow and ice until I reached the cathedral where our youth group met every Wednesday. When I walked into youth group, I reached down, felt my wrist, and realized, in horror: no bracelet.

Seriously God? How many times must I keep relearning this same stupid lesson? That which I already know, but miserably fail to obey?

Most graciously, Henry, who led our youth group, let me leave to go search for that stupid bracelet. The irony of choosing to search for my precious thing rather than spend the next hour and a half with twenty junior high kids seeking Jesus is not lost on me. But, per usual, I began the search by saying "the prayer." It felt manipulative to repeat those same worn-out words asking God to keep the bracelet if it, once again, meant too much to me. Blah, blah, blah . . . I wondered if I even meant the words anymore. Maybe this prayer had become another one of those mindless recitations we Christians love to prattle off: "Now I lay me down to sleep . . ." "God is great, God is good . . ." It felt like a gimmick, a hoax. Except that . . . well, this formulaic prayer worked so well so many times in the past, I had to give it a go again. It may have been purely a rote exercise, but it felt like God was messing with me, so I decided I'd mess back.

Snow- and ice-covered sidewalks can appear an awful lot like diamonds. I bumped into several people on those bustling sidewalks as I walked head down, focused on my search. *Je suis desolee!* I searched the sidewalks, scoured both parking ramps, and returned to the grocery store to retrace my steps down every aisle. Then, last, I walked back to Madame Prudhomme's apartment complex where my day began. There, on the black doormat at the front door—eerily and perfectly arranged in a circle as if it were in the window of a jewelry store—lay my diamond bracelet sparkling in the sun and so conspicuous no soul could have walked through those doors and missed it.

It had been well over two hours since I walked out of that building. That huge apartment building probably housed as many as fifty to seventy-five people. Was I to believe that no one, not a single person, had come in or out of that building in over two hours? I found that unfathomable. I think God miraculously placed that bracelet right there, right at that moment, as a way to say, "Thank you for finally getting it. Now stop this game, will ya?"

And after that, I got a new clasp on the bracelet and stopped wearing it so much. It had taught me a great lesson, I thought, and I decided that was its purpose all along—simply an instrument to teach me surrender. I figured my days of losing it, praying, and finding it back again were over. OVER!

But God had one more final, painfully poignant lesson to teach me.

Epiphany

Somewhat surprising to me, when we were back in Michigan and the "For Sale" sign went up at the big white house, I barely flinched. I couldn't stop thinking of those five-year-old girls in

Cambodia and how we'd now be better poised to donate to IJM. We were going to live simply so that others could simply live. *Ahhhh, blessed to be a blessing. Ahhhh, joy.*

But perhaps I was doing a bit too good with all this rapid change. And perhaps I was feeling a bit too proud of our "sacrificing." Because one day, before the house sold, things came crashing down. My day had been packed with an important meeting at church, a play date for Grace, several errands taking me to two different cities, and a doctor's appointment. I'm not sure why, but I chose to wear my bracelet that day. Late in the afternoon, I returned home and the sun was hitting the white house just perfectly, and I promise you it looked like a postcard. I drove up our long driveway, inching along while soaking in its beauty. My stomach sank faster than a toy thrown down a toilet. Such a beautiful house. My vision was so clouded by tears, I barely found the garage. I had no time that day for an emotional breakdown, so I pulled myself together, and in an attempt to divert my energies, I headed right to the kitchen and started doing the dishes. After draining the sink of the water and suds and running the garbage disposal, I dried my hands and felt my wrist, and realized, once again, the bracelet was gone. I knew instinctively: *This is the final chapter.* Who knew when it fell off? No way would I ever be able to retrace all my steps from that day. No way to get it back if it went down the drain.

It was gone.

For sure.

Everything felt so much heavier than just ten minutes prior, and I couldn't bear the load anymore. My emotions developed a life of their own and proceeded to run away. I sank to the kitchen floor, put my head in my hands, and cried out to God, out loud, not in repentance this time, but in anger: "This is too much, God! Too much! You've simply asked too much of me this time! I admit it, okay? Is that what you want to hear? I *love* that stupid bracelet! Yes—I love it! And this time, God, I really do not think I value it more than people—I just want it back because it's beautiful and I love beautiful things! I don't want to play that silly game and say that silly prayer because I just want that stupid bracelet back, okay already? And one more thing, God, I love this house too! Okay? There, I said it—I love this house! I love how big and impressive it is and how people think we must be smart and important because we have a great house. I love decorating it and showing it off. I admit it, God. Is that what you want? And I love it for more noble reasons too. I love it for the way Paul can hit long fly balls to the boys in the front yard, and how he can hit his nine-iron full out and not even reach the road. I love how the boys made a motocross track and an ice hockey pond in our field. I love how we can dance in our underwear without ever shutting the blinds because we're so far away from neighbors. I love how the rooms form a circle so we can have family chase scenes as cowboys and Indians or Ken in hot pursuit of Barbie. I love the swimming pool and hosting pool parties. I love the way it looks all decorated for Christmas. There, God, I confess! I love this house and I don't want to sell it! And another thing—I'm mad at You for asking such incredibly hard things of us. I'm mad at You, God. You've asked too much of me now. France was hard enough, but now this? This is just too much! And I don't think You love me because this just feels mean. There, God. Yes, it's true. I don't think You love me, and I think You're mean. Amen." (I was still far too much of a good Protestant to not at least add "Amen" to my rebuke of God.)

I bawled until my shirt was soggy, my sleeve was full of snot, and my temples pounded from an ensuing cry-headache. I think I ruined the cherry wood floors in that spot because the installer explicitly said to avoid getting any standing water on them.

And then, out of nowhere, when I had stopped making pathetic, gargling, drowning sounds and I was finally able to hear something other than myself, I heard it. I heard it and knew exactly what it was—there was no mistaking it. As in the past, I don't think it was audible, but it doesn't matter to me either way. I just recognized that deep in my spirit, a visceral feeling in my gut, that God was speaking to me. It felt a repetitive chant saying, "*Cindy, Cindy, Cindy. It's okay. I know. I know. I know.*" As I rocked back and forth on those cherry wood floors, I felt held. I felt the arms of the Almighty around me as he repeated the words, "*I know. I know. I know.*" I suddenly felt very loved, known, and understood—as if no one else in all the world could possibly know how much I loved that house and could possibly understand the sacrifice it would be to give it up—and yet, here was my Lord, completely knowing, completely understanding, and completely empathizing with sacrifice. Sacrifice. Of course! Of course, my Lord understands sacrifice! Who else could possibly better understand? He who sacrificed His very own Son! For me, He gave that incomprehensible gift! No one has ever sacrificed more. He alone really gets me. But what I felt Him say to me next really changed the trajectory of our lives and informed all our countercultural decisions going forward: "*And Cindy, listen carefully my child: You can keep the house if you want to. I never asked you for the house. I only asked that you hold it loosely.*"

I pondered the message—spellbound for the moment—and let it sink in. There was no doubt what I was hearing and what message God had for me. I replayed it over in my mind: *God said we could keep the house if we wanted to. We can keep our house! We can keep our house!*

Owning a nice house was not the problem.

The epiphany was clear. I now understood God's position on possessions. His simple yet profound answer to all that I had been struggling with. He just wanted me to leave behind the tight death grip I had on our stuff, and to be willing at any time to surrender it for something greater. He wanted me to lay down my desires so I could find a piece of life that can only be found in sacrificial giving. He wanted my whole heart—especially the parts where materialism and covetousness had taken up residence. Really, I know now. God wanted to give me a more abundant life, but for me, I needed to receive that additional gift through subtraction.

And in the very next miraculous moment—no lie—I was once again fine with selling the house. It happened that fast. I suddenly understood it's all God's anyway, and *knowing God* had to be my goal, not having the best and most of everything. If selling our home was the thing God wanted to use to draw us closer to Him, then I wanted to do it. I stood up, wiped my face with the kitchen towel and looked out over our massive backyard. I reflected on all the wonderful memories we had made at this beautiful residence and thanked God for them. And I asked God to give us many more wherever he'd take us next.

Then I looked down, and there in the sink on the same side where I had rinsed out the entire basin of suds and ran the garbage disposal—there lay my diamond bracelet.

Addendum

Several years later I stopped wearing the bracelet altogether after watching the movie *Blood Diamond*.

I ran to the bathroom after the movie and stared into the mirror at my bloodshot eyes—the result of two hours of crying. I felt sick to my stomach and not at all sure I could keep from throwing up all over that Celebration Cinema bathroom. I splashed water on my face. And then it was one of those moments when, again, I just knew what I needed to do. I don't know if it was a voice, a feeling, or a force, but I just knew I needed to remove all my diamonds. It didn't take long because I don't have many, but I took off that diamond bracelet and my wedding ring and stuffed them in my pocket.

It took nothing for me to lose myself in the story of illegal diamond exporting in West Africa and how greed and the love of money drove people to the most heinous, despicable, barbaric acts—including forcing children to be soldiers and brainwashing them with drugs, sex, and money to become little killing machines. I felt dissolved into that painfully true story and so now it is a part of my story. Maybe I will and maybe I won't be able to figure out a way to put an end to child soldiers, but wearing my bracelet, which will now always be a symbol to me of evil surrounding the diamond trade, and acting as if life just goes on normally, well, that's not an option for me anymore. What do I do with what I now know after watching that movie? I don't know. And that sometimes beats the hell out of me. But what I cannot do is nothing.

So the stupid bracelet sits in a locked safety deposit box in our basement. And you can easily find it if you're the thieving kind. One of these days I'll just bring that silly thing over to the first dancing highschooler I see wearing one of those "We Buy Gold" sandwich signs along the sidewalk, grab whatever cash they'll give me for it, and send the cash to Sierra Leone to help rescue child soldiers.

CHAPTER 24

Milk Crate Tables

"What do you fear, lady?" [Aragorn] asked. "A cage," [Eowyn] said, "To stay behind bars, until use and old age accept them, and all chance of doing great deeds is gone beyond recall or desire."

J.R.R. TOLKIEN, *THE RETURN OF THE KING*

Four months after putting our house on the market, it sold. We prayed about where God would have us live next. We only knew we wanted something simpler and smaller allowing us to give away more. We had heard of several other families getting out of debt, and so we thought we had good company. When we asked around about it, being debt free to most meant eliminating credit card debt or car loans. But we wanted to get rid of our mortgage too. All the smart people told us no one considers a mortgage as real debt because it's such a given in America to have one! Although we were still young, Paul and I realized we did have options. We were not forced to have a mortgage—we chose to. We chose to buy a house, which cost more than our cash on hand. Accepting that truth was necessary for us as a precursor to eliminating some of our unnecessary middle-class debt.

Everyone we knew had solid justifications why their mortgage was good and necessary and that they couldn't possibly live anywhere cheaper. But we felt a relentless and supernatural nudge to rid ourselves of one.

A few weeks into our search for a downsize, I found it: a little brown rancher about half the size of our white house on a quiet cul-de-sac within the city limits of Hudsonville. The place was a time capsule. Not a single thing had been updated since its 1975 inception. Stalactite spikey plaster dripped down from the family room ceiling, which, if you could jump that high, would probably impale your skull. That same room boasted dark brown paneling, brown, heavy drapes, a brown brick fireplace, and hideous multiloop, multi-shades-of-brown Berber carpeting. The room was so dark, depressing, and poop colored, it felt like walking into someone's bowels. The entire house, both inside and out, sported just two colors: brown and beige. It was a seventies classic. The only missing parts were Ashton and Topher.

Even after making some upgrades to the home, we were able to come away from the deal debt-free. We weren't stupid (I don't think so, anyway). We knew most people considered this a bad financial move. As an accountant and savvy financial planner, Paul knew we were doing something very countercultural and counterintuitive. He admitted that he didn't necessarily counsel his clients to become entirely debt-free. Real estate is generally a solid investment and healthy debt gives you good credit scores and some leverage for investments. But we both had long since stopped caring about such things, and the world's logic just sounded like blah, blah, blah, blah.

Our goal was to position ourselves to be able to give significantly more to those in need. I think we were realistic regarding what "significantly more" means for people like us. We knew that even though we had done fairly well for ourselves, a couple of small-town kids from a rural farming community and no inheritance were solidly planted in the middle of the middle class. We knew that no matter how much money we were earning, we weren't even tickling the underbelly of the upper class. We knew full well that any increase in our philanthropic dollars was not going to rock the world or even the bank account of any small, unsuspecting 501(c)3.

However, a major change in our new understanding of money was that God's economy doesn't always make sense to those of us steeped in American economics. Our pastor often referred to the "upside down kingdom"—where things might not make sense here on earth, but they do in the kingdom of heaven. We realized sometimes we're just asked to do things we know in our souls are true and right. Even though our culture tells us we're screwing up royally, we do it anyway.

I worried what the people in our circles thought of us. I was mad at myself for worrying about it because I just wanted to be past that comparison-jealousy-competition game of life. But I still cared about others' opinions too much and assumed they would assume we couldn't afford the big white house. After all, who would choose to sell their beautiful dream home just as the kids were growing into it and needing and using all the space? I was paranoid that people were talking about us behind our backs. I'm not sure they were. I just worried about it.

And because ours was such a proper Dutch community, people rarely confronted one another if they had concerns. I thought it was odd that no one asked us if we were doing okay or if Paul had just lost his job or something. A few friends who knew we were still okay financially, said things like, "Why would you leave that beautiful home? I'll take it if you don't want it!" or "Are you sure you guys want to do this? Don't you think you'll regret it after a while and wish you had more space again?"

But occasionally, friends would dig a little further to try and understand us. One night while sipping post-dinner wine, a dear friend inquired, "Do you think it's possible you guys just struggle with accepting God's blessings? I mean, it almost sounds as if you're feeling guilty about your beautiful home."

I shot back, "No, that's not it at all!" I had always believed guilt was a bad emotion, in the same camp as lust, greed, and jealousy, and I felt attacked by her comment. So I went on. "It's purely out of conviction. That's all. We just didn't feel right anymore about owning so much house. A smaller home just fits our beliefs better. Some people don't eat pork out of conviction. Some people don't go out to eat on Sunday out of conviction. Some people won't get a tattoo out of conviction. We can't live in a big house out of conviction."

As we drove home that evening I perseverated on her question. What exactly was the emotion that prompted our actions? I wanted to believe it was love for mankind. Or hope for a better world. Or joy in following Jesus. Or, heck, I'd even take excitement that comes with a change! And while I believe all those emotions were part of the concoction that led to our move, I had to admit, guilt played a part. We had reached a point in life when we could no longer be okay with so much abundance when we knew so many others struggled just to stay alive. Yes, I do believe that's called guilt. Because we were guilty! The more aware we became of the world's injustices, the more aware we became of our abundance. And it hurt. I lost sleep many nights thinking of those helpless girls in Cambodia—and for us, doing nothing simply wasn't an option. So we sold our big house and downsized so we could give more money away.

Could it be that God uses guilt to move us? Heck if I know. It's not a motivating factor I observe in too many people's lives, so maybe we've got it all wrong. Honestly, I don't care. To this day, we're unable to shake the thought that maybe we are supposed to feel guilt when our excess and self-centered existence comes at the expense of the oppressed.

I've often wondered if Jesus has waited so ridiculously long to return because he's been waiting for the Internet. I wonder if he is waiting for the time when we all know how the rest of the world is living and fighting and suffering and dying. Certainly, the Internet has linked humanity together like never before in history. In a very real sense, we are all now connected, and maybe now we are all truly each other's neighbor. Jesus had a lot to say about how we're supposed to treat our neighbors. Because of the Internet, we can no longer hide behind our ignorance. Because of the Internet, we know about little girls repeatedly raped in brothels in Cambodia, and we can never stand before our Lord on that final day and say, "I just didn't know."

Selling the big white house was much more than just downsizing and more than freeing up philanthropic dollars. For us, moving down the ladder of house impressiveness was also a symbol of what we wanted our lives to look like in every aspect from then on. We wanted to live simpler, to own fewer things, and to spend less time taking care of our things and more time with our people. We wanted to live beneath our means. We wanted to become more and more generous and less consumed with more, bigger, better, faster—the lie of the American Dream. We were simply trying to come up with an answer to two questions: 1) How much of what we have falls into the category of excess? And 2) Why would God give some people more than they need?

When I stripped away my rationale and justifications for all we owned, I had to be honest and admit that true need is simple to define. We need food, water, shelter, and clothing. That's it. And so, anything beyond that, or extra amounts of any of those things, would be called excess. Since everything is relative, every single one of us can find someone who lives a lifestyle beneath our own. So unless we're unhoused and hungry, every single one of us can find ways to live with and on less. What we're forced to ask ourselves is, "What lifestyle do I choose to live?"

From a rare Taco Bell take-out to regular dinners at Ruth's Chris Steak House, from a flip phone to the newest edition iPhone, from public transportation to a Mercedes, from thrift stores to Prada or Hermes, and to millions of ways up the middle, lifestyle is all about choices. And most of us really do have the wiggle room to choose to reduce.

Our Garage

Recently, I've been volunteering at a ministry in the inner city that serves the unhoused population. They serve meals, offer hot showers, lockers, and laundry services, as well as provide overnight accommodations for women. The ministry employs several social workers who work tirelessly to help these women find housing. I have had the privilege, on more than one occasion, to help a homeless woman pack up all her earthly belongings—typically consisting of one, maybe two garbage bags of moldy, smelly clothes—and move her into her own residence. I've seen the look on her face, that of total disbelief, as she steps through the threshold of a new beginning and into her new apartment. I've seen the tears trickle down her face. I've looked around at the dirty, unfurnished space with broken locks and broken windows, crawling with cockroaches and mice, and thought, *This can only be a step or two above hell. She has nothing. How will she survive in this cramped, stinky apartment in this dangerous neighborhood?* But she, my formerly homeless friend, is in speechless wonder because she is finally home. I even had the privilege of moving one thirty-something woman into an apartment who had spent her entire life living on the streets, even as a child.

One particular day, after helping a young woman search for hours to find an affordable apartment, I drove home to our little brown house—my mind reeling with emotion. When I drove into our garage, I just sat in the car for a long while. I looked around at the stack of lawn chairs and the multiple camp chairs hanging by hooks. I saw the plastic milk crates full of sporting equipment—the same kind of crates the women at the shelter use as chairs and tables. I noticed the black desk in the corner that Josiah couldn't fit into his dorm room. I saw brooms and rakes and shovels and hoses. In the rafters were two large trunks full of seasonal clothing I'd never bothered to donate, an old interior door, a patio umbrella, and several pieces of luggage. A brand-new camping air mattress still in its box sat dusty in the corner. Seven bikes hung from the rafters on hooks—four were old but functional, three were shiny and new.

I looked at all that stuff—stuff that was in our garage alone—and I realized that we are ridiculously rich, and this little brown house is actually huge. We have more belongings in our unfinished, dirty garage than all the homeless women at the shelter put together. In fact, all the homeless women at the shelter would probably happily agree to live in my garage—even if the only household items they had were my garage things. They would most likely be very happy with my garage if it could be called home. Milk crate tables. Lawn chairs for a couch. Castaway clothing. A rickety desk. Suitcases for dressers. An air mattress for a bed. Bikes for transportation.

Just. In. My. Garage.

I realized my vernacular had to change. This house is a freaking mansion. My garage alone could house twenty people! It is not an ugly little brown house at all, and I need to stop calling it that.

Because everything is relative.

For many in the world, our wealth is unfathomable. I sat there that day in the garage and thought, *Am I actually taking pride in the fact that we made one minor adjustment? Do I think we deserve credit for this change we made—as if I'm suffering? Do I really believe this is suffering?* I realized I loved to throw around the phrase "ugly little brown house" just a little too much—perhaps thinking that if I felt it, and others heard it, I'd actually be able to convince myself of how we were suffering for Jesus. But the truth is, we didn't suffer at all with the move to the brown house.

No. This is not suffering.

Giving until It Hurts

I am reminded of an event that happened twenty years earlier at our former rural Reformed Church. It was Thanksgiving, and as a church we decided to collect bags of groceries to donate to a local food bank that in turn provided families in need with all the fixings to have a full-on Thanksgiving celebration. We were proud of ourselves that in just four weeks our little church of only one hundred families had collected one hundred bags of groceries that now neatly lined the back wall of our narthex.

With one week remaining in the food drive, one of our more elderly elders slowly walked up to the pulpit. We anticipated the pat on the back we were about to receive. Instead, in his gentle, crackling voice, he said, "I think it is good that we have collected one hundred bags of groceries. But I think it is safe to say we have all given out of our abundance. We all found some extra cash to buy some extra groceries, and our lives weren't affected in the least. But what if we gave sacrificially? What if we gave until it hurt? What would that look like? Maybe we have to give something up just so others can eat. Maybe we need to give up going out to eat, or Starbucks coffee, or skipping a few meals ourselves. What would it look like if we gave to the point of feeling it? That's my challenge for myself and for this church. Let's not be proud of giving out of our abundance. Let's give until it hurts."

And he slowly walked back off the stage. You could have heard a pin drop in that green carpeted, stained-glass sanctuary as we all stared straight ahead at the cross.

I remember thinking how this was the perfect man from our congregation to give that little rebuke. He modeled sacrificial giving. He and his family weren't fancy or loud about it, they just quietly gave and gave and gave. Although a meager meat packer, every single one of us in that community knew this man and his family lived beneath their means so others could simply live.

The following week, I walked into church and thought it smelled like an orange grove. The entire narthex was piled high with five hundred bags of groceries, and I don't think there was ever a better sermon taught at that church.

So I began to wonder—would we, could we, and how might we continue to simplify our lives and reduce spending? Had Paul and I given until it hurt? The answer was a solid no. What else is there that God might be calling us to leave behind? If we've not reduced ourselves down to the simplest, barest necessities of life, kind of like the way Jesus lived, then there would always be room for further reduction, right? So are we still asking ourselves the right questions? Or upon making a few minor reductions, have we settled in and become comfortable with this new level of excess? Is this the end of the reduction road for Paul and me? Are we supposed to be content with this new, albeit simpler lifestyle we've chosen and just return to tithing 10 percent? Has God stopped asking us to give extravagantly? Was this downsize just a one-off, or should we keep going? And just how far do we go?

Ahhhh—such painful questions and I was not feeling very comfortable with the answers, but to stop asking the questions meant to stop caring.

So I didn't know for sure, but maybe selling the big white house and downsizing to the little brown one was just the first step of many reductions. Perhaps we would be doing it again. And again and again. But one thing we concluded as a nonnegotiable going forward: We will always, always be sure to have people in our lives who are struggling just to survive. We need that constant reminder that we are definitely haves in a world made up mostly of have nots. That sick gut-punch feeling I had that day in our garage, we decided, was probably something we should get used to—not something to live in fear of.

A Trailer Full of Crap

After we were all moved into the brown house, there remained in the driveway a borrowed trailer still full of stuff but nowhere to go with it. The trailer wasn't just a five by eight foot wagon trailer; it was an enclosed trailer for transporting race cars—two cars, in fact. And that whole stinkin' trailer was full of more stinkin' crap. Crap we believed was necessary in our white house. As I roamed from room to room in the brown house, I couldn't think of one thing more we needed. Every person had a bed and a dresser, there were couches and chairs in the two living areas, a dinette set and appliances in the kitchen, bookcases filled with books and plenty of decorative touches everywhere. The house was full. Its diminutive stature said, "No more! No more stuff! I'm full!"

I went back out to that trailer and peered in, wondering what in the world we owned that we didn't need that could fill a whole trailer. Dressers, clothes, exercise equipment, end tables, closet organizers (because the more junk you have, the more you need to organize the junk!), a second refrigerator, floor lamps, bar stools, computer desks, etc. I shuddered in realization at just how excessive our excess had been. I simply could not have known at that moment the journey that God was yet to take us on to teach us so much more about simplification, but what I did feel in that moment was a step in the right direction. In our driveway, in that trailer, I experienced a holy God moment. I felt him smiling down on us. Paul and I contemplated our options on what to do with the stuff, and decided to just give it all away. I felt about fifty pounds lighter that day.

So much easier than Weight Watchers.

But of all the things we purged in that move, there was one new thing we added to the brown house: a simple sign. In my kitchen is a sign with one word: SIMPLIFY. That sign later accompanied us all the way to Morocco. Because, again, I'm just like the grumbling Israelites so inclined to start complaining and forgetting. I can easily forget what I want to be all about and how I want to live my life full of gratitude and contentment, not selfishness and desire. I needed that sign (and still do) as a daily reminder. I also needed to keep a quote board in a conspicuous place and consult it frequently. There are a few quotes that help me when I start drifting back toward materialism. One is "Contentment is not the fulfillment of what you want, but the realization of how much you already have." There's another three-part quote that I'd like to believe I made up myself, but since its theme is frequently found in magazines like *Real Simple* and *Simple Life* I may have borrowed it. In regard to my shopping habits, I want to always remember this:

Think! Think! Think!

Before buying anything ask yourself these three questions:

1. *Is it useful/helpful/functional? Can I honestly say I need it?*
2. *Is it so beautiful that I can honestly say it will enhance my life or the life of others?*
3. *If I buy this new "thing" and bring it into my home, what am I willing to part with to make room for it?*

REMEMBER! Just because you can afford it, doesn't make it right.

A Better Way to Live

The first night in our brown mansion, our bedroom wreaked of paint fumes and had no blinds on the window, but we decided to sleep there anyway. I had painted the walls scarlet red (okay, so maybe not my best decorating decision, okay? Leave it alone), and with the room being so small, it felt mildly cave like. So in the morning, when I rolled over to see Paul lying there wide awake on his back with a small tear trickling down his cheek, I feared the worst. My guy rarely cries. I had a panicky moment afraid he had concluded we'd made a terrible mistake and that he hated waking up in a blood-red bedroom the size of our former walk-in closet.

"Are you okay, hon?" I asked with fear and trepidation.

He took a long pause, wiped away the tear, looked at me with the most peaceful expression I've ever seen on his face, and said, "I cannot tell you how amazing it feels to wake up in the morning and know that you owe no man a thing. We had bought a lie, Cindy. There is a better way to live, and this is it. Spending less on ourselves so we can give extravagantly more is a far, far better way to live."

We'd been liberated from the tyrannical ideology of the American Dream. We realized that the systems we (Americans) construct to create comfort, safety, and security for ourselves are thin, at best, and will always crack with just a little pressure. We realized we could no longer put our trust in those flimsy systems if we wanted to live large and chase Jesus with everything in us. Hard work, wealth, stuff, 401Ks, stocks and bonds, the kids' inheritance, owning a big ol' house that makes others jealous . . . is that the stuff the American Dream is made of? And when you get all that, you'll finally be happy? Nope. It's a lie. It's all a big fat lie.

We had been enslaved to a belief that wasn't true, and once we summoned the courage to name that lie and walk away from it, we finally got our lives back.

Leaving It Behind

On the day we left the white house, the car waiting in the driveway piled high with our last load of stuff, I took one last stroll through our now empty and cavernous mini-mansion, and blessed that home for the next family. I expected the tears to start gushing at any moment—after all, I'm the girl who cries at a good commercial—but they never came. I expected to have that pit in my stomach that comes whenever you're about to embark on something big and scary and unknown, but there was no pit. I expected my kids to get all emotional and want one last look in every room, but they didn't. I expected this move to be hard, but it wasn't.

And that was how we left our white house—with unbelievable, unnatural peace. I cannot explain to you how something that once meant more to me than anything else in the world had now lost all attachment to me except that God had been doing a work in us over the past ten years, patiently teaching us to let it go. Let. It. All. Go.

I felt rescued as we drove away from that house, as if we were leaving a prison and experiencing the outside world for the first time. Each breath felt deeper, fresher, and more beneficial—like we hadn't been fully breathing before today. We were, in a very real sense, coming more and more alive as distance and time grew between us and that home. We weren't naive, I don't think. I believe we were fully cognizant of the sacrifices we were making and that there would be a day, somewhere down the road, when we'd feel the pinch of walking away from a more cushy and comfortable existence. And yes, as time marched on, there were moments when, for example, I cursed my tiny kitchen as I tried to prepare a meal for a large group. I have, at times, missed that impressive home because rich people were coming over and they wouldn't be impressed at all with our little brown house. I have, at times, bemoaned our lack of storage and privacy in the little brown house.

But the underlying truth remains steadfast: I wouldn't trade this new life, in this smaller house, with so much of our time reclaimed, and a large part of our income reclaimed, with our new neighbors and our new goal in life to give away exponentially more than ever before, for anything. Especially—especially for a big white house. To this world that says bigger is better, that more will make you happier, that debt is normal, and that need is anything you can afford, I say, "Keep it." Keep your big houses and big cars and big mortgages and closets full of stuff, because none of that stuff added to my life. In fact, I now know for sure, it subtracted from me.

When the six of us piled into the car that last day and slowly drove down the long, winding driveway one final time, I asked myself, "Don't you want to at least look back and drink in one long, last view of this house that meant so much to you all these years?" My response was quick and sure, "No. I don't." And I didn't look back. Not even a glance.

Because I knew.

I knew there were far, far better things ahead than any we were leaving behind.

One thing I ask from the LORD, this only do I seek: that I may dwell in the house of the LORD all the days of my life, to gaze on the beauty of the LORD and to seek him in his temple.
Psalm 27:4 (NIV)

Epilogue

With only a hint of imagination, I am in Ninevah. Or Bethlehem. Or Corinth. Or any one of the mysterious cities I first heard about in fourth grade Sunday School. Indeed, every part of this crumbling, dusty village—donkeys, mosques, bearded men, women in hijabs—seems to have stepped right off the flannelgraph board in the cinder block basement of the country church of my childhood.

As we wind through this tiny Moroccan village—my husband, our four kids, and our oldest son's girlfriend—I chastise myself for not being more hospitable in this country known for their hospitality. We'd been invited to share a meal at the home of our dear friend Abdel-Kabir. I may stink at math, but I'm pretty sure Abdel-Kabir is around a thousand times poorer than us. Yet he is the one having us over for dinner.

Paul stops our sea-salt-rusted Honda to let a young boy coax a herd of at least a hundred mud-encrusted sheep to cross the road in front of us, and not one of my kids says a word about it. I chuckle to myself and wonder if they even remember that shepherd boys don't lead huge herds of sheep across the streets back in Hudsonville.

Several middle-aged men dressed in traditional long robes sitting on red plastic chairs in front of a tiny *hanut* drinking the country's ubiquitous sugary mint tea look up and nod approvingly as we pass by. A doppelgänger for Old Testament Abraham whacks a stack of fly-covered beef with a shiny machete-like knife as we pass by his walk-up butcher shack. Animal blood covers the floors, the walls, and Abraham's white apron. I make a mental note that the ten or so bloody carcasses hanging around his counter appear less fly-covered than those at the meat stand I typically go to. *It might be time to switch butchers.*

For a moment, I feel bad that our family is ruining this scene of antiquity by puttering down this pockmarked gravel path in a motorized vehicle. We are the epitome of the Sesame Street song, "One of these things is not like the other. One of these things just doesn't belong." In this country, in this village, on this street, with these darker-skinned people who hold fast to their religious Muslim beliefs, our white faces with our Christian faith in this red Honda are definitely "the thing that doesn't belong."

But the most bizarre thing has happened to us over recent years. I totally feel we do belong.

At another time and in another place—so long ago and yet, so fresh—something good, yet painfully weird happened. All that we thought mattered, all that we cherished and held with clenched fists, rather suddenly lost its appeal. When the weird thing happened, we stopped feeling belonging in the place we had always belonged. In fact, we suddenly felt like outcasts in the very place we spent our entire lives trying to get to. And now we belong here—this Ninevah, Bethlehem, Corinth place.

As we near our friend's home, a handful of rambunctious boys jump onto our rear fender and hitch a ride. It's not every day that a vehicle makes its way down these streets, so these boys take advantage of the bouncy thrill. I notice two girls too young to have their heads covered peek out of the doorway from across the street. They smile shyly then duck back inside giggling. It feels like people are expecting us and I wonder if we're more than just Abdel-Kabir's American guests. Is this entire neighborhood excited that we're coming to town for dinner? The thought embarrasses me. I don't like it that our white skin, blue passport, and green money make us anything special.

Abdel-Kabir told us to come at 7:00 p.m. so naturally, we arrived at 8:00. We now know start times in Morocco mean nothing—kind of like their posted office hours, road lane lines, and the labeled price of goods in the market. The Moroccan approach to punctuality (virtually irrelevant) and timekeeping (sporadic, at best) often frustrate Western visitors, but our family's perpetual tardiness made us perfect candidates for this culture. Optional watches and cell phones suit me just fine.

Moments after arriving, Aisha, Abdel-Kabir's wife, enters the living area from the kitchen, which really isn't even a kitchen, nor is it even a separate room, but merely an area in the corner with a hot plate and a spigot. She prattles off something to me in Arabic. I understand none of it, but as she hands me the baby, it's clear she wants me to take the child. I doubt she truly needs my help; she's probably just trying to connect with me somehow since words won't work in this situation.

The baby is slimy, stinky, and looks terrified. I wonder if Aisha asked me to "Please change the baby's diaper" instead of "Would you kindly hold the baby for a bit?" For the millionth time, I wish I would have worked harder at Arabic. I tried. Truly, I did. Yet I'm certain I could have learned how to perform brain surgery, cochlear implants, and heart-lung transplants simultaneously faster than I've learned Arabic.

While waiting for the couple to finish preparing the meal, we entertain the baby and her toddler sister and count the cockroaches that occasionally peek out from under furniture. We've been sitting in their hot, tiny, living-cum-dining-cum-bedroom (it changes depending on the time of day) for what feels like the duration of two back-to-back sermons on a sticky summer Sunday in a sans air-conditioned church in Michigan. I estimate it's after 10:00 p.m. because we've heard the muezzin give the Isha call to prayer. But even for us—a family who has long since ditched our Dutch-heritage early dinner hour and now prefers a late-evening, French approach—this is getting ridiculous.

Not one to censor her words, Yulisa whispers much too loudly, "I'm starving! When are we going to eat?" I don't even acknowledge her complaint but simply give her the glare. I'm thankful Abdel-Kabir and Aisha do not seem to comprehend her words.

The glare easily suffices for this one. We've done this so many times before, I don't need to give her the speech. All the kids know it by heart anyway: "We are guests both in this home and in this country—so we will not fuss, complain, or whine. We'll eat when they say we'll eat, and we'll happily eat whatever they serve us. And then, even if the food turns out to be disgusting, we'll tell them it's delicious." No discussion. She doesn't know differently anyway. She's now lived more of her life overseas than not and has no concept of the American "your way, right away" mindset. She's never been to a Burger King, Taco Bell, or Jimmy Johns and doesn't even know what a Slurpee is. She thinks a Kardashian is a car, and to her, football will always mean soccer.

She's not like the other three—who remember life *before*. Yulisa, has only known the *after*.

Still, we are hungry, and the self-restraint is slowly disappearing in each of us, as the lung-sucking North African heat seems to be melting us. We've been told this indomitable, arid wind (akin to the blast one feels when opening an oven door after four hours of cooking a roast) is called the *Chergui*, originates in the Sahara Desert, and is capable of choking small animals to death. For a brief moment, I worry Yulisa could be considered a small animal. Despite our stellar nutrition since her adoption, she remains virtually doll-sized and holds a six-year run of registering below the zero percentile on every variation of height and weight growth charts. As I spend a little too long on such a bizarre thought, I wonder if I'm going heat crazy—or even slowly suffocating. Some people perhaps spend too much time thinking about their love interests or how to make more money. I spend too much time thinking about the worst way to die, and death by suffocation is in my top ten, for sure. I casually check my own pulse, and I am, in fact, still alive.

We're hot. We're hungry. We're weary. And we're not nice to one another anymore. But still, we wait.

Abdel-Kabir, one of the kindest men we've met since making Morocco our home, deserves no less. He's our street guardian, and his job is to protect residents from bad things on a street where bad things never happen. It's not so much a job as it is Morocco's version of welfare. Moroccans all over the country are employed in nonsensical ways as an alternative to government assistance. Paul met Abdel-Kabir soon after we moved into the neighborhood while walking our tri-lingual Moroccan dog, Buddy.

It was about midnight and the streets were quiet. It was late fall and nighttime temperatures were dipping into the forties. Paul heard wicked, phlegmy coughing coming from a mini shed-like structure on our street corner. These "huts," if you will, dotted most neighborhoods in Morocco, and they looked like a ten-year-old tried to construct an outhouse in shop class. But they are the nighttime homes of our guardians. Paul approached the structure and saw Abdel-Kabir, teeth chattering, looking pale and sickly. Paul's Arabic wasn't what it is today, but he still managed to ask Abdel-Kabir if he was okay. When he shook his head no, Paul ran back to our home, grabbed a blanket, some hand warmers, and a hot cup of coffee and delivered the items to the shivering man. The two were friends from that day forward. I truly believe it's possible Paul saved Abdel-Kabir's life that night.

Despite being "employed," Abdel-Kabir is destitute, and his two children regularly flirt with death from lack of clean water, healthy food, and medical care. Families exactly like Abdel-Kabir's flood Casablanca. Up and down almost every street, every day of the week, every time of day. Although this backdrop of humanity became an annoying staple for most of us, Paul always took the time to talk to the "least of these." After spending a day exploring Morocco with Paul, a visiting American friend made this observation: "Paul humanizes everyone. When poverty is so prevalent and beggars are everywhere, it's logical to decide the only way forward is to ignore them. Paul simply refuses to do that." It's true. It's also a much nicer way of saying what I often say about Paul: "The guy can make friends with a tree."

Eventually, Paul helped Abdul-Kabir secure a much better job at the international school where we worked. After landing that job, Abdel-Kabir was the happiest man ever. He even began to glow. Literally. It could have been because he was just that happy, or it may have been from his healthier skin once his liver stopped acting up. Even in his new job, Abdel-Kabir barely made enough to keep his family of four off the streets (yes, sadly, even the American businesses in the developing world do not pay nationals what they are worth, but instead, what they can get away with). Still, he insisted on hosting all seven of us for a meal of traditional Moroccan couscous to thank Paul for the new job. This dinner easily cost Abdul-Kabir a week's wages.

Several years ago, back in Michigan, I mistakenly thought we had experienced that same level of generosity when some new friends invited us to their second home on Lake Michigan. After taking their Miami Vice style cigar boat for a two-hour cruise down the coast of Lake Michigan, we ate expensive steak and drank expensive wine together. On the way home, I gushed to Paul. "That was so extravagant! I bet the boat gas alone cost $500! They probably spent over $1000 on us tonight!" Characteristically, Paul, unlike me, thought before speaking. Finally he said, "Yeah. Probably. But don't gush. They probably make that much in an hour."

We have come from a world I barely remember, which increasingly feels more foreign than this one.

Dinner finally arrives. It's couscous with beef, and if it wasn't guilt I was feeling before, it surely is now. Meat is such a luxury for poor Moroccans. Aisha beautifully displayed the couscous like a piece of artwork in a large, round, black and red Moroccan pottery bowl that moments before had been hanging above the *froshe* as wall decor. Proper couscous etiquette means every person in the circle digs into the large common bowl and simply plows through the channel of food that is directly in front of them. Abdel-Kabir plops down next to Paul and grabs a large fist full of couscous with his right hand. With a twinkle in his eye, he tells us that we're eating the couscous all wrong. He says, "You must make little balls. Like this." And he shows us how to wad up the couscous like Play-Doh. We make little golf-ball-sized balls of couscous and pop them into our mouths. Abdel-Kabir is beaming.

I summon Aisha, sitting several feet outside our circle, to come join us and eat. I can't find the words in Arabic, but there's no way she could misunderstand my hand gestures. She shakes her head no, indicating that neither she nor her two malnourished children will be eating with us.

We hear footsteps on the creaky stairs and two women bustle in, one with a white headscarf, the other's is green. They take turns using the squatty potty in the corner of the room, and I notice they do not wash their hands afterward. The woman with a white headscarf gives Abdel-Kabir and Aisha an aggressive *bisous*, the traditional greeting of a kiss on each cheek, and smiles at all of us, saying, "*Salam alaikum.*" "*Alaikum-salam,*" we say in return. She proceeds around our circle, kissing everyone. She has an infectious laugh and holds Abdel-Kabir's arm as they chatter away in Arabic. She winks at me, throws her head back, and laughs some more, assuming I got the funny thing she just said. I again chastise myself for not working harder to learn that merciless language. I have no idea who she is, but I love her already.

The older, slightly bent and seriously buxom, green-scarfed woman plops down in the circle next to me, gives me a quick *bisous*, and then digs into the common couscous dish in the channel right next to mine. I remember the glare I gave to Yulisa earlier: "We will eat when they tell us to eat, and we will eat whatever they serve us to eat—joyfully." There is no negotiating these terms. So I joyfully dig into the common bowl next to she with the pee-hands.

Soon, multiple conversations are happening in three different languages. Paul and Andy, now eighteen years old, seem to be having pretty good luck in Arabic with Abdel-Kabir. Josiah with his near-perfect French, is helping me in a conversation with green-scarf woman, who speaks typical Moroccan French. Our girls, Grace and Yulisa, use the universal language of facial expressions and hand gestures to get Abdel-Kabir's daughters to giggle. Couscous is flying everywhere, and every human and cockroach in the room is loving it. I've relaxed now that I've stopped thinking about all the infection control measures I learned in nursing school.

After the traditional dessert of fruit, Aisha presents her ornate silver teapot—the signature symbol of Moroccan hospitality—and serves us the over-sweetened, mint-flavored, piping hot mint tea responsible for rotting the teeth of all Moroccans who lack dental care. By holding the pot a good ten inches above the colorful, shot-sized glass teacups and letting the tea cascade down and form a foamy topping, she elicits several *oohs* and *aahs* from us and forges a half-smile at that. I can tell she's bursting with pride from the admiration of her "wealthy" American guests.

We're not wealthy, of course. Not anymore, anyway. And certainly not by American standards. But compared to most Moroccans, and certainly to this family, we're virtual billionaires.

As we sit in this hot, stinky, crooked-walled home, secretly praying that it won't collapse, digging into the common dish of couscous with our bare hands alongside people who don't wash their hands after toileting, swatting flies and watching for scurrying cockroaches, and as Andy's girlfriend vomits in the corner squatty-potty because her visiting stomach isn't used to Moroccan microbes, and as our family communicates with Abdel-Kabir's family using bits and pieces of three separate languages, I look around this room, at these people, at this moment in time, in this live-flannel-graph country that has become my beloved home, and I feel something deep in my soul:

There is no place in the world I would rather be than right here, right now, with these exact people. I love everything this moment is, and everything it represents—learning about different cultures with their different languages, religions, and societal norms and nuances. I absolutely love making new friends and sharing life with them and loving them deeply while realizing that even though it is hardly possible for us to be more different, we have, with a little time and personal investment, become like family. I love watching my offspring discover God as they experience the richness of this life. And although Paul and I have never been so materially poor in our married life, this moment makes me feel like the richest woman in the world.

Thank you, God. Thank you.

Endnotes

1   Hudsonville High School (HHS) graduated 78 students in 1948, the year my dad graduated. I graduated with 182 students in 1984. Today, HHS is a top-tier, Class A school that graduates over 500 students yearly and consistently wins both regional and state championships in many of their sports programs.

2   I only felt the need to footnote this obvious song reference for the unfortunate souls who are either musically nascent or too young to know the genius of Tom Petty. Google "Free Falling" if you're one of those tragic few. (Half of my beta readers wanted me to remove the extra "too.")

3   The Protestant denomination of my youth is the Reformed Church in America (RCA). As an offshoot of the Dutch Reformed Church, the RCA is rooted in the Reformation of the 1500s under the leadership of John Calvin. Today, the denomination has just over 80,000 members and doesn't even register on lists of largest Protestant denominations in America. In comparison, the Baptist denomination boasts nearly 37 million members in America.

4   Find the story of the widow's mite in Luke 21:1–4.

5    $900 in 2003 is equivalent to about $1,500 in 2025.

6   "I have one life and one chance to make it count for something. I'm free to choose that something. That something—the something that I've chosen—is my faith. My faith demands that I do whatever I can, wherever I can, whenever I can, for as long as I can with whatever I have, to try to make a difference." Jimmy Carter, 39th president of the United States of America (see https://www.crosswalk.com/headlines/contributors/milton-quintanilla/6-inspiring-jimmy-carter-quotes-on-love-prayer-and-faith.html).

Acknowledgments

Well, now this is an odd feeling. I feel exposed, unprepared, and bereft of speech—like an actress at the Oscar's who never in a million years expected to win so she didn't prepare a speech. She slowly ascends the steps, hesitates before approaching the podium, and remains frozen at the microphone for an awkwardly long time. Everyone's staring at her, impatiently waiting. But arriving entirely unprepared, her mind goes blank while the faces and names of people whom she should thank flash through her mind like a cataclysmic lightning storm. With mouth gaping open, drool drips down her chin then trickles down to the front of her $50,000 gown.

That's me. Here, now. Throughout this entire writing journey, I never gave a single thought to writing "Acknowledgments" because that would suggest there would one day be a book. Fear and denial did their best to keep this manuscript buried for an insanely long time. I'm fully aware this book is not award-winning material, and to simply finish writing it isn't even close to the literary equivalent of a Grammy, but still, I'm looking at this page with a chin full of spittle. Good thing I'm only wearing a T-shirt and sweats.

But this is why I must begin with extending my deepest and most heartfelt gratitude to Marcia VanPopering. This book would *still* live only in my computer had it not been for Marcia—a brave, truth-telling friend. Marcia, wearied of my yapping on about a book I was too afraid to release finally blurted, "Well, I can see what needs to happen here—that book holds you captive. You gotta get that book out in the world or you'll never be free. No more excuses, Cindy. Let's get after it. Right now." Sometimes, with someone as blunt as Marcia, people feel intimidated. Not me. I can't get enough of her. I regularly hang out with her just so she can "slap me around" a while (in her most loving and encouraging way, of course). Every insecure person needs a Marcia in their life.

Even with Marcia's gentle yet firm nudging, there still wouldn't be a book if it weren't for Tim Beals and the great team at Credo House Publishers. Thank you so much for taking me on, Tim, and turning my words into this beautiful end-product (and for accepting the swears to let my true voice come through). And Vanessa Carrol, your editing skills are LEGENDARY!!! (See how I'm using BOTH all caps AND punctuation EXCESSIVELY here??? And see how EXHAUSTING that is for the reader???) I think we can all thank God that Vanessa significantly toned me down so that reading this book isn't quite as painful as a week of passing kidney stones.

To my writing coach, developmental editor and true-life Yoda, Chad Allen: Much about the writing life taught me, you have. Have given up long ago, I would. That I could write, you insisted. Quit, you would not let me.

To my bad-ass, incredibly supportive, and truth-telling writing group who all exemplify the kind of courage I aspire toward—Ruth Olsson, Dana Doll, Nurya Parrish, Alicia Waalkes, and Bekah Reese—I am truly indebted to you all, precious friends, for refusing to let me take a match to this manuscript and pushing me forward in the final stages. Also, it's not lost on me what a privilege it is for someone my age to regularly meet with such ridiculously intelligent, world-changing women as yourselves.

To Pat VanderKolk, yet another faithful and brutally honest friend, I thank you with all that's in me for your no-holding-back opinion of my words. Without you, Pat, I fear I would have unfurled some potentially unkind, judgmental and mean-spirited words. Thank you for having the courage to ask, "Are you sure you want to say *that*?"

I simply must roll out an additional vat of wine and a barrel of hugs and kisses to the insanely brilliant and truth-telling Reverend Ruth Bell Olsson for gifting me countless intensive three-hour breakfasts, brunches, and lunches at quirky Eastown eateries where after you'd gently point out my crippling insecurities and remind me how unattractive weak-kneed people are, we'd proceed to solve all the world's problems. #Ruthforpresident. I'm dead serious.

Alicia Waalkes and Lindsay Sisson—my little, yet mighty "team"—I cannot thank you enough for tackling all the things that my geriatric brain couldn't (wouldn't?) learn that often rendered me paralyzed. Thank you for refusing to let me remain crippled. The two of you did more for this book-thing than I ever even hoped or imagined, and you took this meager effort of mine from a slow crawl to a great run.

Stephanie Rouiselle, a thousand Sunday school gold star stickers to you, my precious French friend, for never giving up on me even when, together, we learned that platform building is not for the faint of heart (which, we discovered I am, but you are not!). Also, enormous thanks for accompanying me to writer's conferences and introducing me to oodles of inspiring writers who also write simply for Jesus's sake.

My most sincere thanks to Dana VanderLugt, friend and published author (her book, *Enemies in the Orchard,* is a must read!) who was also our former babysitter, for all the encouragement over the years and for wrangling up a group of wise beta readers who had never met me because I didn't trust feedback from anyone I knew.

To all my beta readers, thank you for your timely and honest feedback. Scott VanPopering (my covert beta reader—are you sure you don't need to be paid?); Julia Lamsen—a phase one beta reader from nearly a decade ago who bravely offered: "There's a lot of words here. Do you think you need them all?" (wiser words have never been spoken); Jenny Schout, Kristin Bakker, Jennifer Owens, Mary Veldink, and Kristen Freiburger who all agreed to read a whole stinkin' memoir of a stranger simply because Dana asked. Wow! I'm indebted. And an all-caps THANKS (sorry, Vanessa) to Mary V. for reaching out to meet up for coffee, then giving me the shot in the arm I desperately needed. I'm so thankful Dana connected us. Your fresh friendship has been life-giving to me.

Once again, sincere thanks to Cal and Laurie Zimmerman for modeling gentle, generous, and gracious parenting long before it was in vogue. You saved us from ourselves.

To my friend and some kind of cousin, Sherry Hoppen (is it once, twice, thrice removed? I can never remember), thank you for paving the way for small town girls from Forest Grove to become authors (her book, *Sober Cycle,* is also a must read!) and especially for exemplifying the way God can use our painful pasts for his glory. This, I believe, makes us related more now than ever. Love you.

Katie Terpstra—because I wrote these stories in my fifties after having lived them in my thirties, I thank you for refreshing my memory on the joys, challenges, and real-life trials of thirty-something mommas to help keep this book relevant to that demographic.

To my fifth grade teacher, Robert Smith, thank you for the way you cleverly excavated the hidden talents in each of your students. You are my earliest recollection of someone I deeply admired telling me, "You're gonna write a book someday, Cindy. I just know it. You're going to have to do *something* with all those words!"

Every author has a quaint café (or seven) that plays some critical role in their writing journey—whether that is late night lattes, quiet places to get creative, or just somewhere to work other than home. To Emmett Bronkema, owner of Eden Café, thank you for providing me and my team the exact right vibe in the exact right location, and often offering the exact right advice when we needed it most.

With deep love and gratitude to some of our amazing friends who nudged me on in the writing journey and never let on if they had, perhaps, grown weary of my incessant book talk: Blaine and Kathy Newhouse, Paul and Leisa Snow, Bill and Donna Terpstra, Jeff and Ruth Olsson, David and Michelle Brouwer, Kel and Pat Vanderkolk, Ryan and Alicia Waalkes, Ben and Bekah Reese, Mike and Karyl Morin, Ernie and Andree Lottman, Harold and Bonnie Price, Mohammed and Khadija Bourouda, Hasnaa Daif.

To all the characters with starring roles in our France story, I thank you for your faithful walk with Jesus that inspired us and animated our family's future in ways you probably never knew:

Keith and Suzann Sparzak, David and Wendy Stoner, John and Rosa Vanderkolk, Fred and Joyce Hoekzema, Henry and Celia Deneen, Mark and Paige Fisher, Alyssa Phillips, Wendy Middleton Chico, David and Danielle Bult, Dan and Carrie Elzinga, Raouf and Carol Ghattas, Melissa Messmer, Darrin and Julie Jones, Daniel Vandellen, Ludovic and Stephanie Alcaraz, Joanne Risnes, Jacques and Marie-Pierre Weiner, Peter and Rita de Waard, Robert and Caroline Coenradi, Stephanie Kolesnikov, Tara Roelofs LaRoche, Emily, Rebecca, Jessica, Christine, and a host of other international students who fearlessly rode in our demon-possessed minivan and shared meals with us in our stable/house.

Deepest love and sincerest thanks to everyone at Servant's Community Church on the west side of Grand Rapids. You came along mere seconds before I'd given up on Christianity here in America. You breathed new breath into my tired lungs and renewed my hope in the Christian church reminding me that the gift of true Christian community is so worth the risk of stepping into something new again. I couldn't imagine there existed a community already living out the Christian values and the way of Jesus in like manner to what Paul and I had discovered over the last twenty years—the same discoveries recorded in this book. But there you were—just waiting for us only six blocks away. I resurrected this story of ours and pursued publication because of all of you. You are living breathing examples of those who know there are far, far better things ahead than any we leave behind.

A million walk-off homeruns of thanks to my sisters: Pam, Diane, and Heidi—my Mary, Carrie, and Grace Ingalls and my Meg, Beth, and Amy March (I know you guys will think it's unfair that I claim *both* Laura and Jo, but hey, none of us *picked* our birth order and they're both the authors—it's only logical!

#writerprivileges) who co-created a kaleidoscope of childhood stories I'd love to share, but who also helped me realize some are better left untold.

And to my precious mother: "Blessed are the pure in heart, for they shall see God," Matthew 5:8. Thank you, mom, for the countless hours of listening to my never-ending stories and incessant chatter. Thank you for telling me I didn't have to keep playing basketball if I didn't want to. Thank you for coming to hear me sing all those many years ago. And thank you for secretly sliding me that tiny piece of paper when I was about thirteen years old that said, "Let no one's unhappiness mar your happy future." If you have days now, which I think you sometimes do, when you look back and wonder if your life mattered, is there any way I can convince you that you made ALL the difference in the world to me? Is there any way I can convey how much your faithful love and support has meant all these years? Do you know how profoundly just one godly mom can change the world by positively influencing future generations? That's you, Mom. That's you.

For my people, the four ridiculously brave souls that made me a mom and the real "stars" of this book—Andy, Josiah, Grace, and Yulisa—I offer you love and gratitude thicker and sweeter than a spoonful of Nutella straight from the jar, hotter and more intense than hiking Saint Victoire in July, and bigger and bolder than the calanques of Cassis for graciously following me and dad to so many far-away places and opening your hearts and minds to experiencing God along the way. You are my heroes, and I could not be prouder of each of you. Also—to the four of you and the delightful people three of you have married, and the offspring two of you have sprung: May you learn from my mistakes, may you always have eyes to see the hurting, oppressed, and marginalized while developing hearts that both care and respond, may you never forget that people are more important than things, may you courageously make good trouble when necessary, and may the God of all creation always lead you home.

And finally, to my best friend, Paul: Thank you for your endless belief in me, for quietly forking over too much of your hard-earned money as I chased a dream, and for always insisting I'm a writer and that it was all worth it. You always fight hard for me—I know it full well, and I thank you with all that's in me. Thank you for being the quiet to my noise, the calm to my storm, and the caution to my impulsivity. I'm fairly certain I'd be dead by now if it weren't for your restraint. I love you and even *I* don't have enough words to express just how much. Now let's go find a new adventure with God and a new beach from where we can worship him, shall we?

A Note on Proceeds

Since this book is rooted in the call to simplify, to give generously, and to honor the lives of those in need, to monetize its story would be missing the point entirely. In fact, it would be a profound contradiction and deeply hypocritical. So, Paul and I have decided to receive no personal profit from book sales and will donate all proceeds to International Justice Mission (IJM), an NGO working tirelessly to rescue individuals and families who are enslaved, abused, and exploited all around the globe. Please visit their website at *ijm.org* to learn more, and maybe even pray about donating more than just the money you paid for this book.

IJM

www.ingramcontent.com/pod-product-compliance
Lightning Source LLC
Chambersburg PA
CBHW062043080426
42734CB00012B/2546